Teaching Effectiveness:

Its Meaning, Assessment, and Improvement

Teaching
Effectiveness:
Its Meaning, Assessment, and Improvement

Madan Mohan and Ronald E. Hull
State University College
Fredonia, New York

Educational Technology Publications
Englewood Cliffs, New Jersey 07632

Library of Congress Cataloging in Publication Data
Main entry under title:

Teaching effectiveness.

CONTENTS: The problem of evaluating teacher effectiveness: Feldman, S. Teacher evaluation: a teacher
unionist's view. Gage, N.L. Can science contribute to
the art of teaching? Ryans, D.G. Teacher behavior can
be evaluated. Flanders, N.A. and Morine, G. The
assessment of proper control and suitable learning
environment. [etc.]
    1. Teaching--Addresses, essays, lectures.
2. Teachers, Rating of--Addresses, essays, lectures.
3. Teachers, Training of--Addresses, essays, lectures.
I. Madan Mohan. II. Hull, Ronald E.

LB1025.2.T416   371.1'02   75-14090
ISBN 0-87778-084-6

Printed in the United States of America.

Library of Congress Catalog Card Number:
75-14090.

International Standard Book Number:
0-87778-084-6.

First Printing: September, 1975.

Preface

Much interest has been shown by researchers in the last decade in the study of teaching effectiveness. Many studies were conducted to identify elements of effective teaching, to specify these elements in terms of teaching behaviors, and to find the relationship of these specific observational behaviors to student growth. It has been a difficult task for the researchers, partly due to lack of conceptual clarity and partly because of the complex nature of the task.

Teachers are being blamed for the failure of the schools. Accountability and teacher evaluation, like motherhood, are enjoying universal approval. Thus "the time has come" when the teaching profession must devise a system of performance accountability. In such a system a teacher will be judged in terms of his or her acts or behaviors that have been consistently found to be related to student achievement.

We have compiled a collection of articles which describe observational behaviors that have been demonstrated to be easy to apply in the classroom by practicing teachers and by professional educators in teacher preparation programs. Criteria used for the selection of articles were: (1) relevance of articles to teaching effectiveness; (2) specificity of teaching behaviors so that results could be applied in classrooms and in teacher education institutions; (3) guidance in the evaluation of classroom instruction; and (4) recency of articles.

It is hoped that the book will provide research-based knowledge to teachers, administrators, parents, students, school boards, and teachers of teachers (both pre- and in-service) so that "teaching effectiveness" will no longer be looked upon as something like the grin of the Cheshire Cat—elusive and unintelligible. If this book contributes toward instructional improvement, we will feel highly rewarded.

Madan Mohan
Ronald E. Hull

February, 1975

Foreword

With more than usual satisfaction, I write a brief word of introduction to this publication.

The Teacher Education Research Center (TERC) of the State University College at Fredonia is a unique agency—the only one of its kind within the State University of New York. Established in 1967, it signaled the changing nature of one area characteristic of the resources traditionally considered essential to the pre-service education of future teachers. At a time when it was unfashionable to do so (in some quarters, even professionally unpatriotic), the College at Fredonia, following considerable study and consultation, determined that the Campus School, with its long history of distinguished service to the teacher education program, had lived out its original mission. Change was needed of a kind that would allow our resources to be utilized fully. A totally different agency, TERC, was created through generous support from the State University of New York. The agency was designed to fulfill a programmatic mission that would allow for intensive research and evaluation of the heralded changes teacher education would undergo during the era of the seventies and beyond. Subsequent events have justified the establishment of TERC. *Teaching Effectiveness: Its Meaning, Assessment, and Improvement* is but one example of the ever-growing significance of TERC as an important research and development arm in the totality of teacher education at Fredonia State.

Most teacher educators readily admit that the research and development efforts of the sixties caused uneasiness in their ranks and set forth many questions and problems. The solutions to these problems need to be implemented in the teacher education programs of the seventies. Professors Mohan and Hull have addressed themselves to a subject that is highly sensitive to practitioners and theorists alike.

Anyone interested sufficiently to open the cover of this book of readings is already well aware that the subject of teaching effectiveness pervades the entire spectrum of the profession. Teacher effectiveness, performance, or whatever else it may be titled, will remain the subject of concern and debate within the profession for a long time.

Through their collection of readings, written by stalwarts in the field, this book contributes significantly to the literature concerning teacher effectiveness. Added together, the writing, the research, the experimentation—indeed, even the debate and conflict which the subject arouses—will, by opening wider class-room doors, enable the professionals and laymen more rationally to direct their combined competencies and responsibilities in a manner that will be of lasting benefit to succeeding generations of children and youth.

I commend this important book to you for thoughtful reading and contemplation.

Dallas K. Beal
President
State University College
Fredonia, New York

Table of Contents

Teaching Effectiveness:

Its Meaning, Assessment, and Improvement

Section One

THE PROBLEM OF EVALUATING
TEACHER EFFECTIVENESS

Introduction to Section One

The Problem of Evaluating
Teacher Effectiveness

We have chosen Sandra Feldman's article, *Teacher Evaluation: A Teacher Unionist's View*, to begin this book because her view of the problem of equitable teacher evaluation seems to be representative of the views of teachers. Also, she presents a realistic view of the problems that beset education in general. She points out that the schools are blamed and scapegoated for countless social ills for which they are not responsible and over which they have no control. Schools are caught in the dilemma of symbolizing the establishment while at the same time the schools are perceived as the vehicle for upward mobility. Unfortunately, expectations for a better life through education have far outdistanced the progress that has been made. Widespread academic retardation still exists.

Feldman claims that the education profession will continue to be vulnerable to vociferous criticism until it has put together a body of knowledge about teaching that is coherent, concrete, and communicable to all. She cites the typical supervisory observation of teaching as a ludicrous ritual which functions only to affirm the teacher's subordinate position in the staff hierarchy. Inasmuch as competencies have not been defined, communicated, and taught to teachers, the evaluation of teaching remains subjective and ambiguous. She contends that poor ratings of teachers by supervisors are not supported by evidence of incompetence and the teacher *never* has received enough help either in pre-service training or on the job to attain the "competencies." Who is incompetent? The professional being rated—or the evaluator?

5

She recommends that teacher evaluation standards (compe-tencies) be identified and validated through research related to pupil achievement, and that teachers be involved in the develop-ment of competencies, "First, because they have a great deal to offer; second, because their very involvement will lead in the process to improvement of their own teaching."

In the next article, *Can Science Contribute to the Art of Teaching?*, N. L. Gage attempts to answer Feldman's plea for a research validation of teaching competencies. Gage begins by acknowledging the summaries of research which show little conclusive evidence that such variables as teacher personality or method of instruction relate to teacher effectiveness; on the other hand, he questions the researchers' generalizations of their findings. He asserts that the research on teaching provides data which support the inference of desirable teacher behaviors and characteristics. He has classified a number of behavioral dimen-sions of teachers that are desirable.

Gage finishes on the optimistic note that science (research) has already contributed greatly to the art of teaching and with added emphasis and resources it will undoubtedly continue to provide useful answers to the difficult questions surrounding the explication of teaching effectiveness.

David G. Ryans, in his article, *Teacher Behavior Can Be Evaluated*, classifies teacher behavior into five categories: (1) motivating and reinforcing behavior; (2) organizing, coordinating, and managing behavior; (3) presenting, explaining, and demon-strating behavior; (4) evaluating behavior; and (5) counseling and advising behavior. He avers that evaluation has to do with judgments as to what is "good" or "bad" teaching, and this good-bad ratio must be defined in terms of the values of the school and community.

In essence, Ryans bases his argument that teaching can be evaluated on these assumptions: (1) teacher behavior is patterned and may be predicted—at least, within limits; (2) empirical study and inductive inference provide a valid approach to understanding teacher behavior; (3) teacher behavior is observable; (4) individual differences exist in observable teacher behavior; (5) teacher behavior is social in nature; (6) the ultimate goal of teacher behavior is to influence the acquisition of pupil behavior of a specified kind; and (7) teacher behavior is relative.

Ryans thinks that teacher behavior can be assessed most reliably by teams of observers, employed for the sole purpose of visiting classrooms throughout the year for observations and assessment of teaching performance. Once teacher behavior has been reliably assessed, evaluation should be based on agreed-upon criteria which are spelled out in behavioral terms, that is, in terms of actual behaviors that can serve as benchmarks against which assessment of an individual teacher's behavior may be compared.

Ryans claims the most important contribution that could be made to the evaluation of teaching and the improvement of the teaching process would be attention on the part of school systems to a "prediction and evaluation research paradigm." This approach would require clear specification of desired qualities of teachers; identification of situations in which "valued" teacher behaviors may occur and in which they may be observed and assessed; operational descriptions of valued teacher behaviors; a cataloging of teacher characteristics and behaviors which occur in the classroom, and research directed at identifying relationships between these valued teacher behaviors and situational variables.

We have selected Ned A. Flanders and Greta Morine's article, *The Assessment of Proper Control and Suitable Learning Environment*, to culminate Section One because it answers some of the questions and provides some alternative solutions to problems posed by the other authors in the Section. In providing concrete recommendations and tangible research evidence that the development of various teaching skills favorably affects pupil performance, the article sets the stage for Section Two, which deals with achievement related to teaching behaviors. The Flanders and Morine paper is a response to California's Stull Bill. The Stull Bill requires the evaluation of the performance of certificated personnel throughout the State of California.

The authors call for, and offer a model for, evaluation of administrative and supervisory personnel as well as for teachers. An important contribution to the academician and the educator in the school setting is the list of sources of materials for developing competencies.

1.

Teacher Evaluation:
A Teacher Unionist's View

Sandra Feldman

It is only slightly more than a decade since teachers achieved collective bargaining after a one-day strike in New York City. In 1960 the teachers' quest for power and dignity was supported and applauded by most of the public and particularly by the liberal press. In those days, teachers were looked upon by those who support "causes" as part of the "oppressed"; and indeed, to a large extent, they were. Salaries were low, working conditions were terrible, school administration was tyrannical at worst, paternalistic at best. Even the *New York Times*, never a friend of trade unionism, was on the side of the teachers' struggle for better pay and improved education.

In pre-collective bargaining days, school administrators had a great deal of arbitrary power over the everyday working lives of teachers, who were required to perform a wide variety of tasks unrelated to their teaching function, and who had nothing to say about their class assignments or the nature of the curriculum, let alone standards for hiring and firing and evaluation.

It took considerable adjustment—experiential learning, one might say—for administrators to come to accept, as many have (though many still have not), such foreign and unspeakable things

Paper presented at the ETS Programs of Continuing Education Course: In-service Teacher Evaluation, at Educational Testing Service, Princeton, New Jersey, November 27, 1972. Copyright © 1972 by Educational Testing Service. All rights reserved. Reproduced by permission. The author is Vice President, American Federation of Teachers.

as contractual rights and grievance procedures, all of which curtailed their long-held prerogatives. The teacher-supervisor relationship has changed in many respects. Teachers are no longer timid or fearful. Armed with their contract and strengthened by the solidarity of a strong organization, they no longer can be arbitrarily assigned to toilet patrol; their preferences in assignments must be taken into account; they cannot be forcibly transferred or dismissed without cause and without the opportunity to bring in their union or association representatives as defense counsel. Administrators have acclimated to monthly consultation with teacher organization committees, to adhering to contractual provisions or facing a grievance, and to a teachers' representative talking to him as an equal.

But there have been other kinds of changes as well. The public, for example, no longer pities the poor teacher. On the contrary, teachers, now considered—and not without reason—to have a good deal of power (although that power is much more limited than the previously sympathetic and now outright hostile editorial pages would have it), are faced daily with criticism, with attacks on their hard-won rights, and with blame—not only for the failure of the schools where they are teaching, but for countless social ills for which they are not responsible and over which they have no control.

Administrators find themselves caught up in the same maelstrom of school conflict. They are subject, in fact, in many cases, to even worse pressures. Superintendents long have been forced to play the game of musical chairs—out of one district and into another. And now principals often find themselves at the mercy of community and parents' groups, with their jobs in continuing jeopardy if they displease one group or another. It is not without significance that in 1971 the New York State Legislature, after a long, fairly bitter session, exempted principals from the right of tenure. Believe it or not, teachers did not applaud their bosses' loss of job security—for a principal without job security too often takes his desperation out on the hides of his faculty in attempting to shift the anger of parents, or the school board, or the community corporation, or some other group, from his back. "It's not my fault; the teachers' contract prevents me from doing what you suggest. . . ." is a refrain we often hear from the principal too fearful to take proper responsibility for the problems brought to him by angry parents, who may or may not be justified in their anger. (If he does this while he has real job security, then he is either cowardly or mean.)

I do not for a moment want to appear insensitive to the problems of a school administrator placed in a rough political situation. I want simply to make two main points: First, these kinds of pressures create very poor atmospheres for the running of schools. And, second, precisely because they have such deep-reaching effects on the schools and particularly on the teacher-administrator relationships within them, we must understand them.

I believe it is important—essential—before turning to the substantive discussion of teacher evaluation, to discuss the dynamics of changing relationships in the schools, the political struggles and the strains the schools are under, where we are, and how we got to this point. Even though the actual evaluative process and procedures have changed very little—which is a problem in itself which I will discuss at length later on—our subject and all of its latest ramifications cannot be clearly understood, in my opinion, without an understanding, an analysis, of the politics of schools. Furthermore, I am here, after all, not just as an educator, but as a teacher unionist, and for me this subject must be discussed from that perspective—an airing of which, I believe, will be of value to your deliberations.

A Brief Look at the Past Decade

In any discussion of almost any sensitive school issue—and teacher evaluation is certainly a sensitive issue—we cannot ignore the fact that for the past decade and longer, schools have been the scene of conflict, standing as they do as symbols, on the one hand, of "the establishment" and on the other hand as the vehicle for upward mobility for the underclasses. Whether or not the role of the schools as providing the path out of poverty has been mythologized—and that alone is an interesting subject—the fact is that working class and lower middle class parents attribute that role to them and place those expectations upon them.

During the early sixties, while teachers were seeking a greater voice, their movement was identified with, and teacher unionists were active in, the integrationist civil rights movement. The teacher union movement continued to grow, continued to succeed. The civil rights movement also had great successes—the Civil Rights Acts of '64 and '66, the voting rights act of '65, the integration of public facilities throughout the South. But all those successes, while they raised expectations throughout the minority communities, left basically unchanged the economic conditions of the poor, particularly in the Northern "inner cities." The joblessness remained; the unlivable slum housing remained; the disgracefully inadequate health care remained; and the poor conditions of the schools remained.

Now, the solutions to unemployment, bad housing, and poor health care can seem ephemeral, intangible. They require enormous political power, a consistent building of forces—votes—to overturn administrations, to elect a Congress. They require consistent, expert, and painstaking lobbying. Job openings cannot be seen, touched, picketed, sat in. But schools are brick and mortar. They are in the neighborhood, approachable, and appear to contain within them not only the solutions to their own ills, but a way out—out of poverty, out of slums, into the mainstream of society. They also contain within them educators—people, teachers in particular, who have made it into the mainstream by virtue of being paid to do a job in those schools, who fought successfully for the decent pay they receive to do that job, which in turn seems not to be getting done. Furthermore, schools are billion dollar operations. Some see in them the opportunity for rebuilding broken patronage machines—or establishing new ones. The struggle over community control ensued—a struggle which deeply involved the hiring, firing, and evaluation of educators.

And so, in the midst of growing social turbulence, with different groups organizing themselves for power, for a voice in decision-making—the poor, the taxpayers, the students, the parents, the teachers, etc.—the schools were immediately in the maelstrom of a storm of social protest.

I should not be misunderstood. I am not for a moment saying that school protest was totally unfocused or misplaced. It is true that thousands upon thousands of poor children are not learning, are leaving school unprepared either for work or higher education—a situation which has helped create what is popularly referred to as the "crisis in confidence" surrounding the public schools. A crisis in confidence, I must add, to which we as educators have contributed—not so much by our own failures as by our ever-willingness, as we should be, to point out our shortcomings in our efforts to highlight the need for educational improvement, as I am doing right now. We are much more hesitant, however, often too defensive, to talk about our successes, which are real and numerous. We have done so good a job, in fact, that we have a highly literate citizenry—a great many of whom feel perfectly capable of doing our jobs as well as, or better than, we do them.

There is no doubt that conflict in the schools, and vociferous criticism of education, has been nourished by the existence of widespread academic retardation. It has been caused, and contributed to in large part, by the changing social conditions I talked about earlier.

But the profession is responsible, too, particularly for the feeling on the part of much of the public that anyone can teach—not because it has taught them so well, not because it is at fault for the inability of the schools to end academic retardation in poor areas, but because it has failed to put together a coherent and concrete body of knowledge about itself, about the teaching-learning process, a body of knowledge which can be coherently communicated and as tangible as medicine or law.

We are defensive not just because of our failures, which hurt us more than our most major successes gratify us, but because without that concrete body of knowledge we cannot defend ourselves.

There is a great sport common to the schools. I call it blame-placing. It used to be played this way: The public blamed the Board, the Board blamed the superintendent, the superintendent blamed his deputy, his deputy blamed the principals, the principals blamed the teachers. Now, we are in a new ballpark and what happens—at least what teachers feel is happening—is that everyone just blames the teachers. Administrators probably feel the same way.

So we have enormous social pressure on the schools for change, and at the same time an atmosphere of blame-placing and scapegoating. We have a situation in which schools, in general, and teachers, in particular, are bearing a great burden of blame for problems they cannot solve, problems caused largely by conditions over which they have no control. Teachers not only suffer the difficulties and strains of the classroom without adequate supports, they are accused of "insensitivity," they are caught in conflicts and power fights, they are constantly criticized, and they are ceaselessly bombarded with "innovations" and new schemes for "accountability" in which they are told they will be judged "objectively"—for example, on the basis of advancement in the standardized test scores of their students.

Or, educators are offered "solutions" like performance contracting, or vouchers. When those do not go over, some school critics, on the basis of research which, instead of seeking answers seeks to establish that the schools make no difference anyway, decide to abandon the schools altogether as a place of learning. As one conclusion of his recent study of the schools (*Inequality*), Christopher Jencks said: "The primary basis for evaluating a school should be whether the students and teachers find it a satisfying place to be."

In other words, forget about achievement. His conclusion, as you know, is that schools have little or no effect on the earning power of adults, and therefore really do not matter all that much. The attitudes of an influential scholar, shared by many school critics, should not be underestimated. They represent a terrible danger to the continued viability of public education. What they are saying—and government is all ears, especially at appropriations time—is "Give up on the schools."

If we are going to counter the attitude that schools do not matter; if, as educators we are going to save the schools—and I believe the job is left to us and we must do it—we must develop a knowledge base.

Now I want to talk about how little we know and how little effort we make in our school systems to know much more. It is in this context that we come to a discussion of teacher evaluation. I will start with the beginning teacher.

The Probationer

Even if he has had student teaching, the new teacher finds himself in a very different situation of sudden and total responsibility for a class. The very logistics involved in a classroom of 25 or 30 pupils (if he is lucky enough to have so few) are frightening; the business of actually teaching them he cannot come to grips with at all until he establishes some authority and order. By authority and order I do not mean hands folded on desks and backs up straight, but a relationship between himself and his pupils, and among the pupils themselves, which allows for mutual respect. If he does not make it in the first few weeks, he is not likely to make it. If he does not make it, one of two things can happen. He can settle into a career in which each day is a terrible strain and struggle just to get through—or he can drop out. When we talk about evaluating competency, we must always remember that the classroom itself—that roomful of youngsters—is a vehicle for accountability. Thousands of new teachers drop out each year, demoralized and defeated. That is a problem for us as educators. We have no way of knowing how many of them might have made good teachers. But there is a bigger problem—the problem of those who are demoralized and defeated but do not drop out. What happens to them and why? Do they lack necessary skills? Do the school or classroom conditions account for the problem? Are there supports not provided which might help? Or is the entire situation beyond the teacher's—or the school's—control?

Then there are the teachers, a majority, who do manage to establish that relationship, who do learn to teach, right there, in the classroom, usually through trial and error. In those classrooms, it appears that teaching and learning is going on. At least it is going on to the uncertain extent that we can measure it.

Where is the administrator while this is happening?

Usually, the new teacher meets him on the first day of school. The teacher is told that if he needs help, he should just ask for it. ("My door is always open" is a standard joke among teachers.) Of course, the last thing a new teacher will do is go to the principal and reveal his inadequacies.

In the first few days or weeks, the teacher probably sees his supervisor pass by his door several times. He may even be visited briefly and, depending on the supervisor and the state of the classroom, he may be either gently or strongly chastised, or he may be told his floor is dirty, his bulletin board is sloppy—or, he may be complimented; the lesson at the moment looks interesting, the children seem happy and orderly, the floor is clean, the bulletin board attractive. Maybe they will meet again at a faculty conference. Perhaps there is an in-service training session after school or during lunch, which the teacher feels is just one more chore unrelated to his problems in the classroom. Or, perhaps in this school, atypically, there is some in-service training which actually has some value.

For the most part, the supervisor or administrator is harried, beset by paper work, parental complaints, community problems, cafeteria mix-ups and disruptions, accidents, or assaults—one could go on. Even if he has been adequately prepared to help new teachers, he hardly has the time. He is much more the school administrator than the principal teacher—and most often this is not of his own making or choice.

Meanwhile, the teacher is developing other relationships in the school. He is recruited to the teachers' organization and is briefed on the nature of the school, its faculty, its administration. The teacher next door offers help—some materials, lesson plans, some knowledge of the youngsters from previous experience. In the coffee shop on the corner or in the teachers' lunchroom he gets a variety of tips and advice. Usually, that is where he brings his teaching problems. And usually, that is where he finds aid. A very important kind of training takes place in this informal way. One of the greatest defects of our school systems is the lack of planned time, available during the school day for teacher-sharing— but I shall talk about solutions after I paint reality.

Sooner or later, before the end of the term, comes "the observation."

After the supervisory observation and the letter of critique which follows, at the end of the term, comes a rating form— different in different districts, but essentially the same throughout our schools, usually with a numerical rating on each item in a checklist. And, most important of all, a small slip with the evaluation—"S" for Satisfactory; "U" for Unsatisfactory—and a recommendation, continuance, or discontinuance.

If you received the "S"—you are doing fine. Breathe easy.

If you received the "U"—you are in trouble; if you also have a "discontinuance," you are really in trouble.

So, what do you do?

A teacher can accept a U rating, and even separation from service. He will do that if he feels the supervisor is correct and he deserves what he is getting.

But very few teachers feel that way.

Most of them will go right to their teachers' organization for advice and aid. The representative could decide, on a review of the situation, that the evidence of incompetency is overwhelming: that the supervisor has followed all procedures properly, that the teacher has been given all the help possible, to no avail—and will advise the teacher to look elsewhere for a career. There actually are occasions when such advice is given.

They are few and far between. The evidence of incompetence is rarely, if ever, overwhelming and the teacher never has received enough help on the job.

And yet, contrary to popular opinion, we are rarely able to overturn U-ratings or probationary dismissals. Probationers appeal their U-ratings and dismissals to an in-house panel of supervisors, and despite our able defense, despite the usual shameful paucity of evidence either of incompetency or help given, that panel usually upholds their colleague supervisor. So, it may be difficult for supervisors to work up a dismissal case against a probationer, but it really does not take much over-exertion to do so. It is easy, procedurally, to "weed out incompetents" during the probationary period.

But substantively, what is incompetence? (I'm not even asking at this point how it is related to learning.) And who is incompetent? The professional being evaluated—or the evaluator?

The Tenured Teacher

Tenure is not a lifetime guarantee of a job.

All it means is that if a teacher has worked satisfactorily for a given period, there is a point at which it is harder to fire him than it was during the previous period. That is, he now has available to him a real due process procedure—in almost all cases, required by state law, and in some, by contract.

In New York City we recently negotiated for teachers in their fourth and fifth year of probation (the legislature last year extended the probationary period from three to five years), the same procedure required by law for tenured teachers. In effect, we negotiated back the three-year probationary period.

The procedure, briefly (and it is probably similar in most states which have tenure laws) requires notice of charges in advance, gives the accused teacher right to counsel, the right to a copy of exact charges and "specifications," the right to cross-examine opposing witnesses and to bring witnesses in his own behalf, and, after a series of hearings through the hierarchy of the school system, the right to a hearing before an impartial trial examiner picked from a list approved by his union as well as by the Board and, finally, recourse to the courts or the Commissioner of Education.

What it means, practically, is that in order for a tenured teacher to be fired for incompetence, his supervisors have to have very good evidence of his incompetence. (There are, of course, other possible causes for dismissing teachers which are not the subject of our discussion, but they too should, and do, require substantial evidence.)

Very few tenured teachers are fired for incompetence. First—and we should not forget this in a discussion of this sort—because within the limits of what we understand teaching competency to be, most teachers who survive the classroom for three years or more are actually competent.

Second, because in order for a supervisor to prove incompetence he has to:

(a) know what it is;
(b) spend a good deal of time in a teacher's classroom to document it;
(c) know what to do in terms of aid and training when a teacher, in his opinion, exhibits incompetence;
(d) document his own efforts to help the teacher; and
(e) show that his efforts at training and helping the teacher were valid, on the one hand, and to no avail on the other.

Since the evaluation of tenured teachers takes exactly the same form, for the most part, as the kind of evaluation I have already described for probationary teachers—"observations" and rating scales—this is very hard to do.

How to Respond?

Given all this, and given the political situation I described earlier, and the demands—understandable, justifiable—being made upon the schools and the profession for achievement, what is the response?

Communities bring pressure for more "accountability." Harebrained schemes for the evaluation of professionals on a piecework product basis come and go; and some, as in California, are enacted into law.

Supervisors and administrators would like to get rid of difficult due process procedures because they think it would make their job of weeding out incompetents easier.

Teachers feel that existing methods of evaluating are subjective, punitively oriented, based on the opinion of supervisors who do not know more about teaching than they do; are easily used in a discriminatory way against the outspoken, the nonconformers, the union activists, the "creative," and, last but not least, are unfair because pre-service teacher education is inadequate and in-service teacher education is poor, if not worthless.

Furthermore, there is confusion about the role of teacher evaluation in the schools. Is it to get rid of incompetents? Teachers want to do that as much as anyone—for they bear the brunt more than anyone when there are incompetent teachers in the school or in the system. Is it to judge performance only—or to improve teaching and education generally?

I feel the need to say a few positive words before going on. There are some good teacher education programs. I have seen a few, particularly those which are public school-based, where microteaching and videotape and other such materials are used, where professors and principals and cooperating teachers and student teachers deal with each other in a non-threatening and fruitful way.

Therefore, believe it or not, despite what may sound to you

like a very negative recital of ills, I am hopeful. I will lose hope only when I am convinced that educators—educators of teachers and of school administrators in particular—are unwilling to look closely and honestly at what is happening in our schools, as I have tried to do so far in this report. And I may lose hope if I do not see a movement away from the "off with their heads" approach to teacher evaluation and toward a view of teacher evaluation which is a total school evaluation. Or if the cacophony of criticism of the schools does not begin to include acknowledgment of successes.

I hope you will bear with me a little longer as I move from the critical to the constructive.

What Should Be Done

Before offering solutions, we must decide on our goal. Is it to get rid of a high percentage of teachers each year on the assumption that a "shape up or ship out" atmosphere in the schools will make things better? If so, then all that needs to be done is to figure out some procedures which make it easier to get rid of people—require less evidence of incompetence, for example.

Or is our goal to improve instruction? If it is—and it is mine—then our job is a little more complicated. Each of the things we must do is dependent on the other things which must be done.

First, pre-service teacher preparation needs vast improvement. It must be made more relevant to the needs of the classroom. It must be more related to the ability of the teacher to perform. It must enable its graduates to demonstrate their competence with confidence.

The Performance-Based Teacher Education movement provides hope for moving in that direction, if it is not killed by the completely Neanderthal way in which most state education departments—including and probably particularly New York's—are going about changing requirements to push universities and colleges toward their (the State Education Department's) own peculiar understanding of Performance-Based Teacher Education. For the most part, teacher education institutions are being asked to change their program to performance-based programs despite the fact that no one knows yet which teacher behaviors affect what learning, and how. In addition, state education departments are changing certification requirements to performance-based, before standards are developed and before competencies are validated. This is being opposed vigorously by the teacher organizations and by most sensible and intelligent teacher educators.

Now, teacher education institutions can do a great deal. They should be involved in research and development as they evolve performance-based, field-centered programs. They can be developing models of teacher performance based on available knowledge, utilizing some of the very limited research and the opinions of experienced classroom educators. And they can be planning comprehensive research to test those models so that the changes they make are based on real knowledge, not on guesses and not on what looks good in a catalogue or brochure.

Second, changes in selection procedures should also be made—but, again, not based on ignorance. So far, we have absolutely no way of knowing whether a teacher candidate will be a good teacher. The fact that he has completed a college program does not tell us. An interview, no matter how well conducted, does not tell us. An examination, while valuable for telling us whether the candidate can read and write and knows his subject matter, cannot predict his performance—at least we have no evidence that it can.

I have grave doubts as to whether we will ever be able to achieve "predictive validity" of selection procedures, but I am in favor of trying to do it to the extent possible. We should be following up to see whether groups of teachers who have been licensed or certified in particular ways are performing satisfactorily, whether a particular preparation program or in-service program, or selection procedure is related to that performance in any way. School systems themselves should be doing this; they should have the capacity and resources for it.

We have had a great deal of controversy over examinations for licensing in New York City, and examinations for licensing supervisors have been stopped by the courts. Judge Mansfield, in enjoining the examination did not say, as most people think, that the exams were discriminatory. He said that in the absence of evidence of their predictive validity, and given the relatively small numbers of Blacks and Puerto Ricans who pass them, their continuance could not be justified in the face of charges of possible discrimination.

So, the exams were ended, and we have had instead widespread favoritism and discrimination in the hiring of supervisors throughout New York City. No one will ever know for sure whether the change has affected school performance positively or negatively, because no effort is being made along those lines.

The problem of just and meaningful selection procedures is not a large-city problem. A look around the country will demonstrate that in the absence of objective standards, discrimination, however subtle, takes place, and to a degree it never did under the merit system in New York City, where minority group after minority group made it into the school system by virtue of an objective examination system. (In fact, one of the last supervisory lists, enjoined by Judge Mansfield, contained the names of over 200 Black and Puerto Rican candidates.)

Changes in selection procedures are needed. State certification, where examinations have not been required, has been totally inadequate—as inadequate as the "approved" teacher education programs on which that certification is based.

Examinations are under attack and are difficult to defend without evidence of their validity.

But selection procedures, certification, and licensing procedures should not be changed on the basis of ignorance merely because there is great political pressure for change. In fact, the highly political situation schools operate under should make us very careful. We should have a selection procedure which is rigorous and objective. Those who argue for a lowering of standards or the discontinuance of examinations altogether so that more minority group candidates can be certified are also seeking a subjective system which is of greater danger to those very groups on whose behalf they demand it. It is—has always been—in the interest of minorities to have selection based on objective standards and merit.

What we need is to make those standards meaningful by basing them on carefully researched and proven knowledge. After all, we have always had standards in education, not only for selection, but for evaluation.

And here I am, at last, getting to evaluation.

Standards have always existed. We have had long checklists for a long time. Those standards have been criticized since time immemorial, for being too general, for being too specific. The real problem with them is that they have not been rooted in a knowledge base backed up by careful research, and so they have had nothing to do with instructional improvement.

And teachers usually have no idea what the standards are.

They should not only know what they are, they should be involved in establishing them. They should have the knowledge, skills, tools, and conditions with which to meet them. They should have confidence in both the standards and the evaluatory system. They should be convinced that there is a knowledge base and that it is a sound one.

They should be evaluated for what they know and for those parts of the educational totality over which they have control. They should be evaluated not on the basis of achievement test scores of pupils—which involve many other factors besides teacher input—but on the basis of their own behavior in the context of knowledge about which teacher behaviors or skills or competencies bring about learning.

As yet, we do not have comprehensive and systematic evidence that any one teaching methodology is superior to any other. We have no conclusive evidence that teachers with x or y particular skill or competency will elicit x or y learning response. Our knowledge is limited and there are grave signs throughout the country that a new fad called "competency-based" is the next educational "innovation." We must not let that happen as it has happened so many times before.

Attempts to apply—simplistically and ignorantly—the management skills developed by business and industry have gotten the schools into trouble before. In the early 1900s the whole notion of "efficiency" was very popular in education. Time and motion studies were being suggested for the schools and they have a frighteningly familiar ring.

Plans for changing and strengthening teacher evaluation must be accompanied by meaningful research. We do not have to wait, to do nothing, until research is completed. We can and should develop teaching models based on the limited available research and on the opinions of experienced classroom teachers; and we can move ahead with those as long as a research design is built in and carried on simultaneously with the development. Such efforts must include the establishment of substantive programs such as teacher internships, so that beginning teachers, instead of learning by trial and error on the job, are given only half a classload in the first year and three-quarters in the second, with the rest of the time spent working with experienced teachers and in relevant in-service training.

In New York City, the United Federation of Teachers has been offering a series of "minicourses." These are courses given by classroom teachers. They are brief two- to four-hour sessions on specific methods and techniques, and they are attended enthusiastically by large numbers of teachers, despite their having no credits attached.

I want to emphasize also that teacher evaluation must not be done in a vacuum. Plans must be made for taking a good, hard look at the entire school program, such as is proposed in the design for "Accountability in the New York City Schools" prepared by Educational Testing Service. We should be attempting to evaluate the total school, taking into account the school environment, the administration, the curriculum, etc., as well as teacher performance, and we should be comparing schools operating under similar conditions in an effort to learn why some appear to be—or are—more effective than others. This should be done not solely for identifying incompetence—a good but negative objective—but for finding out what works in education so that it can be applied and expanded.

Before I summarize and conclude, I want to make a plea—no, a demand, really: Experienced classroom teachers must be involved fully in the development of any program for evaluation of professionals, or of schools, or for changing teacher training programs. First, because they have a great deal to offer; second, because their very involvement will lead in the process to improvement of their own teaching.

In Conclusion

Schools exist in a social and political reality which must be considered and understood by those involved in educational change. Changes in teacher evaluation which take place in an "off with their heads" atmosphere and in the context of school budget-cutting and job shortages will be viewed with suspicion—and justly—by teachers and their organizations. We have learned from history, even if others have not.

There are no "procedural" solutions to improving teaching. For the most part, adequate procedures for weeding out incompetents exist; they are hard for administrators to use primarily because no one really knows what incompetence is, except in extreme cases, and the processes for evaluation now used rely primarily on subjective opinion rather than on proven knowledge.

As teacher unionists, we are vitally interested in better education. Because we are, we will insist that the much-needed, time-consuming, massive research be done to find out what we need to know about teacher behavior and its effects on learning.

We will press for the necessary funds for that research and we will demand that teachers have a meaningful voice in its direction.

We will continue to support the establishment of an on-the-job internship for teachers—whatever their pre-service teaching was.

We will continue to defend teachers subjected to the vagaries and uncertainties of current evaluation procedures.

We will continue to support non-discriminatory high standards for entry into the teaching profession.

And we will cooperate with those institutions which are seeking educational solutions in a meaningful and knowledgeable way.

We are interested in change—we want it—but we have seen too much of change for change's sake. We want educators to stop reinventing the wheel; to stop introducing, with great fanfare, one rehashed "innovation" after another.

We will do our best to see to it that for once in education, change is based on substantive and proven knowledge instead of on public relations and guesswork.

Suggested Readings

Callahan, R.E. *Education and the Cult of Efficiency*. Chicago: University of Chicago Press, 1962.

Dreeben, R. *On What Is Learned in School*. Reading, Massachusetts: Addison-Wesley, 1968.

Dreeben, R. *The Nature of Teaching*. Chicago: University of Chicago Press, 1970.

Fuchs, E. *Teachers Talk*. New York: Anchor Books, 1969.

2.

Can Science Contribute to the Art of Teaching?

N.L. Gage

Can science contribute to the art of teaching? It would be nice if the answer could be a resounding "Yes," followed by a long parade of conclusive evidence and examples of richly useful findings. Unfortunately, that happy paper cannot yet be written in any honest way. Instead, I must offer a rather more complex response to the question. First, I shall define the sense in which I shall use the term "successful" and delimit the setting of the kind of teaching to be discussed. Second, I am going to consider reasons for pessimism on the question of whether research on teaching has any real likelihood of yielding scientific findings that can be used to improve teaching. The third and fourth sections will be an effort to temper some of the pessimism.

Definition and Delimitation

My present definition of "successful" is one based on research on teaching. The findings of such research may or may not accord with common sense. They may or may not accord with the virtues of personality and character, or desirable behaviors, described in writings on ethics, the Boy Scout handbook, or a Dale Carnegie course. Also, a research-based characterization of successful teacher behavior will not necessarily be extremely original, or completely not-obvious. Nor will such a description of successful teacher behavior necessarily be highly systematic, since research findings at any given moment do not necessarily form a coherent scheme. As for validity, it is not inconceivable that in the long run some non-scientific insight or artistic hunch may turn out to be superior to what can now be cited on the basis of research evidence. That is, the truths propounded in the past by novelists, essayists, or skilled supervisors of teachers may eventually outstrip in scientific validity the results of research now available.

Despite the possible limitations just mentioned, we shall consider only what the research literature has to offer. This literature takes the form of reports on empirical studies of one kind or another. In these studies, various kinds of teacher behavior have been related to other variables on which some sort of educational valuation can be placed. So, by the present definition, "successful" teacher behaviors or characteristics are those that have been found through empirical research to be related to something desirable about teachers. The "something desirable" may be improved achievement by pupils or any of the various cognitive, affective, or psychomotor objectives of education. Or the "something desirable" may be a favorable evaluation of the teacher by pupils, a supervisor, a principal, or someone else whose judgment is important.

The empirical relationships between the teacher behaviors and the desirable somethings may be found in two different ways. First, the relationship may be demonstrated in true experiments; if so, they may be considered to be genuine causal or functional relationships. Or they may be found only through correlational studies; if so, the inference that the teacher behavior causes the something desirable may be hazardous. Although it may be urged that conceptual, logical, or historical methods can also establish what is "successful teacher behavior," I am going to exclude such methods from the present argument, i.e., from my present definition of scientific method. That is, I shall assume that scientific knowledge as to what constitutes successful teacher behavior must be based on inference from an experiment or a correlational study that the behavior is related to something desirable.

Now let us specify the kind of setting in which the teacher behavior to be considered takes place. Various innovations being considered by educators may make the setting of teaching one that is not always the conventional classroom. In the future the setting may change in accordance with the needs of the learners and the kinds of learning in which they are engaged. For some kinds of learning, pupils may be taught in large-group settings, such as movie and lecture halls. For other kinds, the setting will be the small-group seminar, programmed instruction, individually prescribed instruction, or independent study. In the future, these settings will, it is said, supplement and perhaps supplant today's conventional classroom.

But these different kinds of settings still lie in the future, for the most part. And my definition of successful teaching requires empirical research demonstrating a relationship between the behaviors of teachers and other desirable things. So this discussion is going to be restricted to the behavior of teachers in the conventional classroom.

Reasons for Pessimism

Let us now consider reasons for pessimism on the question, Can science contribute to the art of teaching? To begin, it should be noted that making positive statements about the results of research on successful teacher behavior is not fashionable among educational research workers. Many reviewers of research on teaching have concluded that it has yielded little of value.

Recent Summary Statements

This disparaging style in appraising research results has had a great vogue. In 1953, as a member of an AERA Committee on the Criteria of Teacher Effectiveness, I rendered the verdict that "the present condition of research on teacher effectiveness holds little promise of yielding results commensurate with the needs of American education."[1] In 1958, Orville Brim[2] concluded from his examination of reviews of the literature that there were no consistent relations between teacher characteristics and effectiveness in teaching. In 1963, in the *Handbook of Research on Teaching*, the authors of the chapter on teaching methods reported an impression that "teaching methods do not seem to make much difference" and that "there is hardly any evidence to favor one method over another."[3] The authors of the chapter on teacher personality and characteristics concluded that ". . . very little is known for certain . . . about the relation between teacher personality and teacher effectiveness."[4] And the authors of the chapter on social interaction in the classroom concluded that "until very recently, the approach to the analysis of teacher-pupil and pupil-pupil interaction . . . has tended to be unrewarding and sterile."[5] It would not be hard to find other summary statements to the effect that empirical research on teaching has not yielded much enlightenment about successful teaching.

Stephens' Theory of Spontaneous Schooling

Some writers hold that all research on school variables, not merely research on teacher behavior, has yielded negative results for the most part. In fact, the view that educational research yields negative findings has even been assimilated into a whole theory of the origins and process of schooling. Stephens[6] has looked at the research reports and the summaries of research and has concluded that practically nothing seems to make any difference in the effectiveness of instruction. Stephens considers this "flood of negative results" to be understandable in the light of his theory of spontaneous schooling. This theory postulates spontaneous, automatic forces to be found in the background of the student—his maturational tendencies, various out-of-school agencies such as the home and the general community, and the reputation of the school as a place concerned about academic matters. The theory also refers to various spontaneous tendencies on the part of humans in the role of the teacher—tendencies to manipulate and communicate. These two kinds of force, the background forces and the automatic teaching forces, account for most of the learning that takes place. Hence, the changes introduced by research variables of one kind or another are inadequate to produce any major difference. Furthermore, the spontaneous powerful forces operate early in the growth process, when influences on learning have greater effects. For this reason, also, administrative factors and pedagogical refinements produce only minor differences, if any.

Stephens documented his position with references to summaries of studies of a host of specific educational variables, procedures, practices, and orientations—namely, school attendance, instructional television, independent study and correspondence courses, size of class, individual consultation and tutoring, counseling, concentration on specific students, the student's involvement, the amount of time spent in study, distraction by jobs, and extracurricular activities, size of school, the qualities of teachers that can be rated by principals and supervisors, nongraded schools, team teaching, ability grouping, progressivism versus traditionalism, discussion versus lecture, group-centered versus teacher-centered approaches, the use of frequent quizzes, and programmed instruction. Studies of all these have failed to show that they make a consistent and significant difference.

Stephens considered briefly the possibility that the negative results are due to methodological errors, such as concentrating on one narrow segment of achievement, using insensitive tests, employing poor controls, exerting overcontrol that holds constant too much and thus restricts the differences, and using too stringent a criterion of statistical significance. But, all in all, Stephens concluded, the negative results are only to be expected, because "in the typical comparison of two administrative devices (such as teaching methods) we have two groups that are comparable in the forces responsible for (say) 95 percent of the growth to be had and which differ only in the force that, at best, can affect only a small fraction of the growth."[7]

At any rate, according to many writers, of whom Stephens is merely the most systematic, the major generalization to be drawn from research is that variations in teaching and educational practice do not make any consistent, significant, or practical difference.

Coleman Report
Apparent support for this view of the effects of educational variables on scholastic achievement can be found in the Coleman Report, *Equality of Educational Opportunity.*[8] According to that report, when the social background and attitudes of individual students and their schoolmates are held constant, achievement is

only slightly related to school characteristics, such as per pupil expenditures, books in the library, and a number of other facilities and curricular measures. Conversely, the report found that family background accounted for a relatively high proportion of the variance in student achievement. Stephens seems to be vindicated by the Coleman Report.

Questioning the Pessimism

So far we have considered the reasons for pessimism about the promise of empirical research on teaching, as offered by reviews of the research, by a systematic theory of schooling, and by the recent and massive Coleman Report. Now let us raise some questions about these lugubrious views.

In the first place, these dismal generalizations may not do complete justice to the research domains for which they have been made. Here and there, in research on teaching methods, on teacher personality and characteristics, and on social interaction in the classroom, it might have been possible to come up with more sanguine judgments about the meaning of the research findings.

The disparaging statements about the yield of past research may reflect the fact that research workers are inveterate critics. Their reflex on hearing about positive findings is to look for flaws in rationale, design, sampling, measurement, and statistical analysis. Only when such a quest for error is unsuccessful are research workers willing to grant credence to positive findings.

This attitude is, of course, all to the good. It protects against fallacies, artifacts, and wishful thinking. But it can also be carried to the point of wholesale and unwarranted rejection of what has gone before. We need more searching reviews of what research on teaching has to offer. Such reviews would piece together the evidence from a variety of approaches to a given problem and determine whether constructive suggestions concerning the practice of teaching might be warranted. The Educational Resources Information Center (ERIC) Clearinghouses, with their improved facilities for tracking down and collating research, ought to make possible "state-of-the-art" papers based on more meticulous sifting of the literature. If so, my guess is that future conclusions about research on teaching will be less melancholy and that Stephens' theory will tend to be disproven as positive results emerge and survive.

What about the Coleman Report? Here also there are reasons for questioning the pessimism. According to Bowles and Levin, the research design of the Coleman study "was overwhelmingly biased in a direction that would dampen the importance of school characteristics."[9] For example, expenditure per pupil was measured in terms of the average expenditure within an entire school district rather than within the given school in which the pupils were located. Hence the expenditure per pupil was overstated for schools attended by lower class students and understated for schools attended by students of higher social status.

Further, as Bowles and Levin have pointed out, the Coleman study used faulty statistical models in estimating the importance of school factors in accounting for achievement. In the report, the importance of a variable was estimated in terms of how much the proportion of variance in achievement explained was increased by adding that variable to the multiple regression equation. But, as Bowles and Levin have indicated, if two predictor variables are correlated, then the additional proportion of variance in achievement that each will explain is "dependent on the order in which each is entered into the regression equation . . . the shared portion of variance in achievement which could be accounted for by either X_1 or X_2 will always be attributed to that variable which is entered into the regression first. Accordingly, the explanatory value of the first variable will be overstated, and that of the second variable understated."[10] Thus when the family background characteristics are entered into the regression first and school resources are entered second, the amount of variance accounted for by the school resource variables is "consistently derogated."[11]

Despite these biases, the Coleman Report found that measures of teacher quality were significantly related to achievement, probably because teacher characteristics were measured individually and averaged for each school. Indeed, the report stated that teacher characteristics accounted for a "higher proportion of variation in student achievement than did all other aspects of the school combined, excluding the student body characteristics."[12] These teacher characteristics were family educational level, years of experience, localism (living in the area most of their lives), a teacher's own educational level, score on a vocabulary test, preference for middle class students, and proportion of teachers in the school who were white. And such factors make a bigger difference, according to the Coleman Report, for Black than for white students, perhaps because their out-of-school environment contributes less of the spontaneous educative forces of which Stephens writes. Accordingly, the characteristics of teachers who work with culturally disadvantaged pupils become all the more important.

These findings of the Coleman Report and the Bowles-Levin analysis indicate that Stephens' view of the relative unimportance of school and teacher variables may be unwarranted. More adequate surveys of educational achievement, analyzed with more sophisticated statistical tools, may show that teacher behaviors and characteristics make a substantial difference.

Some Positive Statements

Now, having emphasized the difficulties of making positive research-based statements about successful teaching behaviors, I wish nonetheless to attempt such statements—to attempt what is altogether unfashionable among students of research on teaching. My procedure will be to present a series of operational definitions of teacher behaviors that seem to belong on the same dimension. These definitions will be drawn from various research procedures and measuring instruments. Then, I shall cite some of the evidence on which it is possible to base the inference that these behaviors or characteristics are desirable. Finally, I shall provide a single summary term that may be used to label this dimension of behaviors and characteristics. (In part, this section is based on an earlier paper.[13]) In short, I shall attempt to piece together some evidence from a variety of approaches. I do not consider my present effort to be very convincing. It is intended merely to illustrate the kind of effort that may alleviate the pessimism stemming from other reviews.

Behavior Dimension A
First, let us consider two of the well-known categories for

analysis developed by Flanders[14] for use by classroom observers. Category 1 is "Accepts and clarifies the feeling tone of the students in a non-threatening manner . . . ," and Category 2 is "Praises or encourages student action or behavior. Jokes that release tension not at the expense of another individual, nodding head or saying 'um hum?' and 'go on' are included." At the end of a period of observation, one determines the number of instances of behavior in these two categories.

A second example of this dimension of teacher behavior can be seen in the responses of teachers to *The Minnesota Teacher Attitude Inventory.*[15] Here, the teacher responds on a five-point agree-disagree scale to such statements as "Most children are obedient," "Minor disciplinary situations should sometimes be turned into jokes," "Most pupils lack productive imagination," and "Most pupils are resourceful when left on their own."

As a third example of the same dimension consider teachers' responses to the California F Scale.[16] Among the items are "Obedience and respect for authority are the most important virtues children should learn," "People can be divided into two distinct classes: the weak and the strong," and "Most of our social problems would be solved if we could somehow get rid of the immoral, crooked, and feeble-minded people."

A fourth example can be drawn from the work of Ryans,[17] who developed a Teacher Characteristics Schedule comprised of such items as the following: "Pupils can behave themselves without constant supervision," "Most pupils are considerate of the teacher's wishes," and "Most teachers are willing to assume their share of the unpleasant tasks associated with teaching."

Now, what is the basis for the proposition that certain patterns of responses to attitude statements of this kind, or behaviors of the kind tabulated in the first two of Flanders' categories, are "desirable"? The answer is that these kinds of attitudes and behaviors tend to be correlated positively with favorable assessments of the teachers by pupils and trained observers, and with pupils' scores on achievement tests. The Minnesota Teacher Attitude Inventory has been found fairly consistently to correlate positively with favorable mean ratings of the teachers by their pupils.[18] The items of Ryans' inventory correlated positively with observers' ratings of elementary school teachers on all three of his teacher behavior patterns—warm, understanding, friendly versus aloof, egocentric, and restricted; responsible, businesslike, systematic versus evading, unplanned, and slipshod; and stimulating, imaginative versus dull, routine.[19] Similarly, Flanders[20] has reported consistent positive relationships between the degree to which teachers behave in accordance with these two categories and their scores on achievement tests adjusted for pupil ability. McGee[21] found that pupils' scores on the California F Scale correlated .6 with previous ratings of the teachers by trained observers on dimensions like aloof versus approachable, unresponsive versus responsive, dominative versus integrative, and harsh versus kindly. Cogan[22] found that descriptions of teachers by their students on similar items correlated positively with the amount of required and also voluntary school work done by the pupils.

In short, a substantial body of evidence justifies two conclusions: (1) Teachers differ reliably from one another on a series of measuring instruments that seem to have a great deal in common. (2) These reliable individual differences among teachers are, by and large, consistently related to various desirable things about teachers.

What term can be applied to the desirable end of this dimension of behaviors and attitudes? Teachers at this desirable end tend to behave approvingly, acceptantly, and supportively; they tend to speak well of their own pupils, pupils in general, and people in general. They tend to like and trust rather than fear other people of all kinds. How they get that way is not our concern at the moment. The point I am making is that it is not impossible to find extremely plausible similarities among the teacher behaviors measured and found desirable by a number of independent investigators working with their own methods, instruments, and concepts. Although any single term is inadequate, it seems safe to use the term "warmth." Teacher warmth, operationally defined as indicated above, seems—on the basis of abundant and varied research evidence—to be quite defensible as a desirable characteristic of teachers.

Behavior Dimension B

To identify a second dimension of teacher behavior, we begin with two more of Flanders' categories. Category 3 is "Accepts or uses ideas of student: clarifying, building, or developing ideas suggested by a student," and Category 4 is "Asks questions: asking a question about content or procedure with the intent that a student answer." In the classrooms of teachers that behave in these ways relatively often, one also finds more instances of Category 8: "Student talk-response: talk by students in response to teacher. Teacher initiates the contact or solicits student statement," and Category 9: "Student talk-initiation: talk by students which they initiate. If 'calling on' student is only to indicate who may talk next, observer must decide whether student wanted to talk. If he did, use this category."

A second example of this dimension of teacher behavior may be seen in the research on what is called "learning by discovery." This research deals with the question, "How much and what kind of guidance should the teacher provide? ... the degree of guidance by the teacher varies from time to time along a continuum, with almost complete direction of what the pupil must do at one extreme to practically no direction at the other."[2 3] This dimension consists of the degree to which the teacher permits pupils to discover underlying concepts and generalizations for themselves, giving them less rather than more direct guidance. The teacher at the higher level of this dimension realizes that it is not always desirable merely to tell the pupil what you want him to know and understand. Rather, it is sometimes better to ask questions, encourage the pupil to become active, seek for himself, use his own ideas, and engage in some trial and error. This kind of teaching represents a willingness to forbear giving the pupil everything he needs to know; it does not mean abandoning the pupil entirely to his own devices.

What is the evidence that this dimension of teacher behavior—exemplified in Flanders' categories and in teaching-by-discovery—has a significant relationship to something educationally desirable? Flanders[2 4] found that what he called indirectness in teachers went along with greater achievement on the part of their pupils in units on geography and geometry. Flanders (in a personal communication) has referred to some dozen studies by various investigators that have yielded positive correlations between his dimension of indirectness and measures of student achievement. Ausubel concluded from his review of the experiments on learning by discovery that the furnishing of completely explicit rules is relatively less effective than some degree of arranging for pupils to discover rules for themselves.[25]

It seems safe to say that a reasonable use of the guided discovery method, or "indirectness," in teaching is desirable. Teachers not sensitized to its desirability typically exhibit too little indirectness. As Flanders[26] put it, "our theory suggests an indirect approach; most teachers use a direct approach."

Behavior Dimension C

The third dimension of teacher behavior to be discussed is more difficult to define operationally, and its connection with desirable outcomes is, despite great plausibility, still not well established empirically. This is the kind of behavior that reflects the teacher's intellectual grasp, or "cognitive organization," of what he is trying to teach.

In one investigation, teachers were tested as to whether they understood the processes and concepts of multiplication; one item measured the teacher's understanding of the reason for moving each sub-product one digit to the left when the multiplier has more than one digit.[27] Studies by B. O. Smith and his co-workers have dealt with the degree to which the teacher's verbal behavior manifests an understanding of the logical properties of a good definition, explanation, or conditional inference.[28] Ausubel has studied the degree to which the teacher, or his instructional material, provides a set of "organizers" for his subject matter that embodies "relevant ideational scaffolding," discriminates new material from previously learned material, and integrates it "at a level of abstraction, generality, and inclusiveness which is much higher than that of the learning material itself."[29] Other research workers express similar ideas in such terms as "cognitive structure" (Ausubel[30] and Bruner[31]), "learning structure" (Gagné[32]), and "logic tree" (Hickey and Newton[33]).

Although the general conception of this aspect of teaching

behavior can be identified, operational definitions are hard to come by. Perhaps the best operational definitions of such variables must be inferred from the procedures of those who develop programmed instructional materials. These procedures call for behavioral definitions of objectives and detailed "learning structures"[34] that analyze the steps involved in achieving a "terminal behavior" into hierarchies of subtasks. Gagné illustrated such learning structures in mathematics and science; Glaser and Reynolds[35] worked out a detailed sequence of sub-behaviors involved in programmed instructional materials for teaching children to tell time from a clock.

In some ways, the injunctions derived from this kind of technical work on teaching and learning have implications for curriculum development rather than for teaching as such. But the curriculum is inevitably shaped through the teacher's behavior in the classroom as well as in the materials that his pupils read. The implications of such instructional research for the behavior of the live teacher in the classroom seem clear: If curricular material should exhibit a valid cognitive organization, so should the behavior of the teacher.

Conclusion

What can we conclude on the question, Can science contribute to the art of teaching? As you will recall, I began by defining successful teaching behavior as that found by empirical methods to be related to something desirable about teachers, and by restricting the discussion to teacher behavior in the conventional classroom in which most of the empirical research on teachers' behaviors and characteristics has been done. I then reviewed some of the reasons for a pessimistic answer to the question, namely, the negative findings and even a general theory that rationalizes the findings of much of the research on teaching and other educational practices. Then, I proceeded to consider some bases for questioning the pessimism, namely, the inadequacies of past analyses of the research literature and errors in statistical weightings of teacher and school variables as correlates of achievement in school. Finally, I attempted to illustrate the kind of collation of the evidence from research on teaching that may yield a better basis for more affirmative answers in the future. My examples of such collations of past research are, of course, far from adequate as evidence of anything. They merely serve at present as bases for hypotheses to be tested by the more valid research designs now available.

The field of research on teaching is today engaged in continuous and intensive analysis of its approaches and theoretical formulations (e.g., Gage and Unruh[36]). More complex research designs capable of taking more categories of significant variables into account are now being propounded (e.g., Siegel and Siegel[37]). The psychological, educational, and methodological sophistication of research workers is being raised by greatly improved pre-doctoral and post-doctoral training programs. And more adequate financial support is providing better organizations and facilities for educational research and development. The faith persists that educationally significant differences can be consistently produced in the future as new intellectual and material resources are brought to bear on educational problems.

Notes

1. American Educational Research Association. "Committee on the Criteria of Teacher Effectiveness," *Journal of Educational Research*, 1953, p. 657.
2. O.G. Brim, Jr. *Sociology and the Field of Education*. New York: Russell Sage Foundation, 1958, p. 32.
3. N.E. Wallen and R.M.W. Travers. "Analysis and Investigation of Teaching Methods." In N.L. Gage (Ed.) *Handbook of Research on Teaching*. Chicago: Rand McNally, 1963, p. 484.
4. J.W. Getzels and P.W. Jackson. "The Teacher's Personality and Characteristics." In N.L. Gage (Ed.) *Handbook of Research on Teaching*. Chicago: Rand McNally, 1963, p. 574.
5. J. Withall and W.W. Lewis. "Social Interaction in the Classroom." In N.L. Gage (Ed.) *Handbook of Research on Teaching*. Chicago: Rand McNally, 1963, p. 708.
6. J.M. Stephens. *The Process of Schooling*. New York: Holt, Rinehart, and Winston, 1967.

7. *Ibid.*, p. 84.
8. J.S. Coleman *et al. Equality of Educational Opportunity.* Washington, D.C.: U.S. Department of Health, Education, and Welfare; Office of Education, 1966. Government Printing Office, Superintendent of Documents, Catalog #FS5-238:38001.
9. S. Bowles and H.M. Levin. "The Determinants of Scholastic Achievement: An Appraisal of Some Recent Evidence," *Journal of Human Resources*, 1968.
10. *Ibid.*, p. 20.
11. *Ibid.*, p. 21.
12. Coleman *et al.* "Equality of Educational Opportunity," *loc. cit.*
13. N.L. Gage. "Desirable Behaviors of Teachers," *Urban Education*, 1965, pp. 85-95.
14. N.A. Flanders. "Teacher Influence, Pupil Attitudes, and Achievement." Minneapolis: University of Minnesota, College of Education, November 30, 1960. (Final Report, Cooperative Research Project No. 397, U.S. Office of Education.)
15. W.W. Cook, C.H. Leeds, and R. Callis. *The Minnesota Teacher Attitude Inventory.* New York: Psychological Corporation, 1951.
16. H.M. McGee. "Measurement of Authoritarianism and Its Relation to Teachers' Classroom Behavior," *Genetic Psychology Monographs*, 1955, pp. 89-146.
17. D.G. Ryans. *Characteristics of Teachers.* Washington, D.C.: American Council on Education, 1960.
18. A.H. Yee. "Is the Minnesota Teacher Attitude Inventory Valid and Homogeneous?" *Journal of Educational Measurement*, 1967, pp. 151-161.
19. Ryans. *Characteristics of Teachers, loc. cit.*
20. Flanders. "Teacher Influence, Pupil Attitudes, and Achievement," *loc. cit.*
21. McGee. "Measurement of Authoritarianism and Its Relation to Teachers' Classroom Behavior," *loc. cit.*
22. M.L. Cogan. "The Behavior of Teachers and the Productive Behavior of Their Pupils: I 'Perception' Analysis; II 'Trait' Analysis," *Journal of Experimental Education*, 1958, pp. 89-105, 107-124.

23. L. Shulman and E. Keislar (Eds.) *Learning by Discovery: A Critical Appraisal.* Chicago: Rand McNally, 1966.
24. Flanders. "Teacher Influence, Pupil Attitudes, and Achievement," *loc. cit.*
25. D.P. Ausubel. *The Psychology of Meaningful Verbal Learning: An Introduction to School Learning.* New York: Grune & Stratton, 1963, p. 171.
26. Flanders. "Teacher Influence, Pupil Attitudes, and Achievement," *loc. cit.*
27. J.S. Orleans. *The Understanding of Arithmetic Processes and Concepts Possessed by Teachers of Arithmetic.* New York: Board of Education of the City of New York, Division of Teacher Education, Office of Research and Evaluation, 1952.
28. M. Meux and B.O. Smith. *Logical Dimensions of Teaching Behavior.* Urbana: Bureau of Educational Research, University of Illinois, 1961. (Mimeographed.)
29. Ausubel. *The Psychology of Meaningful Verbal Learning: An Introduction to School Learning, loc. cit.*
30. *Ibid.*
31. J.S. Bruner. *Toward a Theory of Instruction.* Cambridge: Harvard University Press, 1966.
32. R.M. Gagné. *The Conditions of Learning.* New York: Holt, Rinehart, and Winston, 1965.
33. A.E. Hickey and J.M. Newton. "The Logical Basis of Teaching: I The Effect of Sub-concept Sequence on Learning." Final Report to Office of Naval Research, Personnel and Training Branch, Contract Nonr-4215(00), January, 1964.
34. Gagné. *The Conditions of Learning, loc. cit.*
35. R. Glaser and H.H. Reynolds. "Instructional Objectives and Programmed Instruction: A Case Study." In C.M. Lindvall (Ed.) *Defining Educational Objectives.* Pittsburgh: University of Pittsburgh Press, 1964, pp. 47-76.
36. N.L. Gage and W.R. Unruh. "Theoretical Formulations for Research on Teaching," *Review of Educational Research,* June, 1967, pp. 358-370.
37. L. Siegel and L.C. Siegel. "The Instructional Gestalt." In L. Siegel (Ed.) *Instruction: Some Contemporary Viewpoints.* San Francisco: Chandler Publishing Co., 1967, pp. 261-290.

3.

Teacher Behavior Can Be Evaluated

David G. Ryans

Before discussing the evaluation of teaching and considering the six questions that provide the framework for this paper, I must say something about my conception of teaching behavior.

Note that I say, "my conception," for I will state assumptions about what constitutes teaching that satisfy my logic. These are not necessarily the same assumptions my colleagues may choose.

Some Assumptions About
the Nature of Teacher Behavior

Teacher behavior or teaching behavior may be described as a complexly organized set of behavior variables that interact and combine to comprise the activities of persons as they go about doing what is required of teachers, namely, telesic instrumental activities that take the form of (1) motivating and reinforcing behavior, (2) organizing and managing behavior, (3) presenting and demonstrating behavior, (4) evaluating behavior, and (5) counseling and advising behavior. These behaviors mediate pupil learning in teacher-controlled instructional situations.[1] Learning may take place in the absence of a person who serves as "teacher," and we could extend considerations to include the evaluation of

Reprinted from *The Evaluation of Teaching*, Copyright © 1967, by Pi Lambda Theta, with permission of the author and the publisher. The author is Director, Education Research and Development Center, University of Hawaii at Manoa.

learning mediated by, or teaching performed by, a textbook, a self-instruction program, or any experience that is expected to promote an individual's learning of some specified skill, knowledge, or attitude. But for present purposes the consideration of teaching is limited to the behavior of these persons commonly known as teachers.

The objective of teaching activities or teacher behaviors is to facilitate pupil learning that will contribute to the acquisition and development by the pupil of a repertoire of usable behavior in the form of skills, knowledge, understanding, procedures, and "sets" (including work habits, behaving styles, attitudes, value judgments, and personal adjustment). The ultimate goal of teaching is to provide the individual taught with a behavior base that will help to maximize (a) his personal satisfactions and welfare, and (b) his social productivity, that is, contributions of goods, services, and attitudes of value to society.

I shall assume at least five major categories of teacher behavior to be involved in attempting to achieve the objective just stated: (1) motivating and reinforcing behavior; (2) organizing, coordinating, managing behavior; (3) presenting, explaining, demonstrating behavior; (4) evaluating behavior; and (5) counseling and advising behavior.

By "motivating" or set-establishing "teacher behavior" I mean activities that are intended to maximize the degree to which the learner is appropriately oriented and ready for the intended learning. This involves making as certain as possible that the learner possesses the prerequisite behavior without which the new learning could not take place; and it involves making the situation such that the learner will attend to the directions and materials presented and will actively respond to them. By "reinforcing" behavior I mean teacher behavior directed at changing the probability that the behavior intended to be learned actually will be acquired and will be available for retrieval and use by the pupil.

The "organizing, coordinating, planning, managing teacher behavior" of which I speak relates to the arranging, programming, and integrating of information and methods available to a teacher and to the direction and maintenance of control over the conditions of learning.

By "presenting, explaining, demonstrating teacher behavior," I mean behavior directed at making available to the learner the information intended to be learned—information that is presumed to influence attainment of the educational objectives for which the teaching situation was planned.

"Evaluating teacher behavior" refers to the appraisal of (a) teaching behavior and (b) the effects of teaching behavior on pupil behavior. It involves activities which provide one source of feedback to both teacher and pupil. Evaluation is, of course, a judgmental process and must be preceded by assessment to provide a factual base.

By "counseling, advising, and guiding teacher behavior" I mean provision of information which helps the pupil or learner plan and organize his own behavior; its goal is to make the pupil more aware of his needs and objectives and ways in which he may maximize his personal satisfactions and his social worth.

These categories admittedly are arbitrary and overlap, but they provide one convenient way of breaking down the complex behavior we call teaching as we approach the problems of teaching evaluation.

Now I would like to go still a step further and state some assumptions about the underlying conditions that seem to contribute, in various combinations, to the five major categories of teacher behavior to which I have referred.

For convenience, we may divide the underlying conditions hypothesized to contribute to teacher behavior into two groups: (1) "characteristics of the teaching situation" and (2) "characteristics of the individual teacher." My comments on characteristics of the teaching situation will be brief for the moment, but I have no intention of minimizing the importance of such conditions, as you will observe as the discussion proceeds. Some of the classes of characteristics of the teaching situation which may have marked effect upon teaching behavior and which need be taken into account in teacher evaluation as a backdrop against which to view assessed teacher behavior are: the "milieu," including sociopsychological conditions, economic conditions, ethnic and cultural conditions, administrative policies, grade level or subject matter taught, and the like; the "resources," including physical facilities, teaching aids, available personnel, and so forth; the "pupils taught," including their ability level, motivation level, and expectations with regard to the educational experience; and the expectations held by parents and community. Later I will comment upon the relativity of criteria of teacher effectiveness and we should keep in mind that it is variations in these characteristics of the teaching situation that often determine differences in the degree to which a particular teaching act is judged effective.

Let us turn now to characteristics of the individual teacher that may underlie the kinds of molar teacher behavior I referred to as motivating, organizing, presenting, evaluating, and counseling. I shall assume five major classes of individual teacher characteristics: physical-physiological, abilities and capacities, behaving styles, affective sets, and information possessed by the teacher which is capable of being applied to a teaching situation.

There has been considerable, though still insufficient, research on characteristics of the teacher and we can, indeed, assess a number of generally agreed-upon characteristics with fair assurance.

What are some of the general abilities and capacities of the teacher that have been identified?[2, 3] One that naturally comes to our minds is academic ability. Although the criteria of teacher effectiveness often have been inadequate, time and again investigators have reported substantial relationships between academic ability and judged teaching effectiveness. Another important ability for teaching is what is sometimes known as "verbal-semantic ability"; and certainly we would all agree an important component of teaching is the teacher's ability to express himself clearly and properly in the language adopted by the culture. A third sort of ability important for teaching is what I sometimes call "information-processing ability." Here I am referring to a set of abilities which includes the teacher's ability to call up in his mind information pertinent to the teaching situation and alternative strategies for presenting that information; his ability to apply logical operations necessary for making decisions and to arrive at decisions appropriate to the situation; his ability to properly adapt, channel, and control his own behavior to appropriately communicate the intended cognitive, affective, or psychomotor information to the pupil in a way the pupil can receive it and apply it; his ability to perceive effects of his teaching behavior (to utilize feedback from pupils and others); and to alter his behavior to more effectively achieve the purpose of his teaching. These "information-processing abilities" are more difficult to assess than academic ability or verbal-semantic ability; at least, there has been less progress in the development of instruments that will reliably and validly reflect such abilities.

There is fairly general consensus among educators that behaving styles of the teacher are particularly important—in combination, of course, with relevant abilities and the possession of appropriate information. A large number of researchers have investigated teacher behaving styles and a wide variety of trait names have been attached to characteristics that administrators and investigators believe important. Very substantial evidence has accumulated over the past dozen years suggesting that at least five clusters of teacher behaving styles[4,5,6] seem to be identifiable and capable of assessment.

Let me list the teacher behaving styles that are most supported by research:

X—considerate, understanding, warm, sensitive, nurturant, and supportive teacher behavior;

Y—organizing, managing, orderly, responsible, and business-like teacher behavior;

Z—achievement motivating, stimulating, and imaginative teacher behavior;

E—expressive, attractive, clear, personally, and academically impressive teacher behavior; and

DI—directive, authoritarian (versus non-directive, integrative) teacher behavior.

No attempt will be made to review the literature on characteristics of the teacher, but attention must be called to the very complete volume edited by N.L. Gage[7] on behalf of the American Educational Research Association, the *Handbook of Research on Teaching*, particularly the chapters, "Testing Cognitive Ability and Achievement," "Analysis and Investigation of Teaching Methods," and "The Teacher's Personality and Characteristics." I would be remiss, also, if I did not mention the recent work on teacher behaving styles that is being carried on by Richard L. Turner of Indiana University and the thoroughgoing analytical research of Fred N. Kerlinger of New York University.

A class of characteristics of the individual teacher that is very closely related to the teacher's behaving styles is that which I shall call "affective sets."[8] I refer here to components of the emotional, attitudinal interest, and belief context that appear to operate as "determining tendencies" or "response tendencies" and which help to determine teachers' behavior in particular situations. In this category, again, there has been substantial research and there is considerable agreement on several classes of affective sets that may be identified and assessed. Let me list these:

> B—academic-centered (traditional) as contrasted with permissive child-centered (progressive) educational beliefs or viewpoints;
>
> PI—professional involvement and satisfaction-career motivation;
>
> R—favorable attitudes toward pupils (and, Q-favorable attitudes toward school personnel); and
>
> S—emotional adjustment.

A number of us have conducted analyses and extended research on academic-centered as compared with permissive child-centered teacher-held viewpoints,[9, 10] but the recent work of Kerlinger has been particularly noteworthy in pointing out the importance of this attitudinal domain in determining what people expect teachers to be like, and also in providing a thoroughgoing analysis of these teacher characteristics. Kerlinger[11, 12] infers from a number of studies he has conducted that these affective sets are perhaps the basic factors contributing to what a particular individual or group of individuals believes to be desirable characteristics of teachers. Kerlinger[13] also points out close relationships between these "traditional" and "progressive" viewpoints and descriptions of such behaving styles as warm and friendly, organized and businesslike, and stimulating and imaginative teacher behavior. (High correlation of academic-centered and permissive child-centered educational viewpoints with behaving styles X, Y, and Z were also found by the author in his early studies and more recently by Turner[14] in his closely related research.)

Interest in teaching and professional satisfaction received token attention a number of years ago when I conducted exploratory studies in connection with the administration of the National Teacher Examinations; but when the Teacher Characteristics Study was undertaken this affective set did not attain significance as a separate factor—perhaps because it was submerged among other personal characteristics of the teacher. The recent work of Turner[15] finds substantial and clear evidence of the importance of a factor of career motivation and professional involvement, a factor that Turner has been able to identify and measure successfully. Indeed, Turner feels that for certain purposes of identifying successful as compared with unsuccessful teachers, the scale he has developed to measure "career motivation" may be one of the most significant of those available.

Attitude[16,17] toward pupils is fairly highly correlated with educational viewpoints, that is, permissive child-centered as compared with academic-centered. However, since attitude toward pupils is a rather clearly identified and readily measured characteristic, and since it does appear to relate to the basic underlying opinions of what constitutes good teaching, it certainly should be listed here as one of the important teacher affective sets. It should be noted that attitude toward other school personnel, such as administrators and fellow teachers, and attitude toward parents also contribute to teaching behavior.

Emotional adjustment also is generally agreed to be a significant attribute of the teacher as the teacher is considered in relation to his pupils.[18,19] Adjustment can be fairly readily assessed and research has revealed a number of significant relationships to other characteristics of the teacher.

The last of the classes of characteristics of the individual teacher I shall refer to is that of "information" possessed by the teacher. Here I refer to subject-matter knowledge, to knowledge of professional information and techniques, to understanding of general cultural topics and their relationships, and similar types of knowledge and understanding that are basic to the teacher's performance of his responsibilities. By "information possessed" I am thinking of knowledge and understanding that is accessible for recall and application as the teacher performs the "information-processing" functions mentioned earlier. We do, of course, have relatively adequate means of assessing the information possessed by the teacher.

I think it may be appropriate at this point to comment upon the distinction between teacher assessment and teacher evaluation, and the relativity of teacher evaluation to characteristics of the teaching situation that need to be taken into account.

Assessment relates to quantified or quasi-quantified description. When we *assess* some characteristic of some thing or behavior, we are concerned with the degree to which that characteristic is manifest. In assessing a characteristic of a teacher, we are trying to estimate the extent to which that defined characteristic is manifested by the teacher.

Teacher evaluation has to do with judgment relating to the "goodness" of teacher behavior, judgment that should be derived from assessments of clearly defined, observable teacher characteristics considered in light of agreed-upon educational objectives and the expectancies of individuals or groups with respect to teacher behavior, that is, in light of evaluative criteria approved by the schools and community in which a particular teacher teaches. To adequately carry out evaluation of teaching, we must have evaluative criteria that have been agreed upon, we must have some taxonomy and description of characteristics that comprise teaching behavior, and we must have some means of assessing or measuring those characteristics. Later I shall note that we also should have information about the relationships between observable teacher characteristics and the evaluative criteria—some evidence that the characteristics we may assess are indeed related to the criteria we employ.

When we talk about teacher evaluation we always proceed from the context of an accepted value system. We view teacher behavior in light of a set of attitudes and opinions reflecting the sorts of behavior we approve and prefer, and the kinds of behavior we disapprove and find unacceptable. The use of words like "good" or "superior" introduces value concepts. And value judgments, and the value concepts and systems on which they are based, grow out of highly personal biases, preferences, beliefs, opinions, and attitudes we hold as individuals. To the extent that any group of persons share in common certain expectancies and biases about teachers and teaching, "good" teaching may be defined for that particular group. This means that it is a responsibility of any group that is undertaking teacher evaluation to define what constitutes "good" or "poor" teaching for that group.

What this adds up to is that value systems concerning teaching are relative rather than absolute. So far as specific characteristics of the teacher are concerned, what is judged "good" teaching by one person, one community, or at one time, may not be similarly viewed as "good" by another person, another community, or at some later time.

Based upon his research, Kerlinger[20, 21] has pointed out that the question, "What are the desirable traits of teachers?" is not answerable in an absolute sense; that we should ask, rather, "What traits of teachers do different sets of individuals believe are desirable in teachers?" Kerlinger's investigations[22, 23] suggest that individual perceptions of desirable traits of teachers are often colored by the emphasis an individual may give to such behaving styles as X, Y, and Z that we noted earlier. Kerlinger advises that in trying to determine what is considered effective teaching, one must recognize that any person's opinion about good or poor teaching is a reflection of his basic educational orientation and we must know the underlying criteria (for example, X, Y, and Z) operating to predispose his opinion.

It also may be worth noting that in evaluating teachers the evaluator's concepts of "good" and "poor" teaching behavior may not always fall on the same continuum; that even for a specified group of teachers, such as mathematics teachers, behaviors considered "good" may be qualitatively different from those considered "poor."[24, 25] I found clear evidence of this in trying to determine the factors considered by principals in identifying good and poor teachers.

In Kerlinger's[26] studies he found substantial evidence that the basic attitudes toward teaching of "traditionalism" and "progressivism" constituted two relatively independent dimensions—that they were not necessarily at opposite poles on a single dimension.

Numerous findings indicating variations in teacher characteristics with a variety of conditions of teaching are reported in my book *Characteristics of Teachers*.

Turner[27] recently has reported results which indicate that in appraising beginning teachers, the emphasis of supervisory personnel on teacher "task performance" and "ability to organize" (behaving style Y) materially increases as the proportion of working class to middle class schools in the school system increases. Turner finds this not to be surprising if the supervisor is hypothesized to have a concept of the prevailing type of child with which his system deals and of the kinds of teacher behavior most relevant to teaching children of this type. Among middle class schools the Teacher Characteristics Schedule scales having to do with "friendly, understanding teacher behavior" and "stimulating, imaginative teacher behavior," and the scale devised by Turner estimating "teacher involvement-career motivation" showed particularly large and significant differences.

I also should like to mention the interesting report of G.E. Dickson,[28] *The Characteristics of Teacher Education Students in the British Isles and the United States*. Dickson found significant differences in abilities, behaving styles, affective sets, and information possessed that seem to depend upon cultural influences. One of the most surprising cultural differences was with respect to educational viewpoints or beliefs, with students from the United States tending to be substantially more "learning-centered" and students from the British Isles more "child-centered and permissive" as measured by the appropriate scale of Ryans' Teacher Characteristics Schedule.

I have dwelt upon this matter of relativity of teacher characteristics with cultural conditions, with socioeconomic conditions, and with expectancies of different individuals at some length because this is so fundamental to our thinking as we approach the problem of the evaluation of teaching.

Now, to move on to the questions posed for this paper:

What Are the Assumptions in the Premise "Teaching Can Be Evaluated"?

I would like to state seven assumptions or postulates that seem to me to be required for one to proceed with teacher evaluation and, actually, for any scientific study of teacher behavior or the conduct of teacher education programs. The assumptions which I think need to be made are:

1. *Teacher behavior is characterized by lawfulness and order.*

What we are saying here is that specific teacher acts and characteristics form classes or sets of teacher behavior, the acts and characteristics comprising each class being characterized by common properties which serve to describe that class of teacher behavior. This assumption also implies that classes of teacher behavior are characterized by some degree of stability or consistency. And it implies that the phenomena of teacher behavior are logically related and that it is possible to discover and describe the relationships between different classes. A further implication that is logically consistent is that when the characteristics of teachers, their antecedent and concomitant conditions, and their inter-relationships are identified, teacher behavior may be predicted—at least, within limits.

2. *Empirical study and inductive inference (scientific induction) provide a valid approach to the understanding of teacher behavior.*

I will not dwell on this point, but it does require assumption of the existence and applicability of sampling theory and probability theory, and in general, of the practicability of an inductive approach to the understanding of teacher behavior proceeding from data provided by observation.

3. *Teacher behavior is observable.*

This assumption is an important one if we are to engage in teacher evaluation.[29] It means we assume that classes of teacher behavior have distinguishing features which permit their identification; that samples of teacher behavior and correlates of teacher behavior may be observed in some manner, that is, that teacher behavior is not private, intangible, and unmeasurable; that the conditions of observation of teacher behavior can be controlled, at least to a reasonable degree, making comparability of assessments possible; that teacher behaviors are both qualitatively and quantitatively discriminable—and therefore can be assessed. A number of other implications are involved here; I shall not go into them now.

4. *Individual differences exist in observable teacher behavior.*

With respect to a particular behavior, teachers are not all alike; different behaviors characterize different teachers in varying degrees and in varying combinations.

5. *Teacher behavior is social in nature.*

What I mean here is that in instructional situations where a teacher is involved, that situation is by nature a social situation. In addition to the teacher, there are learners or pupils who are in communication with the teacher and with each other and who are presumably influenced by the behavior of the teacher.

6. *The ultimate goal or end product of teacher behavior is a set of specified pupil behaviors.*

Teacher behavior consists of instrumental operations or activities on the part of the teacher, the objective of which is to influence the acquisition of pupil behavior of a specified kind.

7. *Teacher behavior is relative.*

We already have dwelt upon this point—that there is nothing inherently good or bad in any given teacher behavior or set of behaviors, but that teacher behavior is good or bad, effective or ineffective, only to the extent that such behavior conforms or fails to conform to a particular value system that has been agreed upon.

Perhaps I have not been inclusive, but I think these are some of the assumptions we need to make if we are going to attempt teaching evaluation. Some readers may not be willing to agree to these assumptions, but if not accepted I believe it follows logically that you cannot undertake to evaluate teaching. These are the general assumptions from which we proceed in seeking to identify, describe, assess, consider relationships involved, and evaluate teacher behavior. Personally, I accept them and am willing to be counted as one of those who believes teacher behavior can and should be evaluated.

How Can Teaching Be Assessed and Evaluated and Who Should Be Responsible for Evaluation?

In responding to this question, may I preface my remarks by

asking that you recall the distinction between the assessment of teaching behavior and the evaluation of teaching behavior. Let us turn our attention first to assessment and then to evaluation.

Both commercially available and specially constructed tests and examinations may be used to assess a teacher's abilities and the information he possesses. Paper-and-pencil scales similarly can be used to arrive at usable estimates of the teacher's affective sets—his attitudes, emotional adjustment, educational viewpoints, and the like.

For assessments in the important area of teacher "behaving styles," we usually must resort to direct observation and rating. We may, if we choose, resort to retrospective or *post hoc* ratings, where we ask someone, who is presumed to be competent and to know the teacher who is to be assessed, to make judgments about remembered teacher behavior. Such ratings may be made by principals, fellow teachers, the teacher himself, or they may be made by the teacher's students. Some ratings of this type are useful, but they usually cannot be analytic and very often they are unreliable (unless we have a large number of judges) because of the variety of ways different judges interpret trait names of the behavior to be judged and also because of differences in the interpretation of a particular observed behavior.

Observations and assessments of teacher behavior also may be made as the behavior is actually being performed—"teacher behavior in process" may be observed, interpreted, and recorded. The chief difficulties encountered in following this practice are similar to those involved in retrospective rating, except that observation and assessment make no great demand upon the memory of the judge and instead focus upon particular kinds of teacher behaviors as they occur. Variability in interpretation remains a source of unreliability. Judgmental errors growing out of the ambiguity of language and the variations of observers in perception and judgment can be corrected, however, by the use of trained observers. My own preference is for carefully selected and trained teams of observers, employed in a school system for the sole purpose of observing and assessing on-going teacher behavior. Under such a plan, each teacher may be visited on several occasions throughout the year for observation and assessment of teaching performance. With respect to any characteristic or behavior, the pooling of independent ratings of the judges constitutes a reliable assessment of a teacher's performance. The evaluators must be responsible and informed educators; they must be well trained; and their integrity must be above question. But such a procedure can provide some of the assessment data that are generally inaccessible.

Direct observation is more subjective, that is, more personal, than assessment based upon well-made examinations of knowledge and understanding of subject-matter content, but interobserver reliability of assessments can be substantially increased and the subjectivity and personal impression factors materially reduced (a) through careful development of the observation and observation-recording instruments (involving an iterative process of "preparation, tryout, and revision") carried out to reduce ambiguity of language employed and, insofar as possible, to yield assessments based upon observed teaching (rather than abstract concepts about teaching); (b) through training the observers in the use of the instruments; and (c) by using the observation instruments and trained observers to systematically record teacher behavior in process (rather than resorting to the use of *post hoc* assessments based upon "remembered" teacher behavior).[30]

You will note I have been talking about assessment of teaching behavior per se and have said nothing about judging teaching by assessment of the product of teaching behavior (pupil achievement and pupil change) or perhaps of directly observed pupil behavior. I recognize this as one approach to assessing overall teacher behavior, but at other places and times I have explained the rationale which leads me to prefer assessment of teaching behavior by direct methods rather than approaching it indirectly through observation of pupil behavior or measurement of pupil change.

To this point I have not touched upon the evaluation of teaching as such—the judgment that follows assessment. I believe, if we can achieve usable assessments, we will have taken a long stride toward solving the problem of evaluation. I do not want to imply, however, that the evaluative process should be tossed off lightly. I think the actual evaluation can be accomplished in either of two ways: (1) If the criteria against which assessments are to be judged can be agreed upon and if the weights to be given different components or aspects of teaching behavior can be agreed upon, then the combination of assessments to arrive at an evaluation (either unidimensional or multidimensional) often can be accomplished in a fairly objective manner; and (2) in less formal situations it probably is necessary for some individual, such as a supervisor or principal, to coordinate assessments and arrive at a summary evaluation for each teacher. Indeed, I suspect that in almost all situations some individual, hopefully someone who is adequately trained and capable of exercising objectivity, will need to review the evaluation and make final decisions with regard to action that may be taken in utilizing an evaluation for supervisory purposes, promotion, salary considerations, selection, and the like.

What Are the Components of the Context in Which Teaching Should Be Evaluated?

It would be unnecessary repetition for me to comment further on the components of teaching that can be assessed and should be evaluated. I have mentioned early in the discussion the classes of characteristics I assume to be important in teaching behavior and I also have suggested how certain of these can be assessed. I also have discussed the problem of the relativity of what is considered desirable and undesirable teaching behavior. I will only note, then, that the components of teaching behavior to be evaluated should be those that can be assessed with some assurance and ones that reflect the expectancies of individuals responsible for education in a particular situation.

What Are the Criteria to Be Used in Evaluating Teaching?

Although I have written[31] and spoken at length about the basic importance of the criterion problem and have attempted to classify different kinds of criteria that may be applied in studying teaching behavior, I am going to deal only very briefly with this topic. Indeed, I find in reviewing my earlier remarks there is not much more I can say without getting into a technical discussion of validity. I will comment that insofar as possible the criteria employed for evaluating teaching should be spelled out in behavioral terms, that is, in terms of actual teacher behaviors that can serve as benchmarks against which assessments of individual teacher behavior may be compared. Perhaps this is the most important single thing I can say in this paper.

And I am able to give no advice as to just "what" criteria should be used in teacher evaluation. For this relates to the value system espoused by the individuals responsible for education in a particular community and what they expect of teachers in light of their agreed-upon value system. I believe the selection and detailed spelling out of criteria of teacher effectiveness is a major concern of education; and with our tradition of autonomy of school districts in the United States, this means that it is incumbent upon each school system to think through the problem of what is expected of its teachers under different conditions and describe in behavioral terms the acceptable standards of teaching performance.

What Progress Has Been Made in Assessing the Components of Teaching and in Evaluating Teaching Effectiveness?

Earlier in this discussion we took a fragmentary look at some of the components of teaching behavior that had been identified and for which means of assessment had been developed. For review of the pertinent literature, attention was called to the *Handbook of Research on Teaching.*[32] The sections on "Teacher Effectiveness"[33, 34] in the third edition of the *Encyclopedia of Educational Research* also should be mentioned.

Much of the recent research on teachers and teaching has had to do with the fundamental problem of the description of teacher behavior and conditions with which various teacher characteristics and behaviors appear to be correlated. Considerable effort also has been directed at assessment. But relatively few investigators have attempted to study the evaluation of teaching as such during the last ten years or so. I think this may be due largely to difficulties imposed by the criterion problem and the time and labor required to designate behavioral criteria which reflect expectancies in particular teaching situations. It also is due, I suspect, to the insistence of many of us that we must be able to describe teacher behavior adequately and to have methods of assessing its various components before we tackle problems of evaluation.

Nevertheless, I would like to describe a few efforts with which I am particularly familiar which have approached, albeit tangentially, the problem of teaching effectiveness and which have suggested conditions that may under certain circumstances be correlates of good and poor teaching.

In one investigation carried out as part of the Teacher Characteristics Study,[35] we arbitrarily defined "good" teachers within a framework we had developed through classroom observation and assessment carried out by trained observers. Our research had indicated three prominent patterns of observable classroom behavior or behaving styles: Pattern X—friendly, understanding, sympathetic teacher behavior; Pattern Y—responsible, businesslike, systematic teacher behavior; and Pattern Z—stimulating, imaginative teacher behavior. In the study to which I wish to refer, we selected three groups of teachers who were uniformly high, uniformly average, and uniformly low on these major patterns of classroom behavior. Teachers who had been assessed one standard deviation or more above the mean on all three patterns were placed in the so-called "high" group. Teachers who had been assessed one standard deviation or more below the mean on all three patterns were placed in the so-called "low" group. You may judge for yourselves whether you wish to consider these teacher groups "good" and "poor."

We next proceeded to isolate characteristics of the teachers under study which appeared to distinguish between the criterion groups—between the high criterion group and the low criterion group. I will summarize the results very quickly. The "high" group of teachers as compared with the "low" almost uniformly expressed liking for personal contacts with other people. Members of the "high" teacher group also were very generous in their perceptions of other people—they expressed beliefs that very few pupils are difficult behavior problems, that very few people are influenced in their opinions and attitudes toward others by feelings of jealousy, and that most teachers are willing to assume their full share of extra duties in school. Teachers in the "high" group were predominantly between thirty-five and forty-nine years of age. They were married. They had attained better than average grades while in college. They had belonged to high school and college social groups. As children they had received lessons in dramatics, art, dancing, or music outside of school. They read a great deal. They had visited science museums and exhibitions during the current year. They frequently attended musical concerts and art lectures.

On the other hand characteristics which seemed to distinguish the "lowly assessed" teacher group from the "high" group suggest that the "low" teacher is self-centered, anxious, and restricted—this syndrome being indicated by teacher responses such as: considers favorable prospect of professional advancement an important factor in choice of teaching as a career; thinks a large proportion of teachers suffer from stomach trouble and ulcers brought on by unusual tensions relating to their work; feels a large proportion of people are inclined to worry more than they should; believes a substantial portion of parents' visits to school are made to criticize the teacher or the school; believes a large proportion of people are influenced in their opinions and attitudes toward others by feelings of jealousy. Teachers in the "low" group were predominantly in the late-middle and older age groups (that is, over fifty years of age in elementary school samples and over fifty-five years of age in secondary teacher samples). Teachers in the "low" group indicated preferences for activities which did not involve "contacts with people." With respect to certain kinds of experiences reported, the "low" group was almost the opposite of the "high" teacher group in that they read less and generally manifested less interest in participation in cultural affairs involving science, art, and music.

Now, let me refer to a slightly different study we conducted.[36] In this instance we selected an approximately representative sample of schools throughout the United States and asked the principal of each school to nominate (using a procedure that did not require actual naming of the teacher) the teacher in his school considered most "outstandingly superior" and the teacher considered most "notably poor." After having identified such superior and poor teachers, the principal was asked to give a packet of materials to each teacher who was nominated—an odd-numbered packet to the teacher considered superior and an even-numbered packet to the teacher considered poor. Each packet contained a request from the Teacher Characteristics Study office asking the teacher to complete a Teacher Characteristics Schedule which was enclosed and return it to the central office of the Study. We were thus able to make comparisons of a number of teachers who had been anonymously nominated as "good" or "poor." And we discovered a number of significant differences in mean score on characteristics measured by the Teacher Characteristics Schedule between the teachers judged by their principals to be "superior" and "poor." The more prominent differences were most frequently associated with scores on the Teacher Characteristics Schedule that reflected stimulating teacher behavior (Z), businesslike teacher behavior (Y), verbal ability (I), understanding and friendly teacher behavior (X), and favorable teacher opinion of pupils (R).

I will mention just one more investigation, one of Turner's studies[37] that was directed at the predictive relationship between certain characteristics of beginning teachers and beginning teacher problems.

Pre-test data with respect to characteristics measured by a revision of Ryans' Teacher Characteristics Schedule were obtained for a group of beginning teachers. Subsequently, a questionnaire was sent to each teacher's principal inquiring of areas in which the particular teacher most needed improvement. Teachers were divided into a "no problem" group and into several "problem" sub-groups according to the nature of problem named by the principal, for example, discipline, management, subject matter, social-emotional, and so forth.

A number of significant relationships were suggested. Teachers having management problems differed from those having no problems with respect to the characteristic, "attitude toward school staff" (Q), with the management problem group having less favorable attitudes than the no problem group. Teachers experiencing discipline problems differed significantly from those experiencing no problems on six characteristics: warm, friendly teacher (X); attitude toward school staff (Q); organized, businesslike teacher behavior (Y); stimulating, imaginative teacher behavior (Z); academic-centered versus child-centered educational viewpoints (B); and "problem-solving performance." Teachers with disciplinary problems appeared to be disorganized and unbusinesslike, relatively cool and aloof, "subject-centered," relatively routine in approach, and weak in dealing with skill areas. I cannot go into all of the results of Turner's research, but it is interesting to note that certain characteristics tended to recur as significantly related to more than one problem area, these characteristics of beginning teachers being lack of warmth and understanding (behaving style X), attitude toward school staff (characteristic Q), and organized, businesslike behavior (behaving style Y). Turner comments that "organized, businesslike teacher behavior," as estimated, also was one of the few variables that predicted which teachers would leave their position after the first or second year of experience. He concludes there is much to suggest that low scores on behaving style Y coupled with poor attitude toward other teachers and a distant relationship to pupils portend ill for the beginning elementary teacher.

What Are the Directions in Which Evaluation and Research Must Move if Clarification and Improvement of Teaching Are to Be Effective?

On several occasions I have tried to list what I considered to be "needed research" and future directions in the systematic study of teaching behavior.[38] It is relatively easy to name specific areas of research and even to organize them into classes such as "research growing out of logical analysis of the teaching process," "research stimulated by changing social, economic, and technological conditions," "development of methods and instruments necessary to assess and research teaching behavior," "research suggested by theoretical models of teaching," etc. All of us wish we understood better the relevant aggregates or compounds of teaching behavior, wish we could have a convenient taxonomy of teacher behavior that cataloged and classified the properties or characteristics of teachers, wish we knew how teacher behavior variables relate to observable, operationally defined behaviors of pupils, wish we knew the conditions that motivate and reinforce teacher behavior. We could proceed at length in this way. But I suspect the readers of this paper hoped some suggestions might be made for tackling more directly the problems of evaluation, and I shall limit my remarks accordingly.

In my opinion, the most important contribution that could be made to the evaluation of teaching and improvement of the teaching process would be attention on the part of the individual school systems to what I call the "prediction and evaluation research paradigm."

Although it is recognized that programs of evaluation must often, of necessity, be conducted with a minimum of prior research to provide the desirable basis, in the long run successful evaluation is possible only when a systematic procedure such as outlined by the "paradigm" is followed. The steps involved in this paradigm or model are not particularly unique; consciously or unconsciously every sophisticated researcher who attempts to aid the cause of prediction or evaluation takes them into account. Applied to teacher competency evaluation and prediction, these steps are:

1. Selection and specification of a value system (criterion) framework—the agreed-upon qualities that are desired or expected of teachers in a particular community and in a particular kind of teaching situation. Recall that this process of arriving at a set of such criteria necessarily is subjective and a matter of the value system individuals or groups of individuals may possess in common.

2. Identification of kinds of situations in which the agreed-upon "valued" teacher behaviors may occur and in which they may be observed and assessed.

3. Operational description (that is, description in terms of actual behaviors) of the agreed-upon valued behaviors that are to be assessed.

4. Identification of the properties of teacher classroom behavior that may be related to the operationally described criteria (that is, the descriptive cataloging of teacher characteristics and behaviors that occur in the classroom). Available research findings provide a substantial background of observable teacher characteristics and behaviors, but the taxonomy still is far from complete.

5. Conduct of research directed at identification of relationships between selected, operationally (that is, behaviorally) defined properties of teacher behavior (as noted in Step 4) and selected operationally defined "valued behaviors" in selected situations (as noted in Steps 1, 2, and 3).

When these steps have been taken and the paradigm followed through to its conclusion so that knowledge exists of the extent to which reliable relationships are present between "valued behaviors" and "observable behaviors," then the necessary groundwork has been laid for evaluation.

I have high hopes for the future, but I frankly cannot see how teacher evaluation can be successfully accomplished unless the procedure I have just mentioned is followed in each school system. Certainly, it is true that school systems may possess certain expectancies in common. As experience accumulates, it is reasonable to assume that what has been learned in one school system can be applied to another—provided the criteria that are acceptable and the conditions that obtain are not dissimilar. But at this early stage of the scientific movement in teacher evaluation, I think it will be an obligation of each school system to devote the time and energy necessary to arrive at Step 5 of the prediction and evaluation paradigm and to proceed to an acceptable program of teacher evaluation.

Notes

1. D.G. Ryans. "Assessment of Teacher Behavior and Instructions," *Review of Educational Research*, 33, 1963, pp. 415-441.
2. *Ibid.*
3. D.G. Ryans. "Prediction of Teacher Effectiveness," *Encyclopedia of Educational Research*. New York: Macmillan, 1960, pp. 1486-1491.
4. Ryans. "Assessment of Teacher Behavior and Instructions," *loc. cit.*
5. *Ibid.*
6. Ryans. "Prediction of Teacher Effectiveness," *loc. cit.*

7. N.L. Gage (Ed.). *Handbook of Research on Teaching*. Chicago: Rand McNally, 1963.

8. Ryans. "Assessment of Teacher Behavior and Instructions," *loc. cit.*

9. *Ibid.*

10. Ryans. "Prediction of Teacher Effectiveness," *loc. cit.*

11. F.N. Kerlinger. "Attitudes Toward Education and Perception of Teacher Characteristics: A Q Study," *American Educational Research Journal*, 1966.

12. F.N. Kerlinger. "The Factor Structure and Content of Perception of Desirable Characteristics of Teachers," *Educational and Psychological Measurement*, 1967.

13. F.N. Kerlinger. "The First- and Second-Order Structures of Attitudes Toward Education," *American Educational Research Journal*, 1967.

14. R.L. Turner. "Characteristics of Beginning Teachers: Their Differential Linkage with School System Types," *The School Review*, 73, 1965, pp. 48-58.

15. R.L. Turner. Comparison of teacher characteristics of inner city (working class) and outer city (middle class) teachers falling in upper vs. lower quarters of principals' ratings (personal communication, 1966).

16. Ryans. "Assessment of Teacher Behavior and Instructions," *loc. cit.*

17. Ryans. "Prediction of Teacher Effectiveness," *loc. cit.*

18. Ryans. "Assessment of Teacher Behavior and Instructions," *loc. cit.*

19. Ryans. "Prediction of Teacher Effectiveness," *loc. cit.*

20. Kerlinger. "Attitudes Toward Education and Perception of Teacher Characteristics," *loc. cit.*

21. Kerlinger. "The Factor Structure and Content of Perceptions of Desirable Characteristics of Teachers," *loc. cit.*

22. Kerlinger. "Attitudes Toward Education and Perception of Teacher Characteristics," *loc. cit.*

23. Kerlinger. "The Factor Structure and Content of Perceptions of Desirable Characteristics of Teachers," *loc. cit.*

24. Ryans. "Prediction of Teacher Effectiveness," *loc. cit.*

25. W. Weaver. "Good Teaching," *Science*, 151:3716, 1966, p. 1335.

26. Kerlinger. "Attitudes Toward Education and Perceptions of Teacher Characteristics," *loc. cit.*

27. R.L. Turner. "Characteristics of Beginning Teachers: Their Differential Linkage with School System Types," *The School Review*, 73, 1965, pp. 48-58.

28. G.E. Dickson *et al., The Characteristics of Teacher Education Students in the British Isles and the United States.* U.S.O.E. Cooperative Research Project 2518. Toledo, Ohio: University of Toledo, 1965.

29. D. Wolfe. "The Great Teachers," *Science*, 156:3650, 1964, p. 1421.

30. Ryans. "Prediction of Teacher Effectiveness," *loc. cit.*

31. *Ibid.*

32. N.L. Gage, *loc. cit.*

33. H.E. Mitzel. "Teacher Effectiveness." In *Encyclopedia of Educational Research.* New York: Macmillan, 1960, pp. 1481-1486.

34. Ryans. "Prediction of Teacher Effectiveness," *loc. cit.*

35. *Ibid.*

36. *Ibid.*

37. R.L. Turner. "Beginning Teacher Characteristics and Beginning Teacher Problems: Some Predictive Relationships." Presented at American Educational Research Association meeting, Chicago, 1966.

38. Ryans. "Prediction of Teacher Effectiveness," *loc. cit.*

4.

The Assessment of Proper Control and Suitable Learning Environment

Ned A. Flanders and
Greta Morine

A Point of Departure

This paper is concerned with criteria which can be used to evaluate how supervisors, principals, and teachers perform their adjunctive duties, help to create proper control, and jointly produce a suitable learning environment for the young people who are required by law to attend school. Criteria of evaluation refer to things that can be measured, so we must first ask what measurement techniques are valid and feasible.

If the goal of assessment is a one-time evaluation to be used for purposes of determining retention and merit pay increases, then for assessment to be *valid*, we need:

(1) strong general agreement on the meaning of *proper* in "proper control" and *suitable* in "suitable learning environment";

(2) strong research evidence linking particular teacher behaviors to both control and learning environment;

(3) measurement instruments that are well-developed, that measure most if not all of the facets of behavior related to control and learning environment, and probably

Reprinted with permission of the authors and the Far West Laboratory for Educational Research and Development, San Francisco, California. Ned A. Flanders is Associate Laboratory Director, Teacher Education Division, Far West Laboratory; Greta Morine is Associate Professor, Teacher Education Department, California State University, Hayward. At the time of this writing (October, 1972), Dr. Morine was on leave from CSU, Hayward, and was a Project Director, Teacher Education Division, Far West Laboratory.

instruments that will be administered by *outside* consultants rather than by local school personnel, in order to maintain objectivity of results.

None of the foregoing three requirements is *feasible*, given our multivalued culture, the current state of educational research, and the present financial situation of most school districts. Therefore, assessment viewed as a one-time evaluation *cannot* be valid and feasible at the present time. It is somewhat ironic that the legislative committee hearings on the Stull Bill* apparently provided no testimony (McDonald, 1972) on the adequacy or inadequacy of the currently available evaluation techniques. However, since the Bill makes provisions for counseling and advising certificated personnel after an evaluation, we can assume that there is a strong emphasis on the improvement of performance.

When the goal of assessment is seen as learning how to improve instruction, then a valid assessment requires:

(1) agreement between the teacher and the supervisor on the instructional goals and/or the instructional theory to be utilized;

(2) some research evidence linking particular teacher behaviors to control and learning environment;

(3) some measurement instruments that can be administered by local school personnel as well as by outside consultants; and

(4) some training materials to enable teachers and administrators to improve skills when a need for improvement has been identified.

There are areas of performance for which these requirements can be met. Therefore, assessment aimed at improvement of instruction can be considered to be both valid and feasible. Feasibility will be increased if at least some of the available training materials are self-instructional. This will make skill improvement more individualized and less expensive.

___

*California legislation requiring evaluation of the performance of certificated school personnel. (Editors.)

Clarifying Terms

In order to discuss how the provisions of the Bill dealing with adjunctive duties, proper control, and suitable learning environment can be implemented, it will be necessary to propose a meaning for the various terms that appear in the text. The two terms which stand out, begging for clarification, are *proper* control and *suitable* learning environment. A good deal of space could be assigned to this task, but we prefer to take a shorter, pragmatic approach. The definitions below were determined largely by the limited number of assessment techniques that are available and the mandate of the Bill. Those readers who would prefer to define these terms differently should remember to reconcile their preferences with the operational meanings that the assessment techniques provide.

1. *The goal* of evaluation and of the Stull Bill itself is the *improvement of education*, particularly teaching.

2. *Proper control* ultimately rests on a judgment that the methods of instruction are consistent with the purposes of instruction. Most teachers work in school districts which have a well-established curriculum of study. Yet any curriculum is primarily a guide which a teacher constantly adapts to his instructional purposes, his style of teaching, and his students. When this process of adaptation results in all of the students using the same materials and working on the same assignments under relatively close teacher supervision, a more formal and traditional pattern of active teacher control will seem consistent. When a teacher chooses to create the freedom necessary for independent, individualized learning activities, then a more flexible pattern of control will seem consistent. All teachers exert control. We can define proper control as the *teacher's ability to create and maintain learning activities in which the intended learning can occur without undue disruption*. The judgment of what is proper and what is improper will not be the same for different adaptations of the curriculum. For example, freedom to talk to another student, move about the room, choose one's own learning task, etc., might be considered symptoms of improper control in a formal classroom but they would be proper in a more open classroom. We might further note that proper control is essentially

an adult concept. The values of the parents, the teacher, the principal, or those who provide professional supervision are usually the primary determinants of what is "proper."

3. A *suitable learning environment*, on the other hand, is essentially a child-centered concept. A learning environment refers to the students' opportunity to exploit a situation for the purpose of learning. A suitable environment means that the arrangements for learning match the interests and abilities of the students who are there to learn. One important aspect of a suitable learning environment is that students can participate effectively no matter what their ethnic origins may be and regardless of the socio-economic level of the community. There are many features of a learning environment which we could emphasize, but for it to be suitable, we would at least expect *the students to be interested in coming to class, to look forward optimistically to the work involved, and to obtain a sense of satisfaction from participating, especially in terms of self-respect and self-confidence.*

4. *Adjunctive duties* are presumably to be distinguished from active teaching, administering, or supervising. One might guess they were added to the Stull Bill by those who could remember when teachers also taught Sunday School, principals were expected to plan the Community Chest drive, and supervisors were expected to join a hospital auxiliary. In today's schools, adjunctive duties may involve educators in projects to increase the parents' participation in the school, to revise curricula, or to redesign report cards. The most important adjunctive duty related to classroom control and learning environment is *taking the responsibility for analyzing one's own performance, exploring professional alternatives, and deciding when an alternative is an improvement; to this we add assisting others to do the same.*

5. *Competence and standards* are probably used in the language of the Bill in the simple sense of performing one's job in a satisfactory manner. In this paper we point out that information about an individual's performance can be used in several ways. To invoke standards usually means that criteria of performance can be identified and assessed, that certain minimal levels can be established, and that individual performance measures can be compared with norms from an appropriate reference

group. Unfortunately, it is difficult to invoke standards when adjunctive duties are not consistent from one individual to the next, when proper control varies from one situation to the next, and when a learning environment becomes suitable precisely because it is custom-built to meet the needs of a particular group of youngsters. Faced with this diversity, we suggest that information about *performance can be compared with behavioral descriptors of selected skills* which, in turn, might be derived from a model of teaching. Another alternative is to compare an individual's performance at one point in time with the same performance at another point in time in order to determine the presence or absence of change. These applications of "standards" are likely to improve instruction provided those in the field act wisely by adapting the provisions of the Stull Bill and using research results judiciously.

6. *Student progress* will be discussed here in terms of outcomes other than subject-matter achievement. Attitude inventories can be used to assess student perceptions of the teacher and the learning activities. Such measures are associated with patterns of verbal interaction (Flanders, 1970, p. 389). We would define student progress to include these student perceptions of the learning environment as well as patterns of desirable student behavior that can be observed during instruction.

Adjunctive Duties

Both teaching and non-teaching certificated personnel now face the task of evaluating professional performance. We have defined this task as an adjunctive duty which has been added to all certificated job descriptions. As a result, one can now say that it is the duty of supervisors, building principals, and teachers to participate in the evaluation of their own professional performance and to help evaluate the performance of their colleagues.

The same steps of overall evaluation can be used with a wide variety of adjunctive duties, such as projects to increase parent participation in the schools, to redesign report cards, or to change the curriculum.

Steps For Overall Evaluation

Procedure	Features to be Evaluated
1. The purpose of the project is decided by conferring with those who will participate.	Is the project easy/difficult, significant/insignificant, responsive to current priorities/not responsive, etc.?
2. Plans are made to assess progress at appropriate checkpoints.	Are plans practical (space/time/resources); are objectives specific/ambiguous, consistent with purpose/inconsistent, etc.?
3. Project is carried out.	Were final objectives and checkpoint objectives achieved/not achieved, did a change occur/not occur, can the nature of change be determined/not determined, etc.?
4. The consequences of the project are judged to be an improvement or not an improvement.	Were there sufficient/insufficient data to determine improvement, can results become part of the program/not part of program, etc.?

The above outline is a practical plan of evaluation which would have been appropriate at any point in the history of public education. Given the progress in analyzing teaching which has been accomplished in the 1960s, this old outline can now be implemented with much greater specificity, especially with regard to classroom instruction. The objectives stated in Step Two can be particular skills such as asking questions, using certain responsive acts more frequently, learning how to modify patterns of instruction from one situation to the next, or learning how to write the objectives of instruction in denotative language. This means that the standards of performance which are set are likely to be unique to each project, even though they can be assessed with considerable objectivity.

Teachers, of course, will vary widely in their knowledge of new assessment procedures and their skill in using them. We can expect that evaluation projects designed by less experienced teachers will make use of simple assessment procedures. We can hope that this kind of knowledge and skill will improve with experience so that more extensive evaluation projects may occur as teachers' competence increases.

Non-Teaching Certificated Personnel

The non-teaching certificated personnel who work most closely with teachers to improve both professional performance and instruction are likely to be supervisors and building principals. We propose that it is their adjunctive duty to promote the evaluation of instruction in ways that will contribute to the improvement of education.

Research. Studies of successful and unsuccessful attempts to improve public school education by means of various innovative programs have indicated that the school administrator plays a key role in the change process. Brickell (1964, pp. 503-505), surveying new instructional programs in New York State, noted that introduction of change depended almost exclusively upon administrative initiative. The most successful innovations were those which provided the most elaborate support to teachers as they attempted to change their instructional practice. Fox and Lippitt (1964, p. 297) found a much higher probability of instructional improvement when the efforts of the classroom teacher were accompanied by informed and sympathetic support from both school administrators and professional colleagues. They further noted that channels of communication within a school were needed to enable innovative teachers to share the results of their efforts with colleagues who were facing similar classroom problems. If such channels existed, teachers learned from each other.

California's experience with Title III programs (Johnson, 1964, p. 171) provides additional evidence of the need for administrative leadership. Fifty percent of the elementary schools in California reported extreme difficulty with in-service programs because of the inability of administrative and supervisory staff to provide effective leadership in the substantive content of new programs. As a result, districts were unable to complete their in-service plans, or to conduct adequate evaluation of programs.

The indication of these and other similar studies (Grieder, 1969, p. 1046) is that improvement of control and learning environments is not apt to result from the isolated efforts of individual classroom teachers to change their instructional practices. Support systems are essential.

Recommendations. Since the role of the administrator is such a critical one, evaluation of adjunctive duties could begin with the following questions:

1. Does the principal or supervisor organize space, time, incentives, and resources for the improvement of teaching in sufficient quantity and quality so that a potent change environment for teachers (Flanders, 1970, pp. 336-344) comes into existence?

2. Does the principal or supervisor collect a variety of evaluation procedures and the necessary resource materials so that teachers with different interests and abilities can obtain access to an evaluation procedure that matches their knowledge and skills?

3. Does the principal or supervisor update his own competence regularly? What is the most recent new skill he has acquired? When and how did he acquire it?

4. Does the principal or supervisor facilitate the communication of teachers with their colleagues about their own attempts to improve instructional procedures? Which teachers communicate with whom? How many teachers within the school are involved in this communication network?

5. What outside resources and/or consultant services does the principal or supervisor make available to teachers to provide input about the particular problems they are trying to solve?

It is quite probable that the support system in every school in California needs to be improved if implementation of the Stull Bill is to lead to instructional improvement. Effective support systems will not be established without effort. It will be some time before they are fully developed, if indeed they ever are. But preliminary steps can be taken immediately.

• Providing a model of inquiry. Supervisors and principals who design and conduct Inquiry Projects in which their own skills for supporting teacher evaluation are the objects of inquiry are likely to accomplish several desirable outcomes with the same project. Not only will they learn more about the evaluation of instruction and how they can support it, but even more important, they will provide a model of self-assessment and self-development for the teachers with whom they work. The positive reinforcement effects of providing a model of behavior, which educational researchers at Stanford University have reported, are more likely to be realized if the steps of inquiry which supervisors and principals carry out are similar, if not identical, to the procedures which teachers will use. Consider the following parallels:

Inquiry Projects

Principals or Supervisors	Teachers
1. Identify evaluation activities which you would like your teachers to carry out.	Identify patterns of pupil behavior which you would like your pupils to exhibit.
2. Identify at least two different patterns of supervisory behavior which you think will support the desired teacher behavior.	Identify at least two different patterns of teacher behavior which you think will support the desired pupil behaviors.
3. Practice these supervisory patterns in order to learn them and to develop observation schemes for analyzing them.	Practice these teaching patterns in microteaching and train a colleague to observe these patterns systematically.
4. Try out both supervisory patterns in comparable circumstances and collect data to evaluate and compare the two patterns.	Teach with each pattern in comparable situations and collect observation data to show that the patterns were performed and other data to show pupil reactions.
5. Analyze the data and decide which pattern of supervision works best.	Analyze the data and decide which teaching pattern is more effective.

The parallels in the above outlines are meant to show how teachers, supervisors, and principals can evaluate their own professional performance by following almost identical steps of inquiry. To the extent that this is true, supervisors and principals can take the lead in demonstrating how to evaluate one's own performance under circumstances in which the teacher's behavior is not being evaluated. If the assessment of teachers includes the progress of their pupils, then why not base the evaluation of supervisors and principals partially on the quality and quantity of inquiry projects that are literally carried out by teachers?

• Initiating retraining projects. Supervisors and principals can also initiate projects to develop new skills, and illustrate the process of continuous learning for the teachers with whom they work. The administrator who is actively retraining himself while on the job demonstrates the acceptability, even desirability, of admitting the need to learn new skills.

The Kettering Foundation has developed a design for assisting administrators to retrain themselves. In the Individualized Continuing Education (ICE) system, the school district supports the principal in an individually designed program of self-improvement that will contribute to desired improvements in the school and district (Kettering, 1970). An extension of the ICE program is called SPAR, Self-Performance Achievement Record. In this program the principal's self-development plans are laid out in a contract with specification of behavioral objectives, performance criteria, and acceptable evidence that these have been met (Kettering, 1971). Skill training for administrators and teachers could have the following parallels:

Competency Contracts

Administrators	Teachers
1. Survey faculty communication channels devoted to improving instruction.	Record several segments of classroom interaction, analyze them, and identify the primary characteristics.
2. Determine changes in communication that have highest priority and skills that will implement these changes.	Determine high priority teaching skills to be developed, depending on instructional goals.
3. Select a particular administrative or supervisory skill to be developed; set a performance goal to be reached.	Select a particular teaching skill to be developed; set a performance goal to be reached.
4. Begin a program of training to develop the skill.	Begin a program of training to develop the skill.
5. Collect post-training data to determine whether performance goal has been reached.	Collect post-training data to determine whether performance goal has been reached.

As in the case of inquiry projects, administrators and teachers can follow almost identical steps in planning, conducting, and evaluating a program of skill training. For an administrator who elects this route, one criterion of his effectiveness could be the number of teachers on his staff who have successfully completed some needed skill training through use of a competency contract.

• Skill training materials. The principal who is ready to undertake a training program to develop new skills himself will find some training materials available. The chart which follows indicates some essential skills, training materials, and evaluation instruments.

Administrative and Supervisory Skills	Training Packages	Assessment Measures
1. The supervisor will state behavioral objectives for his own performance as well as the performance of teachers and children.	Developing Effective Instruction (General Programmed Learning, Palo Alto). Behavioral Objectives (Southwest Cooperative Educational Laboratory, Albuquerque).	Evaluation instruments are contained in the training packages.
2. The supervisor will record data on teachers' classroom interaction using an objective observational system.	Interaction Analysis (Far West Laboratory). Systematic and Objective Analysis of Instruction (Northwest Laboratory).	Evaluation instruments are contained in the training package.
3. The supervisor will provide teachers with useful feedback and suggestions on the basis of his observations, in a supportive manner.	Systematic and Objective Analysis of Instruction (Northwest Laboratory).	Evaluation instruments are contained in the training package.
4. The supervisor or administrator will be	Service provides analysis of responses	Administrator Image Questionnaire (Wes-

| perceived by his staff as knowledgeable and supportive. | and suggestions for methods of improving skills. | tern Michigan University. |
| 5. The administrator will demonstrate skill in using group decision-making to determine instructional goals. | Determining Instructional Purposes (Far West Laboratory, Educational Management Program). | Self-evaluation instruments are included in the training package. |

• Providing outside resources. A principal who is not prepared either to model inquiry processes or to demonstrate retraining processes for his staff may still fulfill his adjunctive duty to evaluate and improve instructional competency by providing support to his teachers in the form of outside resources. Outside consultants can be used to identify student entry behavior, desired student terminal behavior, and parameters of teacher behavior which are predictive of student success. Teachers can be observed by trained consultants or technicians, and their goal-directed behavior reinforced.

Two examples of effective systems of this type are the Quality Assurance Specialist Program (QAS) developed by the Southwest Cooperative Educational Laboratory in Albuquerque and the Spaulding Behavior Modification System (Spaulding, 1971). The QAS program is aimed at pupil achievement in learning English as a second language. The Spaulding program is aimed at increasing independent, self-directed behavior of pupils. Both of these systems have been effective in changing teachers' behavior.

In this type of procedure the principal or supervisor is not providing the training or evaluation himself, but he is arranging to have outside consultants work with his teachers to achieve a specific goal of the school. The principal who utilizes this type of support system might be evaluated on the basis of the general improvement shown by the staff in the instructional skills being reinforced.

Certificated Teaching Personnel

The adjunctive duties of teachers pertaining to evaluation of professional performance are basically similar to those of principals and supervisors. We propose that it is the teacher's adjunctive duty to: (1) evaluate and improve his own performance; and (2) assist his colleagues in the evaluation and improvement of their performance.

Recommendations. The processes by which the teacher can evaluate and improve his own performance have already been discussed in illustrating the parallel procedures that could occur when a supervisor models an approach to inquiry or demonstrates an approach to retraining. The effectiveness of Inquiry Projects has been demonstrated in one study that involved the use of operant conditioning procedures, and labeled the process "precision teaching self-evaluation." Teachers identified their immediate and long-range goals, collected baseline data on their own behavior and on pupil behavior in microteaching situations, planned a strategy to bring about desired changes in pupil behavior, and tested the effectiveness of the strategy in further microteaching situations. Subjects were able to change both their own behavior and the behavior of their pupils.

While the process of inquiry or of competency contracting may be the same for both teachers and principals, the skills that teachers need to learn may differ markedly. Self-instructional training materials available to develop new teaching skills will be discussed in the section on Evaluation of Proper Control and Suitable Learning Environment.

The process of assisting one's colleagues to evaluate and improve their performance was mentioned in the explanation of inquiry for teachers, but merits some additional discussion here. The Fox and Lippitt study cited earlier stressed the need for innovative teachers to share their problems and discoveries with colleagues (Fox and Lippitt, 1964, p. 296). Schmuck reported on alternative intervention strategies designed to help teachers improve informal group processes in the classroom, and noted that an effective procedure was to have pairs and trios of teachers plan and conduct Inquiry Projects (Schmuck, 1971, pp. 33 ff). The Teachers College, Columbia University Pre-Service Program has made extensive use of peer feedback as student teachers are trained to use a number of different instructional models in classroom interaction with children. The peer feedback is effective in helping student teachers learn to display measurably different patterns of teaching behavior as they play different instructional roles (Joyce *et al.*, 1972).

At least two school districts in California have experimented successfully with dyadic peer relationships for the support of self-improvement programs (Fox, 1972; Wallace, 1972). One advantage of a support system involving peer observation and evaluation is that the teacher is less apt to put on an "act" in order to achieve a high rating, and is more apt to learn from the evaluation process. Peer feedback may be less threatening than evaluation by one's employer. As an added bonus, the teacher who is assisting a colleague by observing and providing feedback is also learning himself by developing new perceptions of the teaching act.

The assessment of a teacher's performance of adjunctive duties could include consideration of the quality and quantity of his own inquiry projects. It should also give some weight to the quality and quantity of his assistance to his colleagues in the conduct of their inquiry projects.

Summary

The adjunctive duties most closely related to assessment of proper control and learning environment are those which involve evaluation and improvement of one's own professional performance and assistance to one's colleagues in evaluating and improving their professional performance. Three possible organizational procedures for carrying out these adjunctive duties, and consequently for carrying out the assessment of professional performance, have been identified as use of inquiry projects, use of competency contracts, and use of outside consultants. These three procedures can be used separately or in conjunction with each other. Each procedure has been tested in use in at least one pilot project.

It has been suggested that the role of non-teaching certified personnel in providing proper control and suitable learning environment be evaluated in part on the quality and quantity of inquiry projects carried out by teachers, and the number of teachers successfully completing competency contracts. The assessment of a teacher's performance of adjunctive duties could be evaluated in part by the quality and quantity of his own inquiry projects and competency contracts, and by the quality of his assistance to his colleagues in their attempts to improve professional performance.

Evaluation of Proper Control
and Suitable Learning Environment

We have defined *proper control* as the teacher's ability to create and maintain a climate in which the intended learning can occur without undue interruption. A *suitable learning environment* was said to exist when students are interested in coming to class, look forward optimistically to the work involved, and obtain a sense of satisfaction from participating, especially in terms of self-respect and self-confidence. These definitions represent goals that probably cannot be achieved for all students, all of the time. Yet working toward these goals as if they could be accomplished is a crucial element of professional teaching. It is our position that standards for assessment of teachers' achievement of these goals should refer to identifiable levels of performance associated with particular teaching skills, and should be selected and defined by the teacher whose performance is to be evaluated.

Earlier, we identified four criteria to be met if assessment of proper control and learning environment, viewed in terms of improvement of instruction, was to be considered valid and feasible. The criteria were: agreement between teacher and supervisor on instructional goals; some research evidence linking teacher behavior with control and learning environment; measurement instruments that can be utilized by local school personnel as well as outside consultants; and skill training materials, at least some of which are self-instructional.

Three sources of data for evaluating proper control and suitable learning environment are teacher planning activities, student attitudes and perceptions, and the verbal interaction of teachers and pupils. Each of these data sources will be considered in light of the above criteria, and appropriate organizational procedures for the assessment of each will be identified.

Planning

On the basis of common sense we expect that classroom control and learning environment are better when a teacher plans for instruction than when he does not plan. Planning for adaptation of curriculum materials to fit the needs of a particular class and particular children within a class may be taken as evidence that a teacher is *attempting* to provide proper control and a suitable learning environment. But can it be taken as evidence that a teacher is *achieving* proper control and a suitable learning environment? We think not.

Criteria for Valid and Feasible Assessment. Consider teacher planning activities in terms of the four criteria restated above. The first step in assessment is to reach agreement between a teacher and supervisor on instructional goals. This agreement is likely to be facilitated by the statement of instructional goals in terms of specific behavior. Thus, one criterion of effective planning is the teacher's ability to specify objectives in behavioral terms. When specific objectives have been agreed upon, teacher performance can be assessed in terms of how well other planning activities contribute to achievement of those objectives.

• Research evidence. We know of no research projects which have the purpose of showing that making plans for instruction (versus not making plans) results in the improvement of desirable learning outcomes. Perhaps such studies do not exist because the answer seems self-evident. Relevant research with regard to planning does provide some suggestions with regard to the particular aspects of teacher planning that might be most closely related to control and learning environment. Berlyne reports that novelty, complexity, and "surprisingness" all contribute to attending behavior (Berlyne, 1960). Other studies indicate that provision of a variety of learning activities reduces "satiation" and is conducivé to appropriate classroom behavior (Kounin, 1966). Biddle and Adams (1967) note that classroom arrangements in which the teacher occupies center stage and pupils are encapsulated in small areas tend to be settings of some boredom for pupils. These studies suggest the possibility of evaluating the teacher's planning of both the physical arrangement of the classroom and the instructional materials available for use, with variety as an important criterion in both instances.

Planning for variety of instructional materials makes more sense when class formations and plans for the role of the teacher are also taken into consideration. For example, as work begins on a unit of study, the first task is to identify individual learning goals for students. There is a stage of teacher-student planning which calls for an appropriate class formation and particular patterns of teaching behavior. Later on, as work gets underway, another class formation, a shift in the role of the teacher, and the use of a variety of learning materials can be expected. Some suggestions about expected changes in teaching behavior as individual learning goals are clarified have been reported by Flanders (1970, p. 327) in mathematics and social studies classes. Joyce and Weil (1972) identify and discuss different teaching models or strategies as appropriate for different instructional objectives. Taba (1966) also proposes particular changes in teaching behavior designed to support and encourage skill in inductive thinking.

We might note, in passing, that changes in the instructional materials do not necessarily ensure complementary changes in the patterns of teaching behavior. There is evidence that modern mathematics curricula (Wright, 1967) and the new physics curriculum designed by the Physical Science Study Committee (Moore, 1968) failed to promote more independent patterns of student participation primarily because old patterns of teaching behavior were continued when new patterns were required.

• Measurement instruments and training materials. There is no available supply of tested measurement instruments for the assessment of teacher performance in planning for variety of classroom arrangements and instructional materials. There are both assessment instruments and training materials to deal with teacher performance in stating behavioral objectives. We have been unable to locate any training materials dealing with skills in planning for variety of classroom arrangements and use of instructional materials, though a training format for such materials has been proposed (Morine, 1972). Some books explicating the process of planning for use of different instructional models are available (Joyce and Weil, 1972; Morine and Morine, 1973) as well as self-instructional materials to develop the interactive skills associated with such models (Joyce, Weil, and Wald, 1972).

Skill-training materials related to two other facets of teacher planning have been produced. The Far West Laboratory's Mini-course on Independent Learning deals with teacher-pupil planning of independent learning contracts, and emphasizes teaching behaviors related to providing for individual differences in academic interests and self-direction, both of which are relevant to control and learning environment. The training package on team teaching developed by the Austin, Texas, Research and Development Center deals with teacher-teacher planning, and emphasizes behaviors that may be most closely related to the adjunctive duty of providing support and assistance to one's colleagues.

Appropriate Assessment Procedures. Given this state of affairs, it seems evident that improvement of some planning skills is an achievable goal, but that assessment in terms of normative standards would be indefensible. We recommend that assessment of planning proceed through use of competency contracts. A particular planning skill to be assessed can be identified jointly by teacher and administrator. Baseline data on teacher performance of this skill can be gathered by some objective means mutually agreed upon. Performance criteria that represent skill development in a particular direction can then be specified. Training materials would be made available to the teacher. Final assessment would be based upon attainment of the specified performance level.

Student Attitudes

The point was made earlier that a suitable learning environment was essentially a child-centered concept, referring to arrangements which maximize a child's opportunity to exploit a situation for the purpose of learning. It follows that students' attitudes toward the learning environment will be an important indicator of the suitability of that environment for them. Student attitudes toward themselves and toward their peers are apt to be related to their patterns of social behavior, and thus may have an effect on classroom control.

Criteria for Valid and Feasible Assessment. Agreement on attitudinal goals that may be related to control and learning environment can probably be achieved by most teachers and supervisors. Most educators support goals such as the student will value learning, enjoy school, believe in his own ability to achieve, accept responsibility for helping his peers, value and display independence, be willing to accept group decisions, and obey group rules. Where disagreements occur frequently is in the identification of instructional procedures to implement these goals.

• Research evidence. It is encouraging to note that a large group of studies, totaling more than twenty,* showed that when teaching behavior was more responsive, students had more positive attitudes toward the teacher and toward learning, often learning more as shown by achievement tests, and often showed more desirable patterns of behavior in the classroom.

There are also a few studies relating student attitudes toward themselves and their peers to classroom control and learning environment. Wide sociometric dispersion in a group is related to higher group cohesiveness and stronger group norms supporting educational goals (Schmuck, 1966). Low sociometric status is related to negative self-esteem and hostility toward others (Lippitt and Gold, 1959). Teacher praise is likely to increase the sociometric status of the particular students toward whom it is directed (Flanders and Havumaki, 1960). While this latter research is rather meager, it does suggest that sociometric patterns may indicate the existence of problems in the area of control and learning environment. It does not suggest many solutions to such problems or point strongly to a particular direction for teacher improvement.

• Measurement instruments and training materials. There are a variety of instruments available to measure student perceptions of the teacher, their peers, and themselves. Twenty-three different diagnostic forms of obtaining student perceptions are discussed by Fox *et al.* (Fox, Luszki, and Schmuck, 1966) in a very interesting

*Amidon and Flanders, 1961; Birkin, 1967; Emmer, 1967; Filson, 1957; Flanders, 1965 (four separate studies); Flanders, 1970 (three separate studies); Furst, 1967; Johns, 1966; LaShier, 1965; Measel, 1967; Morrison, 1966; Pankratz, 1967; Powell, 1968; Samph, 1968; Schantz, 1963; Snider, 1965; Soar, 1966; and Weber, 1968.

little pamphlet called *Diagnosing Classroom Learning Environments*. The development of microteaching at Stanford included a student reaction form called the Stanford Teacher Appraisal Guide (STAG) to obtain student perceptions of teaching performance. The Michigan Student Questionnaire has been used in several of the studies relating pupil attitudes to teaching behavior, and has demonstrated reliability (Flanders *et al.*, 1969, pp. 169-179). The Educator Feedback Center of Western Michigan University provides a service for teachers that includes distribution and analysis of questionnaires dealing with pupil perception of teacher effectiveness, and preparation of a Teacher-Image Profile. One instrument collects pupil descriptions of their actual and ideal teacher and permits the teacher to compare himself with a "pupil-designed" model teacher.

The reactions of students who cannot respond by using a paper-and-pencil reaction form can be obtained by asking them or by using an observation system that includes non-verbal student observation. Fairly reliable ratings have been reported by Soar (1966) on such matters as "at work/not at work," "interest/boredom," "participating/not participating" at younger age levels.

While assessment measures for student attitudes exist, there are no training materials specifically designed to help teachers improve pupil attitudes toward school, toward each other, or toward themselves. Thus, assessment of student attitudes will not lead easily into a skill training program.

Appropriate Assessment Procedures. Assessment of student attitudes *can* lead to use of inquiry projects. When data on student attitudes have been collected, the teacher can identify alternative patterns of teaching behavior that might support a change in pupil attitudes, practice these teaching patterns with different groups of pupils, and collect further data from students to determine which pattern was more effective in bringing about the desired change. Final assessment of teaching performance would be based upon the teacher's ability to plan, conduct, and evaluate the inquiry project, as well as the ability to learn new patterns of behavior and to bring about some change in pupil behavior. Possible designs for inquiry projects are discussed in the next section.

Interactive Behavior

The interactive events between a teacher and his students, as well as those that occur among students, create a major part of the learning environment and also reveal patterns of classroom control. In fact, as students "interact" with instructional materials, which are inanimate objects, the adaptation of these materials for purposes of learning, the "humanizing" of these materials so to speak, is created by what teachers and students say to each other and how they coordinate their actions. It follows that an analysis of interactive behavior should give us considerable insight into the qualities of the learning environment and the processes of control. This kind of evaluation can be based on many different systems of interaction analysis. Perhaps the first analysis of this kind was made some 60 years ago, with the study of teacher questions from written transcripts recorded in stenographic shorthand. An extensive inventory of the observation procedures now available can be found in Simon and Boyer's (1970) *Mirrors for Behavior*, in which eighty systems for encoding interactive events are reported.

One general conclusion from all of the research which uses some form of interaction analysis is that when experienced teachers or college students take the time to analyze their own patterns of verbal interaction, they are likely to change these patterns. Many different changes have been reported, but among those which occur most frequently are less teacher talk, more responsive teacher talk (e.g., reacting to ideas students express), and less teacher initiation (e.g., lecturing, giving directions, and criticizing students). This generalization is supported, to one degree or another, by no less than twelve* different research projects. One possible reason for these consistent results is that interaction analysis, with proper feedback, helps a teacher compare what actually happened during classroom interaction with what he wanted to have happen. When a teacher analyzes his

*At the pre-service level, Bondi, 1969; Finske, 1967; Furst, 1967; Kirk, 1963; Lohman, Ober, and Hough, 1967; Moskowitz, 1967. At the in-service level, Emmer, 1967; Flanders, 1963; Hill, 1966; Jeffs, 1968; and Soar, 1966. Others have reported similar findings since this survey was made, such as Borg *et al.* (1970).

own chain of interactive events, he is more likely to discover appropriate opportunities to react to students and this increases the average incidence of responsive acts. Additional explanation has been proposed by Wagner (1971), whose study suggests that practice in discriminating among responsive acts may be more important than practice in performing these acts.

As noted earlier, there is also a large group of studies linking responsive teaching behavior to positive student attitudes, higher pupil achievement, and more desirable patterns of classroom behavior. There are, of course, reservations and exceptions to be made to these two rather sweeping generalizations. They are of the sort that not every teacher can benefit equally from the study of his own interaction (Zahn, 1965, p. 297); cause and effect are not yet clearly established (Flanders, 1970, p. 426); the relationships may actually be curvilinear, which means a teacher can become too responsive (Soar, 1966); and not all classes, subject matter, age levels, and ways to quantify variables are properly represented in the research reported (Rosenshine and Furst, 1971, pp. 37 ff.). However, the line of research is still impressive and deserves attention in terms of implementing the Stull Bill.

Criteria and Inquiry Design. The problem of evaluation is to obtain information that is based on fairly objective criteria and then to use this information to make intelligent comparisons that, in turn, lead to valid conclusions. In research we say that variables should be carefully quantified and the data should be analyzed within a logical research design. Evaluation under the Stull Bill may only approach the quality of carefully conceived research, yet attention to the principles of good research is inescapable.

• Criteria for interactive events. The criteria of evaluation when some system of interaction analysis is used will depend on the nature of the category system. In the Flanders (1970, p. 197) ten-category system, the criteria can include ratios of different verbal statements made by the teacher (e.g., the i/i + d ratio); direct percentages of teacher talk, student talk, or silence/ confusion; or subdivisions of the main categories. Other systems such as Parsons' (1970) *Guided Self-Analysis* and Morine, Spaulding and Greenberg's (1971) discriminate different kinds of questions and different ways that a teacher can respond to student statements. Spaulding's CASES and STARS (1971) discriminates types of pupil behavior and teacher use of positive or negative reinforcement.

Coding and analysis of total classroom interaction require extensive time and training. It is possible for evaluation to focus on one or two aspects of interaction and for coding to be limited to particular types of behavior. It is our recommendation that initial assessment of verbal interaction skills focus on teacher questions and directions, which occur just before pupils participate, and teacher responsive behaviors, which occur just after pupils participate (Flanders, 1972). Such assessment will require the following procedures:

1. A trained observer will encode interaction analysis data by visiting live classroom settings, or will have access to an intelligible voice and/or video magnetic recording.

2. The encoded data will be tabulated or placed into a display which permits questions, directions, responsive statements, and criticism to be identified, along with various kinds of student statements. Additional ratings of the situation and data from student inventories can also be utilized.

3. Fairly simple ratios or summary percentages can be calculated in order to provide scores for subsequent comparisons.

The trick, if we can call it that, is to avoid superficial, unreliable indices which have questionable value, and to focus, instead, on features of the interactive events which are more likely to have pervasive consequences for the learning environment. For example, counting particular kinds of words, such as an "I/We" ratio, may seem to be related to Martin Buber's observations and philosophy about personal relationships, but we do not have convincing evidence that such word counts are related to educational outcomes, either desirable or undesirable. On the other hand, the proportion of responsive teacher statements to all teacher statements (the i/i + d ratio) has been shown to be associated with positive student attitudes.

• Inquiry designs. Considerable attention should be given to the situations in which interaction analysis data are collected. The main problem is to choose an inquiry design which permits logical comparisons that are consistent with the purpose of the evaluation.

One-time evaluations for the purpose of rating the quality of teaching were rejected in the second paragraph of this paper. One reason for this recommendation is that a single visit is not likely to be representative of what normally occurs in a classroom. More representative data may require at least six one-hour visits, well spaced (Flanders, 1970, p. 100) in order to collect reliable data. Samph (1968) has shown that the presence of an observer does influence interaction. The use of "standardized" lessons shows some promise of producing more reliable data (Finske, 1967), but more research will be necessary to demonstrate that such lessons represent average interaction. Most of us who conduct research using interaction analysis have discovered that it is not difficult for a teacher to put on an act which cannot be detected by most interaction analysis procedures. The final blow to one-time evaluation is that we simply do not have enough normative data to evaluate a teacher's performance by comparison with reasonably similar populations. Comparisons over time for the same teacher and the same class may be the best type of design for the diagnostic evaluation of learning environment and the control processes.

One design could involve comparing interaction data with a model. A profile of interaction analysis data can be used to represent a particular model of teaching, such as a model of inquiry teaching. Examples of such a model can be found in Morine *et al.* (1971). A teacher can then practice using this model and, on successive occasions, compare his profile based on a specimen of interaction with the model display itself. With this method he can determine when his teaching matches the model. The primary purpose of this design is the improvement of instruction, rather than some kind of rating.

A second design would require a colleague or older student who is a trained observer to visit the class and obtain a general profile of interactive events at a first point in time. The teacher who was observed may identify some feature of this profile that he would like to change. He can then practice making these changes in microteaching or short-lesson sessions. He finally invites his colleague-observer back for an observation at a second point in time. A comparison of the data, collected at two different points in time, can often lead to useful insights. Again, this design is directed primarily toward the improvement of instruction.

The five-step inquiry model for teachers, outlined earlier, is perhaps the most advanced level of inquiry in which one's own behavior is the object of study. It is more advanced because in Step Two the teacher proposes his own model. These five steps are discussed in considerable detail, including proposed systems for displaying the interaction data, in *Analyzing Teaching Behavior* (Flanders, 1970, Chap. 9).

Combining Interaction Analysis with Other Data-Collecting Procedures. The generalization that teachers tend to change interaction patterns when they study and analyze their own verbal statements is most easily explained by recourse to "feedback" and the effects of feedback on a behavior system. More adequate feedback to teachers is likely to occur if more adequate information is obtained. One way that this can be accomplished is to help teachers develop the skills necessary to collect other kinds of information as well as information about interaction.

Two kinds of data, such as interaction data and student perception data, are essential to adapting teaching methods to one's own class. The interaction data permit a teacher to determine the extent to which his interaction matched his intentions. The data on student perceptions help to associate student reactions with the patterns of instruction. The combination permits inferences about how well a given strategy works for a particular class.

• Regular feedback. Incidental feedback to the teacher goes on constantly. Systematic feedback occurs less frequently. Change is more likely to result from the latter because it is planned.

An effective, easy way to obtain feedback from students as part of an inquiry project is to ask them. It may be both more tactful and more effective to divide the class into groups of four or five students, ask them to form opinions about some phase of instruction, and then have a "summarizer" report for the sub-group, not naming individual students. After opinions are rewritten to reflect the various sub-group discussions, a show of hands to indicate the amount of agreement and the strength of conviction helps to quantify class opinion.

Short forms for written or scaled student reaction which take only a few minutes to fill out can be created by most teachers. Many examples are shown in Fox, Luszki, and Schmuck (1966).

Feedback on interactive behavior is not quite so readily obtained. Time, space, incentive, and resources are necessary to learn to encode and decode classroom interaction. This kind of activity is not easily accomplished if it is an extra burden added to the load of an already busy teacher or supervisor.

One deterrent to the learning of interaction analysis systems may be exaggerated demands for reliability of observations. Both authors of this paper have worked with teachers as they learn some form of interaction analysis. We have found that the standards of reliability required for research projects need not necessarily be reached in order to benefit instruction. When two teachers disagree on how to code an event and they discuss their differences, it probably helps them to improve their discrimination.

Other factors will affect the success of training attempts. At the Far West Laboratory, we have some unpublished information from our field tests to indicate that teachers working alone are less likely to complete training in interaction analysis than teachers working with one or more partners. The Northwest Laboratory's materials are purposely designed to fit the format of a weekend workshop for a reasonably sized group of teachers. If such a workshop is not feasible, then self-instructional training packages should probably be used by several teachers in the same school for maximum effectiveness. There are quite a few training materials for learning one or another form of interaction analysis.

Skill Training

Any assessment of teacher performance that is aimed at improvement of instruction will eventually lead to the identification of new teaching skills to be acquired. Not all teachers will be ready to conduct inquiry projects or write competency contracts. For many the route to improvement of instructional skills will be the use of training packages that identify skills to be learned, provide carefully designed materials to assist the teacher in skill acquisition, and include assessment measures to determine the extent of learning that has occurred.

It is probable that training in stating behavioral objectives will be necessary for many teachers before they can write competency contracts. Training in coding interactive behaviors will be essential for many teachers before they can begin inquiry projects. Some teachers will move rapidly from skill training projects to more complex assessment procedures. Others will remain at the level of skill training for longer periods of time.

One of the more powerful approaches to the improvement of interactive teaching skills is the development of minicourses, which are products of the Far West Laboratory for Research and Development (Borg *et al.*, 1970). Minicourses combine the techniques of microteaching with work on providing models of behavior. A minicourse provides a coordinator's manual, a teacher's manual, color films, or video recordings to demonstrate particular teaching skills, all organized around a series of lessons. Individualized training is possible for a single teacher or a group of teachers. Each minicourse is the product of an extensive sequence of product development and evaluation.

Other regional laboratories and university centers are currently developing and testing instructional materials designed to improve particular skills of teaching. The advantage of most of these products is that they are designed to assist those teachers who do not care to design their own self-development programs. The procedures of interaction analysis, discussed in the previous section, require considerable teacher initiative and often the ability to invent a model of teaching (e.g., "What pattern of teaching behavior will support the desired pupil behavior?"). The self-contained minicourses and the instructional materials from laboratories and centers have the advantage that skills are usually specified in advance and the materials also specify a series of steps which will permit a trainee to improve his skill providing he follows the sequences of instruction.

Space does not permit an exhaustive list of the possible skill training materials that could contribute to the improvement of classroom control and learning environment. We include below a sampling of skills and training materials to indicate something of the range of possibilities that exists.

Teaching Skills	Training Packages
1. The teacher will state performance objectives for the instruction of his pupils.	Developing Effective Instruction (General Programmed Learning) Behavioral Objectives (SWCEL)
2. The teacher will record data on his own classroom interaction using objective observation system.	Interaction Analysis (FWL) Interaction Analysis (Northwest Laboratory)
3. The teacher will interact with pupils in ways that encourage high level thinking skills.	Facilitating Inquiry in the Classroom (Northwest Laboratory) Effective Questioning: Elementary Level (Minicourse 1, FWL) Higher Cognitive Questioning (Minicourse 9, FWL)
4. The teacher will organize the classroom for individualized instruction.	Organizing for Independent Learning (Minicourse 8, FWL) Individualizing Instruction in Mathematics (Minicourse 5, FWL) Teaching in IPI Mathematics (Research for Better Schools)
5. The teacher will increase the students' interest in learning.	Teaching Achievement Motivation (Education Ventures)
6. The teacher will expand the language and thought of young children.	Developing Children's Oral Language (Minicourse 2, FWL)

Summary

Assessment of proper control and suitable learning environment can proceed through collection of data related to teaching planning, student attitudes, and interactive behavior of teachers and pupils. The use of such data for improvement of instruction can provide valid and feasible assessment procedures. Directed skill training, competency contracts, and inquiry projects are all appropriate means of assessment and improvement at this stage in our development of techniques for evaluation of teacher effectiveness. Inquiry projects ·can involve comparisons of behavior with a model, comparisons of behavior with stated behavioral objectives, and comparisons of behavior over time. Peer cooperation in collection of interactive data is apt to contribute to development of skills in coding interactive behavior, and therefore to lead to greater behavior change.

A Beginning

The educational community of California has been issued an ultimatum to evaluate the performance of certificated personnel throughout the state. We do not have the necessary knowledge base nor the required measurement techniques and tools to respond to this ultimatum by instituting a system of rigid evaluative criteria for purposes of retention or merit pay. We do have the opportunity to respond by instituting systems of assessment that can contribute to the improvement of instruction.

Improvement of the educational process is a goal to which we all aspire. Perhaps we wish that we had not been placed under such immediate pressures to achieve this goal as the Stull Bill seems to exert. But if we marshal our resources, we can make an important initial attack on the problems of accountability, effective teaching, and improvement of instruction.

There are those who will view the Stull Bill as an obstruction or a dead end. We could make it a beginning.

References

Amidon, E.J. and N.A. Flanders. "The Effects of Direct and Indirect Teacher Influence on Dependent-Prone Students Learning Geometry," *Journal of Educational Psychology*, 52, 1961, pp. 286-291.

Berlyne, D.E. *Conflict, Arousal, and Curiosity*. New York: McGraw-Hill, 1960.

Biddle, B.J. and R.S. Adams. *An Analysis of Classroom Activities*. Columbia: Missouri University, 1967.

Birkin, T.A. "Toward a Model of Instruction Processes." Unpublished manuscript, School of Education, University of Birmingham, England, 1967.

Bondi, J.C., Jr. "The Effects of Interaction Analysis Feedback on the Verbal Behavior of Student Teachers," *Educational Leadership*, 26, 1969, pp. 794-799.

Borg, W. *et al. The Minicourse: A Microteaching Approach to Teacher Education*. 8701 Wilshire Boulevard, Beverly Hills, California, Macmillan Educational Services, 1970.

Brickell, H.M. "State Organization for Educational Change: A Case Study and a Proposal." In M.B. Miles (Ed.) *Innovation in Education*. New York: Teachers College, Columbia University Bureau of Publications, 1964.

Emmer, E.T. "The Effect of Teacher Use and Acceptance of Student Ideas on Student Verbal Initiation." Unpublished doctoral dissertation, University of Michigan, 1967.

Filson, T.N. "Factors Influencing the Level of Dependence in the Classroom." Unpublished doctoral dissertation, University of Minnesota, 1957.

Finske, Sister M.J. "The Effect of Feedback through Interaction Analysis on the Development of Flexibility in Student Teachers." Unpublished doctoral dissertation, University of Michigan, 1967.

Flanders, N.A. *Helping Teachers Change Their Behavior*. Final Report, N.D.E.A. Projects 1721012 and 7-32-0560-171.O, U.S. Office of Education. University of Michigan, School of Education, 1963. (Out of print.)

Flanders, N.A. *Teacher Influence, Pupil Attitudes, and Achievement*. Cooperative Research Monograph No. 12 (OE-25040), U.S. Office of Education, University of Michigan, School of Education, 1965. (Out of print.)

Flanders, N.A. *Analyzing Teaching Behavior*. Reading, Massachusetts: Addison-Wesley, 1970.

Flanders, N.A. "Basic Teaching Skills Derived from a Model of Speaking and Listening." Paper presented at Basic Skills Seminar, American Educational Research Association Annual Meeting, Chicago, 1972. (Available from author.)

Flanders, N.A. *et al.* "Teacher Influence Patterns and Pupil Achievement in the Second, Fourth, and Sixth Grade Levels." Cooperative Research Project No. 5-1055 (OE-4-10-243), U.S. Office of Education. University of Michigan, School of Education, December, 1969. (Available from Far West Laboratory, San Francisco, California.)

Flanders, N.A. and S. Havumaki. "The Effect of Teacher-Pupil Contacts Involving Praise on the Sociometric Choices of Students," *Journal of Educational Psychology*, 51, 1960, pp. 65-68.

Fox, R.S. and R. Lippitt. "The Innovation of Classroom Mental Health Practices." In M.B. Miles (Ed.) *Innovation in Education*. New York: Teachers College, Columbia University Bureau of Publications, 1964.

Fox, R.S., M. Luszki, and R. Schmuck. *Diagnosing Classroom Learning Environments*. Chicago: Science Research Associates, 1966.

Fox, S.L. "The Sponsor/Colleague System," *California School Boards*, 31, 1972, p. 19.

Furst, N. "The Effects of Training in Interaction Analysis on the Behavior of Student Teachers in Secondary Schools." In E.J. Amidon and J.B. Hough (Eds.) *Interaction Analysis: Theory, Research, and Application*. Reading, Massachusetts: Addison-Wesley, 1967.

Grieder, C. "Public School Administration." In Robert L. Ebel (Ed.) *Encyclopedia of Educational Research*, 4th Ed. American Educational Research Association, New York: Macmillan, 1969.

Hill, W.M. "The Effects on Verbal Teaching Behavior of Learning Interaction Analysis as an In-Service Education Activity." Unpublished doctoral dissertation, Ohio State University, 1966.

Jeffs, G.A. *et al.* "The Effects of Training in Interaction Analysis on the Verbal Behavior of Teachers." Mimeographed research report. Ed. W. Clark High School, Las Vegas, Nevada, 1968.

Johns, J.P. "The Relationship Between Teacher Behavior and the Incidence of Thought-Provoking Questions by Students in Secondary Schools." Unpublished doctoral dissertation, University of Michigan, 1966.

Johnson, D.W. "Title III and the Dynamics of Educational Change in California Schools." In M.B. Miles (Ed.) *Innovation in Education*. New York: Teachers College, Columbia University Bureau of Publications, 1964.

Joyce, B.R. and M. Weil. *Models of Teaching*. Englewood Cliffs, New Jersey: Prentice-Hall, 1972.

Joyce, B.R., M. Weil, and R. Wald. *Three Teaching Strategies for the Social Studies*. Chicago: Science Research Associates, 1972.

Joyce, B.R. *et al*. "Models of Teaching as a Paradigm for Teacher Education." Paper presented at the American Educational Research Association meeting, Chicago, 1972.

Kettering Program Associates. "Individualized Continuing Education for School Administrators—One Approach." A CFK Ltd. Occasional Paper. Englewood, Colorado, 1970.

Kettering Program Associates. "A Quality Performance Program for Individualizing Continuing Education for School Administrators." A CFK Ltd. Occasional Paper. Englewood, Colorado, 1971.

Kirk, J. "Effects of Teaching the Minnesota System of Interaction Analysis to Intermediate Grade Student Teachers." Unpublished doctoral dissertation, Temple University, 1963.

Kounin, J.S. *et al*. "Managing Emotionally Disturbed Children in Regular Classrooms," *Journal of Educational Psychology*, 57, 1966, pp. 1-13.

LaShier, W.S. "An Analysis of Certain Aspects of the Verbal Behavior of Student Teachers of Eighth Grade Students Participating in a BSCS Laboratory Block." Unpublished doctoral dissertation, University of Texas, 1965.

Lippitt, R. and M. Gold. "Classroom Social Structure as a Mental Health Problem," *Journal of Social Issues*, 15, 1959, pp. 40-58.

Lohman, E., R. Ober, and J.B. Hough. "A Study of the Effect of Pre-Service Training in Interaction Analysis on the Verbal Behavior of Student Teachers." In E.J. Amidon and J.B. Hough (Eds.) *Interaction Analysis: Theory, Research, and Application*. Reading, Massachusetts: Addison-Wesley, 1967.

McDonald, S.C. "The Passage of AB 293, The Stull Act of 1971." Unpublished report, 1972. (Available from Ned Flanders, Far West Laboratory, San Francisco, California.)

Measel, W.W. "The Relationship Between Teacher Influence and Levels of Thinking of Second Grade Teachers and Pupils." Unpublished doctoral dissertation, University of Michigan, 1967.

Moore, J.R. "An Analysis of Teacher and Pupil Verbal Behavior and Teacher Procedural and Evaluative Behavior in Relation to Objectives Unique to the PSSC and Non-PSSC Physics Curricula." Doctoral dissertation, University of Michigan, 1968.

Morine, G. "Basic Teaching Skills: Identification of Preactive Skills." Paper presented at Seminar on Basic Skills, American Educational Research Association meeting, Chicago, 1972.

Morine, H. and G. Morine. *Discovery: A Challenge to Teachers.* Englewood Cliffs, New Jersey: Prentice-Hall, 1973.

Morine, G., R. Spaulding, and S. Greenberg. *Discovering New Dimensions in the Teaching Process.* Scranton, Pennsylvania: Intext Educational Publishers, 1971.

Morrison, B.M. "The Reactions of Internal and External Children to Patterns of Teaching Behavior." Unpublished doctoral dissertation, University of Michigan, 1966.

Moskowitz, G. "The Attitudes and Teaching Patterns of Cooperative Teachers and Student Teachers Trained in Interaction Analysis." In E.J. Amidon and J.B. Hough (Eds.) *Interaction Analysis: Theory, Research, and Application.* Reading, Massachusetts: Addison-Wesley, 1967.

Pankratz, R. "Verbal Interaction Patterns in the Classrooms of Selected Physics Teachers." In E.J. Amidon and J.B. Hough (Eds.) *Interaction Analysis: Theory, Research, and Application.* Reading, Massachusetts: Addison-Wesley, 1967.

Parsons, T.W. *Guided Self-Analysis System for Professional Development: Guidelines for Implementation.* G.S.A. Education Series, Berkeley, 1970.

Powell, E.R. "Teacher Behavior and Pupil Achievement." Paper presented at American Educational Research Association meeting, Chicago, 1968.

Rosenshine, B. and N. Furst. "Research on Teacher Performance Criteria." In B.O. Smith (Ed.) *Research in Teacher Education: A Symposium.* Englewood Cliffs, New Jersey: Prentice-Hall, 1971.

Samph, T. "Observer Effects on Teacher Behavior." Unpublished doctoral dissertation, University of Michigan, 1968.

Schantz, B.M.B. "An Experimental Study Comparing the Effects of Verbal Recall by Children in Direct and Indirect Teaching Methods as a Tool of Measurement." Unpublished doctoral dissertation, Pennsylvania State University, 1963.

Schmuck, R.A. "Some Aspects of Classroom Social Climate," *Psychology in the Schools*, 3, 1966, pp. 59-65.

Schmuck, R.A. "Improving Classroom Group Processes." In R.A. Schmuck and M.B. Miles (Eds.) *Organization Development in Schools*. Palo Alto, California: National Press Books, 1971.

Simon, A. and E.G. Boyer. *Mirrors for Behavior*. Philadelphia: Research for Better Schools, 1970.

Snider, R.M. *A Project to Study the Nature of Effective Physics Teaching*. Cooperative Research No. S-280, U.S. Office of Education, Cornell University, 1965.

Soar, R.S. *An Integrative Approach to Classroom Learning*. Final Report, Public Health Service Grant No. 5-R11 MH 01096 to the University of South Carolina and Grant No. 7-R11 MH 02045 to Temple University, Temple University, 1966.

Spaulding, R.L. *Educational Intervention in Early Childhood*. Durham Education Improvement Program Final Report, Volume I. Durham, North Carolina: Duke University, 1971.

Taba, H. *Teaching Strategies and Cognitive Functioning in Elementary School Children*. Cooperative Research Project #2404, San Francisco State College, February, 1966.

Wagner, A.C. "Changing Teaching Behavior: A Comparison of Microteaching and Discrimination Practice." Unpublished doctoral dissertation, University of Michigan, 1971.

Wallace, C.E. "Self-Appraisal: Systems for Improvement," *California School Boards*, 31, 1972, p. 14.

Weber, W.A. "Relationships Between Teacher Behavior and Pupil Creativity in the Elementary School." Unpublished doctoral dissertation, Temple University, 1968.

Wright, M.E. "Teacher-Pupil Interaction in the Mathematics Classroom." Technical Report No. 67-5, Minnesota National Laboratory, Minnesota State Department of Education, 1967.

Zahn, R. "The Use of Interaction Analysis in Supervising Student Teachers." Unpublished doctoral dissertation, Temple University, 1965.

Section Two

ACHIEVEMENT RELATED
TEACHING BEHAVIORS

Introduction to Section Two

Achievement Related Teaching Behaviors

Many problems in evaluating teaching effectiveness were mentioned in Section One. The papers included in this section deal with teaching behaviors that have been found to be related to student achievement. Barak Rosenshine, in his article, *Enthusiastic Teaching: A Research Review*, reviews the studies investigating the relationship of enthusiasm to pupil achievement, and specifies the behavioral components of enthusiasm. Rosenshine also discusses the relevance of the results of the studies to teacher education programs and suggests directions for educational research in validating the connection between low-inference and high-inference behaviors, studying the frequency and type of teacher questions, exploring teacher remarks about the importance of certain material, and in studying the feasibility of training teachers to teach with more enthusiasm.

Berj Harootunian's paper, *Research on Teaching Effectiveness*, deals with promising strategies for the study of teaching effectiveness. The author underscores the importance of matching strategies with contextual or situational variables. This article spells out the matching of teacher characteristics with characteristics of pupils which Ryans calls for in his chapter. He suggests that in order to study effective teaching we should ask the question in a narrower way: What characterizes the effective teacher for students with characteristic A as opposed to one for students with characteristic B? Harootunian's approach appears to be rational and based on empirical evidence and demands attention for evaluation of teaching effectiveness across situations.

In *One in Five Made Us Think*, Garnar V. Walsh reports a survey study conducted to seek reactions of college students to three broad areas of teaching: (1) instructors who made students "think" and their characteristics; (2) qualities of the instructors which students felt triggered their thought process; and (3) the percentage of instructors who made students think beyond the facts and data level. The three qualities of the instructors which the students felt had a major impact in raising their level of thinking were found to be: (1) expert knowledge of subject; (2) ability to stimulate student interest; (3) enthusiastic attitude toward subject.

Madan Mohan's paper, *Specifying Behavioral Components of Some Higher-Order Concepts of Teaching*, is concerned with teaching behaviors which have demonstrated positive relationship with pupil achievement. Mohan draws an important distinction between higher-order teaching concepts and their behavioral components. It is hoped that the specification of higher-order teaching concepts in what teachers will be doing to bring about a desirable state or condition in their students will provide the handle on effective teaching and will serve as a reasonable yardstick for evaluating teaching effectiveness.

5.

Enthusiastic Teaching: A Research Review

Barak Rosenshine

In the folklore of education, the teaching behaviors considered desirable include enthusiasm, energy, and surgency. Even educational psychologists have endorsed teacher enthusiasm. For example, Ausubel wrote, "It is . . . important that teachers be able to communicate a sense of excitement about the subjects they teach."[1] But this idea was one of the few for which Ausubel did not cite evidence. After pages of documentation on the ineffectiveness of structural innovations in education, Stephens hypothesized that effective teaching depends upon the "lively interests of teachers."[2]

This paper is a review of the attempts to assess the relationship of enthusiasm to pupil achievement and to specify the behavioral components of enthusiasm. Correlational and experimental studies in classrooms ranging from elementary school to college will be examined. I shall discuss the results of the studies, estimate the relevance of the results to teacher training programs, and suggest directions for future research. An important element of this paper is the discussion of how high-inference and low-inference measures can be used together in the study of teaching.

High- Versus Low-Inference Measures

The correlational and experimental studies to be cited here

Reprinted from *School Review*, 1970, pp. 499-515. Reprinted by permission of the author and the publisher. The author is Associate Professor of Educational Psychology at the University of Illinois.

are divided into studies of high-inference and low-inference measures, following conventions described by Ackerman[3] and Gage.[4] "Inference" here refers to the process intervening between the objective data seen or heard and the judgment concerning a higher-order construct of cognitive or social interaction. It is similar to "extrapolation" as used by Gage and Cronbach.[5] High-inference measures are those which require considerable inferring from what is seen or heard in the classroom to the labeling of the behavior, such as ratings of the teacher on such scales as "partial-fair," "autocratic-democratic," or "dull-stimulating." Low-inference measures are those which require the observer to classify teaching behaviors according to relatively objective categories. Examples of these measures are words per minute, movements per minute, and the behaviors in relatively objective category systems, such as Interaction Analysis.[6]

Ratings on high-inference variables are particularly useful in exploring new ideas, and they have generally yielded higher correlations with teacher effects than more specific, or low-inference, behavioral measures,[7] probably because such measures allow a rater to consider more evidence before making a decision. But the results of studies using low-inference measures are easier to use in teacher training programs, because the variables are easier to translate into specific behaviors.[8]

High-Inference Studies

Six studies were located which contained high-inference variables and measures of adjusted pupil achievement; some significant results were obtained in each of the six studies. Solomon *et al.*[9] studied the behaviors of twenty-four teachers of evening college courses in introductory American government. Two criterion measures were used: scores on a test on the American constitution (factual gain) and scores on a passage on political philosophy (comprehension gain). (Both residual gain scores and raw gain scores were computed, but because these correlated .90 or above, for simplicity the investigators used the raw gain scores as the criteria.) In all, 169 independent variables were investigated: sixty-one frequency measures developed from an analysis of the tape recordings of two class sessions for each teacher; thirty-eight observer ratings of the same two sessions; mean student ratings on fifty-two items, and the teachers' responses to eighteen items on a questionnaire. Scores on these 169 variables were factor analyzed by the principal components method with varimax rotation and yielded eight factors accounting for sixty-six percent of the variance.[10]

The factor labeled Clarity had a significant[11] relationship with factual gain (r = .58), and the factor Energy had a significant relationship with comprehension gain (r = .44).[12] The factors Energy and Clarity appear to describe a stimulating or enthusiastic teacher. Energy contained high loadings for observer ratings on "energy," "enthusiasm," "relaxation," and "mobility." Clarity contained loadings for student ratings on "expressiveness" and "enthusiasm," as well as a loading for observer ratings on "enthusiasm." The low-inference variables will be discussed below.

Additional evidence for the validity of the student ratings of "expressiveness" and "enthusiasm" may be seen in a subsequent study by Solomon[13] in which a similar student questionnaire was used to describe the classroom behavior of 229 teachers of a broad range of adult evening courses at five schools throughout the country. The criterion measure was the mean student rating on the question: "Considering everything, how would you evaluate the instructor in this course?" This criterion measure had been found in the previous study[14] to correlate significantly (r = .46) with factual gain. Factor analysis of the data in the 1966 study yielded ten factors, two of which were significantly related to the criterion rating. Of these two factors, the one labeled Energy versus Lethargy contained high loadings (.75 or higher) for student ratings of the teacher's "enthusiasm," "energy," and "expressiveness." This factor contained equally high negative loadings for "monotony" and "dullness."

Fortune[15] asked student teachers in social studies, mathematics, and English to teach three ten- to fifteen-minute lessons to randomly selected halves of their fourth-, fifth-, and sixth-grade classes. The average class size for each lesson was fourteen pupils. After each lesson, the teacher was rated independently by two supervisors on two scales, a bipolar adjective checklist similar to that used by Ryans[16] and a modification of the Stanford Teacher Appraisal Guide.

Of the eighteen bipolar adjectives, only one is of interest in this review: dull-stimulating. The simple correlations between ratings on this dimension and the adjusted class achievement scores on a twelve-item test were significant (p < .01): the more stimulating teachers had pupils who achieved higher scores. Although none of the items on the Appraisal Guide was similar to animation, it is noteworthy that the ratings of all forty-two teachers on the variable dull-stimulating had significant correlations (r's ≐ .30—.61) with seven of the eight items on the Appraisal Guide.

Wallen[17] studied the relationship of teaching behaviors to class scores in vocabulary, reading comprehension, and arithmetic, as measured by the California Achievement Test. Post-test scores were adjusted for initial reading ability. Separate analyses were made for thirty-six first-grade teachers and forty third-grade teachers.

The behaviors of the teachers were measured with rating scales, Q-sort ratings, and counts of the frequencies and proportions of specific behaviors recorded by trained observers in the classroom. No factor analysis was made. Of the twenty-five independent variables measured, three had nearly significant to significant correlations with pupil gain scores on all six dependent variables. These variables were the Q-sort ratings of behaviors labeled "stimulating," "intellectual effectiveness," and "achievement oriented." The variable relevant to this review—"stimulating"—had significant correlations with adjusted achievement scores in arithmetic in both grades. The stimulating teacher was defined as one who was "interesting and/or dynamic in her role as a teacher."[18]

This investigation by Wallen[19] was intended to clarify the results obtained in an earlier study by Wallen and Wodtke.[20] In their investigation, sixty-five teachers of grades 1 through 5 were observed, and separate correlations were reported for each grade; the number of teachers of each grade was "approximately 12." The highest correlations were those between observer ratings on "recognition" and adjusted pupil reading achievement scores (r's = .29-.65); four of the five correlations were significant. Recognition was defined as the "degree to which the teacher is the center of attention."[21] According to the investigators, the correlations suggested that "the more stimulating teacher . . . obtains a greater growth in reading achievement regardless of grade."[22] Because the term "recognition" was ambiguous, Wallen used "stimulating" as the observational variable in his concluding study.[23]

In a series of independent analyses of the same data,[24] Rosenshine,[25] Unruh,[26] and Dell and Hiller[27] sought correlates of effective "explaining behavior." In the basic investigation, forty-five social studies teachers gave two lectures—one on Yugoslavia and one on Thailand—on successive days to their twelfth-grade classes. Immediately after each lecture, the pupils took a ten-item comprehension test. The lectures were ranked according to the residual mean scores of the pupils in each class, after statistical adjustment for (a) the relevance of the material in each lecture to the criterion test and (b) the pupils' ability as measured by comprehension scores on a tape-recorded lecture on Israel.

Unruh[28] assigned thirty high school students to observe and describe the videotapes of the lectures on Yugoslavia, and an additional thirty to observe and describe those on Thailand. After viewing each videotape, the raters were asked to write at least six adjectives or phrases describing strengths and weaknesses of the teacher. The frequency of free-response mentions of "enthusiasm, vitality, energy, etc." was clearly related to the adjusted class mean achievement score on the Thailand lectures, but the corresponding results were not consistent or significant for the Yugoslavia lectures.[29]

Unruh then showed six-minute segments of the videotapes to the raters and asked them to rate each teacher on a series of twenty-seven seven-point, bipolar scales consisting of adjectives and phrases selected from the research literature. In this analysis the results were the opposite of those obtained using the free-response data. The ratings on items such as "enthusiastic-unenthusiastic" and "energetic-lethargic" correlated significantly with the achievement measure for the Yugoslavia sample (r's = .35 and .42), but the correlations were significant and negative for the Thailand sample (r's = -.33 and -.35). The studies by Unruh thus provide some support for the relevance of animation; but they raise difficult questions about the consistency of results when free-response and fixed-response rating procedures are used.

In an experimental study by Mastin,[30] teacher enthusiasm was manipulated as the independent variable. Twenty teachers of sixth-grade and seventh-grade pupils were asked to give two illustrated lectures to their classes; one lecture dealt with ancient Egypt, and the other, with ancient Rome and Pompeii. Each lecture was accompanied by a set of fifteen mounted photographs and a map of the Mediterranean area. The report of the study did not indicate the length of the lectures, nor whether a control was applied for differences in length. Each teacher was instructed to teach one lesson with enthusiasm, that is, "in such a manner as to convey to his pupils the impression that he was enthusiastic about the ideas and illustrative materials of the lesson and the subject covered by the lesson."[31] Each teacher was instructed to teach the other lesson with indifference, that is, "in such a manner as to convey to the group a feeling that he had an indifferent attitude about the ideas, etc." Every teacher taught one randomly chosen lesson with enthusiasm and the other with indifference. The pupils took a 102-item, multiple-choice test after each lesson. The fact that the two lessons and the tests were of unknown relative difficulty and may not be comparable was presumably taken into account by the random assignment of lessons to treatments (enthusiastic vs. indifferent) for each teacher.

The class mean for the lesson which was taught with enthusiasm, whether that lesson was presented first or second, and whether that lesson was the lecture on Rome or on Egypt, was higher for nineteen of the twenty classes than the mean of the lesson presented with indifference. Of the nineteen comparisons, fifteen were significant ($p < .01$); in one class, the lesson presented with indifference was significantly superior. Apparently, no observation of the teachers' performances during the lessons was made, and no behavioral definition of enthusiasm and indifference was obtained.

With the possible exception of the study by Unruh,[32] the results of which are not clear, these high-inference studies provide strikingly consistent results. They suggest that one of the patterns of effective teaching behavior identified by Ryans,[33] namely,

Pattern Z, described as "stimulating, imaginative, surgent vs. dull, routine teacher behavior" is significantly related to pupil achievement.

The results above are not particularly useful for teacher training programs because they do not tell us how a teacher should behave in order to be stimulating. To determine the specific behaviors, we must review studies that use low-inference measures.

Low-Inference Studies

The ideal design for low-inference studies to determine the behaviors which comprise stimulating teaching would be one in which both rating scales and objective observation instruments are used in the same study, and the results are examined in a table of intercorrelations. Administrative difficulties and cost factors frequently preclude these arrangements. Nevertheless, Solomon *et al.*[34] and Wallen[35] have conducted such studies.

In the study by Solomon and his co-workers[36] the factor Energy versus Lethargy contained loadings for several low-inference variables. There were high loadings for teacher requests interpretation, teacher requests opinions, teacher requests facts, and amount of gesturing; positive reinforcement also had a positive loading, and there was a negative loading for teacher factual statements. Thus, the teacher who scored high on the Energy factor appears to exhibit three types of related behaviors. First, he is energetic, a rapid speaker, mobile, and enthusiastic, but relaxed. Second, he asks varied questions of interpretation and opinion as well as factual questions. Third, he praises frequently.

Wallen[37] correlated Q-sort ratings with the frequency or percentage of specified teaching behaviors. The behaviors were tabulated by means of a modification of the Flanders[38] Interaction Analysis (IA) categories. In grade 1, the ratings on the behavior "stimulating" had significant correlations with four of the low-inference measures: asking questions, praise and encouragement, personal control, and hostility and reprimands. In grade 3, the ratings for "stimulating" were significantly correlated with two behaviors: praise and encouragement, and personal control. These correlations are not impressive. The lack of clearer evidence on the objective behaviors representing stimulating teaching may be due to the socioemotional orientation of the IA categories, and the lack of cognitive variables in the IA system.

More studies are needed which contain both high-inference and low-inference measures; it is hazardous to draw conclusions from two studies in which the pupils were of widely different ages. The results are similar in that counts of teacher use of praise or approval were related to ratings of "stimulating" or "enthusiastic" in both studies; however, in neither of the two samples studied by Wallen were frequencies of "praise and encouragement" significantly correlated with any of the three criterion measures. (Frequencies of "personal control" were significantly related only to growth in vocabulary in grade 1.)

Mobility and Animation

In two of the studies, low-inference behaviors representing mobility or animation may have been components of the high-inference behavior, stimulating. In the study by Solomon *et al.*,[39] the factor Energy contained high loadings for student ratings on "rapidity of speech" and "mobility." This factor structure was replicated in the subsequent study by Solomon.[40] In the study by Mastin,[41] teachers were limited to the technique of lecturing in both the enthusiastic and indifferent presentations; movement and variation of voice may have been the only behaviors which teachers could use in order to show enthusiasm.

Some additional correlational and experimental studies illustrate the effects of animated behavior. Rosenshine[42] studied lectures in order to determine the correlates of effective explaining behavior. One variable which discriminated significantly between the high-scoring and low-scoring classes with both lecture topics was the frequency and amount of time the teacher gestured or moved: the teachers of high-scoring classes moved and gestured more.

In an ingenious study, McCoard[43] investigated the relationships between certain "speech factors" of the teacher and pupil achievement. Although no details were given concerning the criterion measure, it was described as a "composite of pupil-change scores" in "measurable attitudes, ideals, and information in the social studies field."[44] These criterion tests were administered to the seventh- and eighth-grade pupils of forty teachers in one-room, rural Wisconsin schools. Each of the teachers prepared two audio recordings, a three-minute recording reading standard materials (reading), and a three-minute talk on the topic, "My Preparation for Teaching" (speaking). Twenty-two speech teachers listened to each recording twice and rated each recording on fourteen seven-point speech variables.

The results were remarkably consistent. On the reading tapes, all fourteen rated variables had significant correlations (r's = .34-.46) with the criterion measure. On the speaking tapes, eleven of the fourteen variables were significantly correlated with achievement (r's = .32-.42). Of the fourteen rated variables, ten can be analyzed as pairs: The first variable in a pair was a rating of a speech characteristic; the second variable was a rating of variation in that characteristic. Thus both "pitch" and "variation of pitch," and "volume" and "variation in volume" were rated. Ten comparisons of these pairs of variables can be inspected—five each for the reading tapes and the speaking tapes. In eight of the ten comparisons, the rating of the variation correlated more highly with pupil achievement than did the rating of the characteristic itself. These results suggest that inflection is an important correlate of achievement.

The results of four experimental studies support the importance of animation in enhancing comprehension. Coats and Smidchens[45] had two teachers present two ten-minute lectures in two ways—statically and dynamically. The static speaker "read the entire speech from a manuscript. He made no gestures, had no direct eye contact, and held vocal inflection to a minimum. However, he did speak with good diction and sufficient volume." The dynamic speeches were "delivered from memory, with much vocal inflection, gesturing, eye contact, and animation on the part of the speaker." The college students took a ten-item multiple-choice test after each lecture; the mean score of the students who heard the dynamic lecture was significantly higher (p < .01) than that of the students who heard the static lecture.

Similar conclusions on the importance of inflection can be drawn from part of a study by Gauger.[46] Two independent variables were investigated in this study: (a) the high school students only heard, or heard and saw the speaker; and (b) the speaker gestured or did not gesture. No significant differences in achievement were reported between hearing and seeing compared with only hearing the speaker, but those students who heard and saw or only heard a speaker who gestured achieved significantly higher adjusted post-test scores than those who heard and saw or only heard a speaker who did not gesture.[47] In addition, when the results in the hearing-only condition were analyzed separately, there was a nearly significant (p < .10) effect for gesture, even when the audience could not see the speaker.

In two studies, the use of gestures was experimentally manipulated. Both Jersild[48] and Ehrensberger[49] varied the method of presenting approximately fifty statements. The speakers varied their presentations by speaking in a loud or soft voice, pausing, saying, "Now get this," and gesturing, defined as a "simple gesture with hand, or pointing with the first finger."[50] The criterion was the score on a fill-in test (Jersild) or a multiple-choice test (Ehrensberger) on each of the statements in the presentation. Both experimenters found that statements were remembered significantly more often when accompanied by gesture than when presented in a neutral manner.

Summary and Discussion

In summary, the results of high-inference studies provide evidence that ratings given to teachers on such behaviors as "stimulating," "energetic," "mobile," "enthusiastic," and "animated" are related to measures of pupil achievement. The results of low-inference studies suggest that the frequencies of such variables as movement, gesture, variation in voice, and eye contact are related to pupil achievement.

These results may occur because animated behavior arouses the attending behavior of pupils. Because it is content-free, animated behavior enhances learning instead of distracting the pupils. It is possible, of course, that extreme animation would distract the pupils from the lesson because the pupils might focus upon the animation rather than on the content. But apparently, such extremes did not occur in the studies reviewed. Animated behavior may also serve as a secondary reinforcer: hearing and seeing an energetic speaker may positively reinforce certain responses of the pupils during the lesson.

In some of the correlational studies, the animated behavior may have been a by-product of either the teacher's superior organization of the material or his greatest task orientation. Although such an explanation is plausible, the experimental studies demonstrate that superior organization is not necessary, because merely instructing a teacher to increase his enthusiasm[51] or manipulating the amount of teacher animation[52] without modifying content resulted in superior achievement.

Future Research Using High-Inference and Low-Inference Variables

Although the high-inference variables and the low-inference variables discussed above appear to be similar, we must be cautious in claiming that high frequency of movement, variation in voice, and use of eye contact represent all, or even a significant part, of high-inference dimensions such as "energetic" and "stimulating." The task of validating the connection between the proposed low-inference and high-inference behaviors will be difficult. In addition, there is a need to search for additional low-inference behaviors in this area.

One relevant area for future research on low-inference behaviors which form part of the dimension labeled "stimulating" might be the study of teacher questions. The study by Wallen[53] suggests that the frequency of questions might be important, and the research of Solomon and his associates[54] suggests that the types of questions may be related to ratings of "energetic." Additional low-inference behaviors may include teacher responses to pupil answers, and teacher use of phrases about the importance or relevance of certain material.

There is a need for future studies similar to those conducted by Wallen and Solomon in which both high-inference and low-inference variables are included in the observation schedules. The correlations between these two sets of variables can then be studied more intensively. For example, in the study by Wallen,[55] very little of the potential of the relatively objective IA was utilized in the analysis, nor was there a classification of questions.

More intensive comparison of high-inference and low-inference variables may result in a better understanding of the correlates of teacher effects.

Future Research on Animated Behaviors

The identification of such low-inference teacher behaviors as frequent movement and gesture, variation in voice, and use of eye contact as correlates of pupil achievement suggests that these low-inference behaviors might be employed profitably in teacher education programs. At the same time, three types of studies could be conducted to add evidence about animation to that already gathered. First, replications of the original studies could be made with improved controls; second, correlational and experimental studies could be made to compare animation with other behaviors of teachers that are known to increase the comprehension of pupils; third, experiments could be conducted using the denotable, operationally defined behaviors included in the category, Animation.

A note about controls is appropriate. The experimental studies should include teaching in a manner described as "regular," in contrast to "enthusiastic" and "indifferent." That is, a test should be made of the possibility that the effect of enthusiasm is really the effect of novelty. A test should also be made of the possibility that indifference detracts from learning more than enthusiasm enhances learning.

Can teachers who characteristically teach without animation, whose pupils achieve low comprehension scores, be trained to increase the comprehension of their pupils by teaching with more animation? An experiment to test this question should include measures of retention for both teachers and pupils, to show whether teachers trained to increase their animation maintained this new behavior. Pupils could also be tested periodically to determine whether they maintained their improved comprehension while the teachers continued to use animation.

Notes

1. D.P. Ausubel. "How Reversible Are the Cognitive and

Motivational Effects of Cultural Deprivation? Implications for Teaching the Culturally Deprived Child," *Urban Education*, 1964.

2. J.M. Stephens. *The Process of Schooling: A Psychological Examination.* New York: Holt, Rinehart, and Winston, 1967.
3. W.I. Ackerman. "Teacher Competence and Pupil Change," *Harvard Educational Review*, 1954.
4. N.L. Gage. "Teaching Methods." In R.L. Ebel (Ed.) *Encyclopedia of Educational Research*, 4th Ed. New York: Macmillan, 1969.
5. N.L. Gage and L.J. Cronbach. "Conceptual and Methodological Problems in Interpersonal Perception," *Psychological Review*, 1955.
6. N.A. Flanders. *Teacher Influence, Pupil Attitudes, and Achievement.* U.S. Office of Education Cooperative Research Monograph No. 12, OE-25040. Washington, D.C.: Government Printing Office, 1965.
7. B. Rosenshine. "Objectively Measured Behavioral Predictors of Effectiveness in Explaining." In N.L. Gage *et al.*, *Explorations of the Teacher's Effectiveness in Explaining.* Technical Report No. 4. Stanford, California: Stanford Center for Research and Development in Teaching, School of Education, Stanford University, 1968.
8. Gage. "Teaching Methods," *loc. cit.*
9. D. Solomon, W.E. Bezdek, and L. Rosenberg. *Teaching Styles and Learning.* Chicago: Center for the Study of Liberal Education for Adults, 1963. The major results of the study are more readily available in these two articles: D. Solomon, W.E. Bezdek, and L. Rosenberg, "Dimensions of Teacher Behavior," *Journal of Experimental Education*, 1964; and D. Solomon, L. Rosenberg, and W.E. Bezdek, "Teacher Behavior and Student Learning," *Journal of Educational Psychology*, 1964.
10. One difficulty with this approach is that the ratio of variables (169) to subjects (24) tends to invalidate the assumptions of the factor analytic method. Because there are so many behaviors to observe, and administrative difficulties preclude the use of 200-300 classrooms, every study in this area contains more variables than classrooms.

11. In this paper, the level of significance is p<.05 unless otherwise noted.

12. The procedures used to determine factor scores and factor loadings for each teacher appear to be incorrect (G.V. Glass and T.O. Maguire, "Abuses of Factor Scores," *American Educational Research Journal*, 3 [1966]: 297-304). These procedures yielded factor scores which correlated highly with the true factor score (r's = .85 or above), but the resulting factor scores are not independent of one another.

13. D. Solomon. "Teacher Behavior Dimensions, Course Characteristics, and Student Evaluations of Teachers," *American Educational Research Journal*, 1966, pp. 35-47.

14. Solomon *et al.* "Teaching Styles and Learning," *loc. cit.*

15. J.C. Fortune. *The Generality of Presenting Behaviors in Teaching Preschool Children*. Memphis, Tennessee: Memphis State University, 1966.

16. D.G. Ryans. *Characteristics of Teachers*. Washington, D.C.: American Council on Education, 1960.

17. N.E. Wallen. Relationships Between Teacher Characteristics and Student Behavior: Part 3. U.S. Office of Education Cooperative Research Project No. SAE OE5-10-181. Salt Lake City: University of Utah, 1966.

18. *Ibid.*, p. 2.18.

19. *Ibid.*

20. N.E. Wallen and K.H. Wodtke. Relationships Between Teacher Characteristics and Student Behavior: Part 1. U.S. Office of Education Contract No. 2-10-013. Salt Lake City: Department of Educational Psychology, University of Utah, 1963.

21. *Ibid.*, p. 3.02.

22. *Ibid.*, p. 4.07.

23. Wallen. "Relationships between Teacher Characteristics and Student Behavior," *loc. cit.*

24. N.L. Gage *et al. Explorations of the Teacher's Effectiveness in Explaining*, Technical Report No. 4. Stanford, California: Stanford Center for Research and Development in Teaching, School of Education, Stanford University, 1968.

25. Rosenshine. "Objectively Measured Behavioral Predictors of

Effectiveness in Explaining," *loc. cit.*

26. W.R. Unruh. "The Modality and Validity of Cues to Lecture Effectiveness." In Gage *et al.* "Explorations of the Teacher's Effectiveness in Explaining," *loc. cit.*

27. D. Dell and J.E. Hiller. "Computer Analysis of Teachers' Explanations." In Gage *et al.* "Explorations of the Teacher's Effectiveness in Explaining," *loc. cit.*

28. Unruh. "The Modality and Validity of Cues to Lecture Effectiveness," *loc. cit.*

29. *Ibid.*, pp. 26-27.

30. V.E. Mastin. "Teacher Enthusiasm," *Journal of Educational Research*, 1963.

31. *Ibid.*, p. 385.

32. Unruh. "The Modality and Validity of Cues to Lecture Effectiveness," *loc. cit.*

33. Ryans. "Characteristics of Teachers," *loc. cit.*

34. Solomon *et al.* "Teaching Styles and Learning," *loc. cit.*

35. Wallen. "Relationships Between Teacher Characteristics and Student Behavior," *loc. cit.*

36. Solomon *et al.* "Teaching Styles and Learning," *loc. cit.*

37. Wallen. "Relationships Between Teacher Characteristics and Student Behavior," *loc. cit.*

38. Flanders. "Teacher Influence, Pupil Attitudes, and Achievement," *loc. cit.*

39. Solomon *et al.* "Teaching Styles and Learning," *loc. cit.*

40. Solomon. "Teacher Behavior Dimensions, Course Characteristics, and Student Evaluations of Teachers," *loc. cit.*

41. Mastin. "Teacher Enthusiasm," *loc. cit.*

42. Rosenshine. "Objectively Measured Behavioral Predictors of Effectiveness in Explaining," *loc. cit.*

43. W.B. McCoard. "Speech Factors as Related to Teaching Efficiency," *Speech Monographs*, 11, 1944, pp. 53-64.

44. *Ibid.*, p. 57.

45. W.D. Coats and U. Smidchens. "Audience Recall as a Function of Speaker Dynamism," *Journal of Educational Psychology*, 1966.

46. P.W. Gauger. "The Effect of Gesture and the Presence or Absence of the Speaker on the Listening Comprehension of

Eleventh and Twelfth Grade High School Pupils." Ph.D. dissertation, University of Wisconsin, 1951.

47. No significant main effect for gesture was reported in the original study. However, I reanalyzed the data using a 2 x 2 analysis of covariance design in place of the one-way analysis of variance design reported by Gauger. The covariates were IQ and pre-test score, and the criterion was the post-test score. The data were obtained from the original dissertation by Gauger.

48. A.T. Jersild. "Modes of Emphasis in Public Speaking," *Journal of Applied Psychology*, 12, 1928, pp. 611-620.

49. R. Ehrensberger. "An Experimental Study of the Relative Effectiveness of Certain Forms of Emphasis in Public Speaking," *Speech Monographs*, 12, 1945, pp. 94-111.

50.· *Ibid.*, p. 97.

51. Mastin. "Teacher Enthusiasm," *loc. cit.*

52. Coats and Smidchens. "Audience Recall as a Function of Speaker Dynamism," *loc. cit.*

53. Wallen. "Relationships Between Teacher Characteristics and Student Behavior," *loc. cit.*

54. Solomon *et al.* "Teaching Styles and Learning," *loc. cit.*

55. Wallen. "Relationships Between Teacher Characteristics and Student Behavior," *loc. cit.*

6.

Research on Teaching Effectiveness

Berj Harootunian

This paper focuses on teaching and teacher behavior rather than curriculum and instruction as such. No claim is made for either the comprehensiveness or the objectivity of this review. I want to stress, on the basis of available evidence, strategies which are promising for the study of effective teaching.

The problem I am concerned about can be illustrated best by a true story. A few years ago a colleague of mine bemoaned the fact that very few of his students knew who Comenius was. When I asked him why it was particularly necessary for prospective teachers to be able to identify Comenius, he became very indignant and accused me of all kinds of anti-intellectual sins.

Recently, teacher educators have placed much emphasis on performance criteria. There is no doubt that this is a desirable step, but given the present state of what we know about teaching, we may entrap ourselves into the same situation we are trying to get out of. We may in effect be requiring teachers or would-be teachers to demonstrate behaviors which may have the same sort of validity for their teaching as does the ability to identify Comenius. Rosenshine and Furst (1970), for example, point out that the Far West Regional Laboratory uses Minicourse I to train teachers to repeat student answers *less* often. The Northwest's Regional Laboratory's training program in Flanders' Interaction

Reprinted from *The Researcher*, Vol. 9, No. 1, February, 1971, with permission of the author and the publisher. The author is Professor of Education at Syracuse University.

Analysis requires teachers to repeat student answers *more*, since this will help establish the preferred indirect teaching style.

Which behaviors are most appropriate for teachers, and which are not? This question is an extremely stubborn one, but which nonetheless is the focus of this review.

There are, of course, some investigators who dismiss the study of effective teaching as an activity with little payoff. Stephens (1967), for example, theorizes with considerable empirical justification that all schooling, including teaching, is relatively ineffectual when compared to other more potent societal forces that bear upon the learner. As Gage (1968) notes, such a view is probably too pessimistic. For example, despite the statistically biased analysis of the Coleman Report (1966), measures of teacher characteristics accounted for a "higher proportion of variation in student achievement than did all other aspects of the school combined, excluding student body characteristics." Moreover, these teacher characteristics make a greater difference with black students. This differential effect of teacher characteristics for black students is an important point to which reference will be made again.

Gage (1968) attempted to make some "positive research-based statements" about successful teaching by (1) presenting a series of operational definitions of teacher behaviors that seem to belong on the same dimension, (2) citing the evidence in support of his inferences, and (3) labeling the dimensions of teacher behavior and characteristics. Gage was thus able to specify three dimensions on which teachers differ reliably from one another and on which differences are rather consistently related to "various desirable things about teaching." These dimensions are the warmth of the teacher, the guided discovery or indirect method of teaching, and what might be termed the teacher's grasp or control of the cognitive organization of the learning material.

Warmth of teachers is evidenced by such diverse operations as Categories 1 and 2 from Flanders' System of Interaction Attitude Inventory, the California F Scale, and Ryans' Teacher Characteristics Schedule.

Indirectness in teaching or guided discovery is defined by Flanders' Categories 3 and 4 and 8 and 9 and the degree to which teachers permit pupils to discover underlying concepts and generalizations for themselves.

The teacher's grasp or control of the cognitive organization of what he is trying to teach is more difficult to define. Gage cites as examples the work of Orleans (1952), Smith (1961), Ausubel (1963), Bruner (1966), and Gagné (1965). The efforts of these individuals have had important implications for curriculum. These would appear to be as crucial for teaching.

The three characteristics of teaching which Gage sketched out are, of course, only very rough approximations of what may be. Gage was careful to point this out himself, but we in education seem to be ever so attracted by easy answers, irrespective of the grossness of the evidence. One example should suffice to clarify this point.

Indirectness of teaching has been so stressed by various teacher educators that there are many people in education who are convinced that "direct teaching" is bad and "indirect teaching" is good. Indeed Soar (1966), through factor analysis, has found that the indirect categories (1, 2, 3) load on a factor orthogonal to the direct categories (6, 7). The factor containing the direct categories is inversely related to student achievement, but note also that the factor containing the indirect categories is *not* related to achievement. Moreover, when Soar (1968) reanalyzed his data, he found the relationship between indirectness and achievement tends to be curvilinear, not linear, and is a function of the nature of the achievement criterion. To quote Flanders (1970):

> . . . The pupil growth index which involves memory, a relatively low level cognitive task, can tolerate lower levels of teacher indirectness. . . . Yet higher levels of cognitive reasoning are associated with more indirect . . . teacher influence patterns: Creativity appears to flourish most with the most indirect patterns.

It would appear that indirectness in teaching, when matched with certain contextual or situational variables, is an appropriate teaching strategy but in other contexts and situations it is ineffective. I want to underscore at this juncture the idea of matching strategies and situations, since the implications of such interactions will come up again.

Perhaps, the most comprehensive attempt at synthesizing the relationships between teaching process characteristics and student achievement has been the continuing effort of Rosenshine (1970a), and Rosenshine and Furst (1970, 1971).

After finding and reviewing some fifty studies of classroom behavior, Rosenshine was able to identify tentatively eleven classes or constellations of teacher behavior that are promising. These studies employed both low- and high-inference measures. Low-inference measures are specific, denotable, and relatively objective. Flanders' System of Interaction Analysis is an example of a low-inference instrument. High-inference measures lack specificity and require an observer to make many more judgments. A scale, rating the enthusiasm of a teacher from 1 to 5, would be an example of a high-inference measure (Gage, 1969).

Rosenshine's tentative findings are best comprehended in their original context. What will follow here is in effect a review of a review and as such will probably not be very satisfactory. The original source (Rosenshine and Furst, 1971) should be consulted to get the full meaning of this synthesis and a specific listing of the citations. Only a brief description is feasible here. The eleven variables are:

1. *Clarity*. Teacher clarity has been found to be related to student achievement in at least seven studies. But teacher clarity has been for the most part assessed by high-inference instruments so that it is not quite clear just what is meant when we say, "a teacher is clear." "Organization" is a variable similar to clarity and has also been assessed in non-specific ways. Organization refers to such things as the amount of confusion in a lesson and the coherence of the lesson and has been found to be significantly and positively related to student achievement in four of six studies.

2. *Variability*. When teachers use different cognitive levels of discourse, vary the levels of student tasks, or employ a variety of instructional materials and classroom techniques, they are exemplifying the teaching behavior "variability." Significant relationships between variability, as measured by student ratings, and various criteria of student achievement have been found in at least five different studies. In three studies where specific counts were made, similar findings were reported.

3. *Enthusiasm*. A teacher's enthusiasm has been operationalized through the use of such devices as observer ratings on paired adjectives, observer estimation of amount of teacher vigor and power, and students' ratings of teacher involvement or excitement about his subject. Enthusiasm has been found to be significantly related to at least one criterion of student achievement in five studies, and all non-significant results have been in the positive direction. Rosenshine (1970d) suggests that more specific low-inference measures of enthusiasm might be elicited through the teacher's movements, gestures, and voice inflections.

4. *Task Oriented and/or Businesslike*. Teacher behavior which can be classified as task oriented, achievement oriented and/or businesslike has been variously measured. It is not clear at present whether these different behaviors can be lumped together. However operationalized, these behaviors have been found to be significantly related to student achievement in six of seven studies.

5. *Student Opportunity to Learn Criterion Material*. Only a few attempts have been made to determine the relationship between the material covered in a class and the criterion instrument. Opportunity to learn can be assessed by the overlap between transcripts of verbal classroom behavior and items on the criterion test, by amount of actual time spent on topics, or by teachers' estimates of the number of students who have been provided the opportunity to learn the content elicited by test items. Significant relationships between "opportunity to learn" and student achievement have been found in three of the four studies that have thus far looked at this variable.

6. *Use of Student Ideas and Teacher Indirectness*. Flanders' System of Interaction Analysis has generated this variable. Use of student ideas refers to Flanders' Category 3, while indirectness of teaching refers to Categories 1, 2, and 3. The latter contains the former; hence the reason for its inclusion here. Teacher use of student ideas is positively and consistently, but not significantly, related to student achievement. Investigations of indirectness of teaching have yielded similar results.

7. *Criticism*. Criticism by teachers and its effect on achievement have been studied extensively (seventeen studies). Criticism has been measured by simply counting the incidents and by

counting and then rating the event (e.g., strong, mild, or neutral). The surprise is that criticism has not yielded more significant findings. Six studies have found negative relationship between teachers' use of criticism and some achievement criterion. The relationship between criticism and achievement is more impressive when only the direction of the relationship is considered. Twelve of seventeen studies found negative correlations. In those studies where the intensity of the criticism was considered, the evidence from ten of seventeen studies suggests that teachers who are extreme in their criticism tend to achieve less with their studies in most subject areas.

8. *Use of Structuring Comments.* Teacher statements made at the beginning or end of a lesson which provides an overview or a summary are one example of structuring comments. But this variable has included other types of variously defined teacher statements. The lack of consistent definition makes this variable somewhat elusive, but teachers' structuring statements have been significantly related to student achievement measures in four studies and have been considered as important in at least two more.

9. *Types of Questions.* A number of studies have looked at the cognitive levels of teacher questions. Most of these studies have simply dichotomized the questions as higher order or lower order, but a few have attempted a multilevel classification. Teachers' questions have been categorized on only two cognitive levels in seven studies; only three of these found significant results which are at best ambiguous. It is not clear what kind of questions should be asked.

The three studies of multilevel teacher questions all have yielded significant results. However, with these studies, as with the two-level studies of questioning behavior, generalizations are difficult to make. The studies are too different in design, instrumentation, and objectives.

10. *Probing.* When a teacher responds to a student's comments by encouraging him or another student to elaborate further, he is engaging in probing behavior. The problem is that this variable is defined in other ways as well, so it may not be a single or unitary phenomenon. Whatever the definition, the three

studies that have identified probing as a variable have found it to be significantly and positively correlated with student achievement.

11. *Level of Difficulty of Instruction.* The difficulty of the course or lesson, as perceived by the students, has been a variable in a handful of studies. Strictly speaking, this variable, as it has been assessed, includes more than the teacher's behavior in the classroom. It may be more of a reflection of the brightness or abilities of the students in a class rather than the "toughness" of the teacher. In two of four studies there has been a significant positive relationship between student perception of difficulty and student achievement. Future research on this variable ought to clarify its function.

Taken in their entirety, Rosenshine's (Rosenshine and Furst, 1971) attempt at synthesizing research on teaching effectiveness represents a Herculean task. Of the eleven variables he has identified, it would appear at this time that five seem to be rather relevant to good teaching. These five are clarity, variability, enthusiasm, task orientation, and student opportunity to learn. Each of these variables needs more precise definition and further exploration. Two variables, use of student ideas and/or teacher indirectness and criticism, have not been as significant in the statistical sense but have occurred consistently enough over a wide range of studies to merit consideration. Finally four variables: use of structuring comments, use of multiple levels of discourse, probing, and perceived difficulty of the course need much more study to understand their role in effective teaching.

Perhaps, Rosenshine's effort is as important for what the research has not revealed. Rosenshine and Furst (1971) have summarized the situation as follows:

> At first glance, the above list of the strongest findings may appear to represent mere educational platitudes. Their value can be appreciated, however, only when they are compared to the behavioral characteristics, equally virtuous and "obvious," which have *not* shown significant or consistent relationships with achievement *to date*. These variables . . . are listed below, and the method by which they were assessed follows . . . non-

verbal approval (counting), praise (counting), warmth (rating), ratio of all indirect behaviors to all direct teacher behaviors, or the I/D ratio (counting), flexibility (counting), questions or inter-changes classified into two types (counting), teacher talk (counting), student participation (rating), number of teacher-student interactions (counting), student absence, teacher absence, teacher time spent on class participation (rating), teacher experience, and teacher knowledge of subject area. It is possible that future studies employing improved designs and improved analysis of the data, or future reviews of the same literature may yield somewhat different conclusions. However, such caution works both ways— one cannot claim that the above non-significant variables are correlates of student achievement until he can marshal supportive data.

Why has it been so difficult to identify the elements of effective teaching? Is teaching per se relatively unimportant as Stephens (1967) suggests? Or is it so complex that any attempt to take hold of part of it gives a false and unreliable picture? These questions are not new, and a number of people, such as Flanders (1970), Herbert (1970), Rosenshine and Furst (1970), and Turner (1970) all have recently addressed themselves to these and other similar questions.

As a finale to this review, I want to provide still another perspective for viewing studies of teacher effectiveness. This view suggests that as long as teacher effectiveness studies continue in the same vein, there is little likelihood of payoff and even Rosenshine's excellent synthesis may be misleading. The formulations which follow owe a great debt to the theoretical conceptualizations of Lee Cronbach (1957; 1967), David Hunt (1970), and Bruce Joyce (1968).

It was noted earlier that the characteristics of teachers had a differential effect for the achievement of black and white students (Coleman, 1966). Cronbach has formulated what has been called the Aptitude-Treatment-Interaction Model (ATI) to explain such differences. According to the ATI model what one should look for are combinations of learner aptitudes and educational treatments which will produce learner effects. Differences in teacher effects then are more likely to occur by looking at the effects of different treatments on students varying in aptitude than by simply taking the mean class achievement of the two or more alternative aspects of teaching that are being compared.

Hunt (1970) has reconceptualized the ATI model into a "matching model" by which he "aimed to set forth principles which specify those approaches most likely to facilitate certain objectives for different kinds of persons." In Hunt's application of the matching model, the basis for the match between learner characteristics and educational approaches is the student's conceptual level (CL). In Hunt's (1970) words:

> Given the characteristics of low CL learners—categorical, dependent on external standards, and not capable of generating their own concepts—the prediction follows that they will profit more from educational approaches providing a high degree of structure. Given the characteristics of high CL learners—capable of generating new concepts, having a greater degree of internal standards, and being capable of taking on different perspectives—they should profit more from approaches which are low in structure . . . the heart of the CL matching model is a generally inverse relation between CL and degree of structure: *low CL learners profiting more from high structure and high CL learners profiting more from low structure, or in some cases being less affected by variation in structure.*

Several studies have recently been completed that support Hunt's conceptualization (McLachlan, 1969; Rathbone, 1970; Tomlinson, 1969; Tuckman, 1968). Because of time and space constraints, only two of these studies will be described here. McLachlan (1969) investigated the interactive effects of learner CL and variations in structure as represented by a discovery (low structure) and a lecture (high structure) approach. High and low CL students matched on ability were assigned to the two conditions. The content of each treatment involved the presentation of visual materials designed to acquaint the student with the Picasso painting "Guernica." Students in both conditions were shown the same materials—a slide of the total picture plus a series of component parts of the picture on separate slides. The dependent variable was the student's subjective integration of the picture; i.e., whether a student was able to give his own ideas of the central meaning of the picture and how the parts fit together into this meaning. Results showed an ordinal interaction; low CL students performed significantly better under high structure (lecture) than low structure (discovery). High CL students did not differ under the two conditions.

Rathbone's (1970) recent study is particularly revealing vis-a-vis teacher behavior. Rathbone matched students and teachers on the basis of CL and looked at what happened to the teacher's handling of information. As predicted, the two matched groups, high CL students and high CL teachers and low CL students and low CL teachers, showed the greatest divergence in the teacher's verbal behavior. The mis-matched groups fell in between. Thus, anyone studying how the style of these teachers affected student achievement would be oversimplifying and masking the problem if he concluded that teachers with varying levels of CL handle information differently. It was not the teachers' CL per se that resulted in the greatest differences; it was the teachers' CL interacting with the students' CL.

Hunt has extended his matching model to include learner characteristics other than CL, so that it can handle various person-environment combinations. Basically the student is viewed in terms of his "accessibility channels." As Hunt notes, "taking account of accessibility channels is almost unavoidable when working with a physically handicapped student. Though less apparent, it seems equally important to consider any student in terms of channels of accessibility so that the form of educational approach can be most appropriately 'tuned in' to the student."

Thus, while the CL matching model considers only the cognitive orientation of the learner, others might be based on the motivational, value, and sensory orientations of the student. For example, the long-term work of Atkinson and Feather (1966) on motivation suggests that different kinds of feedback and rewards are required for students with affiliative motives than for students with achievement motives.

What the ATI and matching models mean is that the study of teaching and teaching effectiveness has a new set of ground rules. The question, "What characterizes an effective teacher?," has to be asked in a narrower way: "What characterizes the effective teacher for students with characteristic A as opposed to one for students with characteristic B?" We have probably intuited this all along, and now it is explicit.

In the past decade, such terms as interaction analysis, I/S ratio, indirect teaching, process-product variables, and many more have entered the vocabulary of researchers. In this new decade, those of us who study teaching would do well to become just as familiar and comfortable with "matching model," "ATI," "accessibility channels," "disordinal interactions," and the like. It sounds like a lot of fun, and we just might begin to unravel the murky complexities of teaching in the bargain.

References

Atkinson, J.W. and N.T. Feather. *A Theory of Achievement Motivation*. New York: John Wiley, 1966.

Ausubel, D.P. *The Psychology of Meaningful Verbal Learning: An Introduction to School Learning*. New York: Grune & Stratton, 1963, p. 171.

Bruner, J.S. *Toward a Theory of Instruction*. Cambridge: Harvard University Press, 1966.

Coleman, J.S. *et al. Equality of Educational Opportunity*. Washington, D.C. U.S. Department of Health, Education, and Welfare: Office of Education, 1966, Government Printing Office, Superintendent of Documents, Catalog #FS 3-238; 38001.

Cronbach, L.J. "The Two Disciplines of Scientific Psychology," *American Psychologist*, 12, 1957, pp. 671-684.

Cronbach, L.J. "How Can Instruction Be Adapted to Individual Differences?" In R.M. Gagné (Ed.) *Learning and Individual Differences*. New York: Macmillan, 1967, pp. 23-44.

Flanders, N.A. *Analyzing Teaching Behavior*. Reading, Massachusetts: Addison-Wesley Publishing Company, 1970.

Gage, N.L. "Can Science Contribute to the Art of Teaching?" *Phi Delta Kappan*, 49, 1968, pp. 399-403.

Gage, N.L. "Teaching Methods." In R.L. Ebel (Ed.) *Encyclopedia of Educational Research*, 4th ed. A project of the American Educational Research Association. London: Macmillan, 1969, pp. 1446-1458.

Gagné, R.M. *The Conditions of Learning*. New York: Holt, Rinehart, and Winston, 1965.

Herbert, J. "A Research Base for the Accreditation of Teacher Preparation Programs." Paper presentation at the AERA, Minneapolis, Minnesota, 1970.

Hunt, D.E. "A Conceptual Level Matching Model for Coordinating Learner Characteristics with Educational Approaches," *Interchange*, 1970.

Joyce, B.R. *The Teacher Innovator: A Program to Prepare Teachers*. Washington, D.C. Bureau of Research, 1968. U.S. Government Printing Office, FS5, 258:58021.

McLachlan, J.F.C. "Individual Differences and Teaching Methods in Student Interpretation of Modern Art." Unpublished master's thesis, University of Toronto, 1969.

Orleans, J.S. *The Understanding of Arithmetic Processes and Concepts Possessed by Teachers of Arithmetic*. New York: Board of Education of the City of New York, Division of Teacher Education, Office of Research and Evaluation, 1952.

Rathbone, C. "Teacher's Information Handling When Grouped with Students by Conceptual Level." Unpublished doctoral thesis, Syracuse University, 1970.

Rosenshine, B. *Teaching Behaviors and Student Achievement*. Stockholm, Sweden: International Association for the Evaluation of Educational Achievement, 1970a (mimeo).

Rosenshine, B. *Interpretative Study of Teacher Behaviors Related to Student Achievement*. U.S.O.E. Project No. 9B-010. Temple University, 1970b.

Rosenshine, B. "Evaluation of Instruction," *Review of Educational Research*, 40, 1970c, pp. 279-301.

Rosenshine, B. "Enthusiastic Teaching: A Research Review," *School Review*, 78, 1970d, pp. 499-515.

Rosenshine, B. and N. Furst. "Research Issues and Problems in

Didactics." Paper delivered at the Annual Meeting of the American Educational Research Association, Minneapolis, 1970.

Rosenshine, B. and N. Furst. "Current and Future Research on Teacher Performance Criteria." This article appears as Chapter 2 in B.O. Smith (Ed.) *Research on Teacher Education: A Symposium*. Englewood Cliffs, New Jersey: Prentice-Hall, 1971.

Smith, B.O. *et al. The Logic of Teaching*. Bureau of Educational Research, College of Education, University of Illinois, Urbana, c. 1961.

Soar, R.S. *An Integrative Approach to Classroom Learning*. Final Report, Public Health Service Grant No. 5-r11 MH 01096 and National Institute of Mental Health Grant No. 7-r11-MH 02045, Temple University, 1966.

Soar, R.S. "Optimum Teacher-Pupil Interaction for Pupil Growth," *Educational Leadership*, 26, 1968, pp. 275-280.

Stephens, J.M. *The Process of Schooling*. New York: Holt, Rinehart, and Winston, 1967.

Tomlinson, P.D. "Differential Effectiveness of Three Teaching Strategies for Students of Varying Conceptual Levels." Unpublished master's thesis, University of Toronto, 1969.

Tuckman, B.W. *A Study of the Effectiveness of Directive vs. Non-directive Vocational Teachers as a Function of Student Characteristics and Course Format*. Final Report, U.S. Office of Education, 1968.

Turner, R.L. "Conceptual Foundations of Research in Teacher Education." Paper presented at the AERA, Prentice-Hall Symposium, Minneapolis, Minnesota, 1970.

7.

One in Five Made Us Think

Garnar V. Walsh

Teaching at best is a difficult task, rewarding but far from easy. Experts have not as yet reached consensus as to what constitutes good teaching. What one group of theorists says is good, another group disputes. Teacher preparation often suffers from lack of direction and a sparsity of evidence as to how a good teacher is developed and trained. This can also be said of other academic areas of preparation. When one asks a chemist and/or historian, for example, "What have you done to a student in three or four years of training so that you can now say he is a chemist and/or a historian?" the persons asked will invariably be defensive and evasive. There will be little chance of receiving a well-structured and definitive answer. Other academicians will respond in similar manner.

This paper reports a research study conducted on two campuses, a State University College and a State University Center. The mechanical aspects of good teaching have been studied so many times that they were dismissed as the basis for this research project. Instead, it was decided to deal with the thinking processes of students and their reaction to what occurred in classes. Good teaching was thus defined as that which caused a student to raise his thought processes above the facts and data level. He mentally conceptualized, theorized, made general-

Reprinted from *Improving College and University Teaching*, Summer, 1972 with permission of the author and the publisher. The author is Assistant to the President of New York State University College at Potsdam.

izations, and drew conclusions. Answers were sought for the question: "What did an instructor do to cause you to conclude that the higher levels of thought occurred in his interaction with you in the classroom?"

A questionnaire was developed and mailed to a State College sample of 200, selected in a random fashion. A total of 117 students responded. A total of 184 at the University Center responded via the Direct Contact Approach. The results herein are thus drawn from data provided by a total population sample of 301 individuals.

The instrument covered three broad areas: (1) selected instructors who made students "think" and characteristics of these men and women; (2) qualities of the instructors which students felt triggered their thought processes; and (3) the total number of instructors in contact with the two student samples, and how many of these made students think beyond the facts and data level.

Before discussing some of the results of the survey, one point should be stressed. The results should be taken for what they are. These students (male and female) attended a State College and/or State University Center. They all reacted to an instrument and made value judgments. Their responses provide us with interesting information, and we may make generalizations and draw con- clusions. However, the reader is cautioned to remain "open" to the results of other similar studies, some of which may be contradictory.

Only the most significant data will be reported here. Table 1 contains information about the students and instructors they selected. A few comments will suffice. The reader will note that students often selected instructors from outside their own academic major (thirty-nine percent in the State College sample, fifty-one percent of the University Center sample). The question follows, "Why?" Are not students so engrossed in their majors that selection of one of their own would be almost automatic? On the other hand, do instructors in elective areas offer more in the way of variety and newness and are therefore more successful in raising the thought levels of students? The reason or reasons for instructor selections by students are not reported here, but the data do say that 139 students of the 301 picked "outside."

Table 1 data also indicate that higher thought processes may occur within lower level course interactions. The level of the course apparently has little to do with stimulation of thought. Other factors appear to be more important. A word of caution here: a number of students indicated more than one course level with their chosen instructors. This accounts for the discrepancy in total selections.

Table 1

Responses to Selected Student and Instructor Questions:
Sample Comparisons

	State College	University Center
Sample Totals	117	184
Student Academic Area Same as Instructor Chosen	71	91
Student Academic Area Different from Instructor Chosen	46	93
Level of Course (some multiselections)		
Lower Division	105	161
Upper Division	56	39
Does Instructor Have a Doctoral Degree?		
Yes	57	143
No	57	39
Did Not Answer	3	2

Finally, the doctoral degree data raise an interesting question. Have the rigorous doctoral degree programs with their emphases on the acquisition of greater knowledge neglected a factor or factors which are vital to the classroom interaction process? Almost one-third of the total number of instructors did not possess the doctorate, with the State College sample weighting the combined results.

Included in the instrument and fundamental to the study are thirteen qualities (see Table 2) which many people believe are necessary in the teaching process. Possibly the reader may see each of the thirteen as part of his own conception of teaching. All are admirable, desirable, and scarcely disputable. Participants in the study were asked to select the qualities which they felt had a major impact in raising their level of thinking in the classroom situation. The qualities are presented and ranked in Table 2. Participants were also asked to indicate qualities which they felt had a minor impact on their thought processes. These qualities were ranked. The results are not reported since the correlation was so high with the previous ranking that they do not add to the knowledge to be gained from this research.

Table 2

Qualities of "Greatest Impact"
by Ranks

State College Sample Qualities	University Center Sample Qualities
Rank	**Rank**
1 Expert Knowledge of Subject (f)	1 Expert Knowledge of Subject (f)
2 Ability to Stimulate Student Interest (d)	2 Enthusiastic Attitude Toward Subject (g)
3 Enthusiastic Attitude Toward Subject (g)	3 Ability to Stimulate Student Interest (d)
4 Ability to Explain Clearly (c)	4 Ability to Explain Clearly (c)
5 Encourage Active Participation in Classroom (k)	5 Systematic Organization of Subject Matter (a)
6 Systematic Organization of Subject Matter (a)	6 Encourage Active Participation in Classroom (k)
7 Warm, Outgoing Personality (j)	7 Warm, Outgoing Personality (j)
8 Maintains a Balance Between Theoretical and Practical (l)	8 Maintains a Balance Between Theoretical and Practical (l)
9 Sympathetic Attitude Toward Students (e)	9 Good Speaking Ability (mechanics) (b)
10 Good Speaking Ability (mechanics) (b)	10 Sympathetic Attitude Toward Students (e)
11 Fairness in Marking and Grading Tests (h)	11 Fairness in Marking and Grading Tests (h)
12 Attempts to Use Individualized Instruction (m)	12 Tolerance Toward Student Disagreement (i)
13 Tolerance Toward Student Disagreement (i)	13 Attempts to Use Individualized Instruction (m)

Table 2 shows the exceptionally high correlation between the two sample groups in their choices of those qualities exhibited by instructors who made them think. The data almost appear rigged. The table raises rather interesting questions. Why do students minimize the importance of individualized instruction? Why do they feel that a theoretical-practical balance is not as important as an enthusiastic attitude toward a subject, expert knowledge of subject matter, the ability to explain clearly, etc.? Is not a good speaking ability really one of the most important qualities of good teaching? It may be to many instructors, but are the students in agreement? Careful study of Table 2 will stimulate other questions.

The final area of the study dealt with all of the instructors with whom the 301 students came in contact during their years at their College and/or University Center. Results are reported in Table 3.

Table 3

Instructor Total, Quality and Percentage

	Instructors	"Thought Provokers"	Percentage
State College Sample	3,956	740	18.7
University Center Sample	4,194	912	21.7

The data in Table 3 are quite significant, and a number of questions arise. Why are the percentages of "thought provokers" so low? Are many instructors really that unsuccessful in triggering the thought processes of their students? Are many classroom situations that stupefying and stultifying to thought? Students seem to think so, and their responses are hardly complimentary to many of their instructors.

In conclusion, it is not the intent of this research study to generalize, recommend, criticize, or complain. Rather, its purposes are threefold: (1) to report on the opinions of a sample of students about instructors who have made them "think," (2) to raise questions which should cause instructors to look more closely and carefully at the classroom processes with which they are intimately involved and concerned, and (3) to seek a closer correlation between instructors and students as to what constitutes good teaching.

The only possible result is a better teaching-learning situation, and who can argue against that?

8.

Specifying Behavioral Components of Some Higher-Order Concepts of Teaching

Madan Mohan

Educators generally agree that there is a need to reform teacher education programs. It is pointed out that many teacher education programs emphasize telling rather than doing; deal with generalities rather than systematic development of specific skills; and provide little effective feedback. As a result of evaluative statements about teacher education, both by professionals and others, the structure and content of the education of teachers are being examined and in many instances recast.

Many teacher education institutions are getting away from an emphasis on meeting certain course requirements; rather, they are serving time to a system which emphasizes performance. Many projects have been launched to develop performance-based criteria for teacher certification. These projects are designed to provide models for helping teacher education break away from certifying teachers on the basis of completion of a certain number of courses; the new programs propose moving toward certifying them on the basis of how they perform in the classroom.

Inasmuch as performance is the outcome of behavior, the question naturally arises: What teaching behaviors make a difference in desired pupil outcomes? Many teaching behaviors have been suggested in research studies on teacher effectiveness, but there is little research relating teaching behaviors to pupil

This chapter was written at the special request of the editors of this book. The author is Associate Research Professor, State University College, Fredonia, New York.

performance (Harootunian, 1971). Though this caution by Harootunian is worthy of note, it is the contention of this writer that there are some basic teaching behaviors whose utility in promoting behavior changes in learners have been validated. Such behaviors combine the worthwhile characteristics of both goal-referenced instructional models (Glaser, 1965; Popham, 1964) and means-referenced instructional models (Flanders, 1965; Hughes, 1959). It is further contended that there are a few simple teaching behaviors of which all complex behaviors are made. It may be hard to imagine this. Just think: everything in the universe, from stars to snowflakes, is built up from just 100 or so basic "building blocks." Think of it this way. There are only twenty-six letters in the alphabet. Yet every book and article ever written in English is made up of different combinations of those twenty-six letters. In much the same way, all complex teaching behaviors may be made up of some combinations of the simple teaching behaviors which have a measurable and significant effect on pupil performance and pupil self-concepts and attitudes.

The problem is to identify teaching behaviors considered desirable, state criteria (speed of learning, retention, transfer, problem-solving, attitude change) against which desirability was established, specify conditions appropriate for the use of a specific teaching behavior, and specify these identified teaching behaviors so that practicing teachers can apply them in their classrooms and professional educators can determine the nature of teacher preparation programs. In this paper, an attempt is made to list teaching behaviors which have demonstrated positive relationship with pupil achievement in many studies reported in the educational literature. It is hoped that the specification of higher-order teaching concepts in terms of what teachers will be doing to bring about a desirable state or condition in their students will provide a handle on "effective teaching." These behaviors also will provide a reasonable yardstick for evaluating teaching effectiveness. Some of the higher-order concepts and their corresponding indicator teaching behaviors are as follows:

1. **Enthusiasm**
Teacher enthusiasm has been considered a desirable teaching

behavior by laymen, educational psychologists, practicing teachers, students, and even by critics of the process of schooling (Stephens, 1967). Many other higher-order concepts have been used to convey the same meaning: (a) teacher communicates a sense of excitement about the subject; (b) teacher creates lively interest; (c) teacher stimulates; (d) teacher is interesting and/or dynamic in her role as a teacher; (e) teacher does not convey a feeling that she has an indifferent attitude about ideas; and (f) teacher is stimulating, imaginative, and surgent.

However, all these descriptors of enthusiastic teaching are loaded with surplus meaning and do not tell teachers what they should do in order to be stimulating. Rosenshine (1970) suggests the following teacher behaviors to describe enthusiastic teaching:

1. Teacher requests interpretation.
2. Teacher requests opinions.
3. Teacher requests facts.
4. Teacher praises frequently.
5. Teacher makes gestures.
6. Teacher is a rapid speaker.
7. Teacher moves about in the classroom.
8. Teacher asks varied questions.
9. Teacher makes eye contact.
10. Teacher raises and lowers vocal inflection.

In discussing these behaviors, Rosenshine suggests that these behaviors facilitate stimulus reception because they arouse the attending behavior of pupils. It is also suggested that this enthusiastic behavior of the teacher may have been a by-product of either the teacher's superior organization of the material or his greater task orientation.

2. Warmth

Very important in what we do is the one-to-one relationship. Trust is the pre-condition for the relationship to be an effective interaction between the teacher and the child. We cannot interact fruitfully with people we scorn or hate. A review of research indicates that teacher warmth is consistently related to student achievement and favorable supervisor ratings (Gage, 1968). Other descriptors, such as "friendly," "understanding," and "sensitive" also have been used. Some of the low-inference behaviors that go to make up the meaning of the concept "warmth" are:

a. Teacher accepts the feeling tone of the students in a non-threatening manner.
b. Teacher clarifies the feeling tone of the students in a non-threatening manner.
c. Teacher praises student action or behavior.
d. Teacher encourages student action or behavior.
e. Teacher jokes to release tension.
f. Teacher turns minor disciplinary situations into jokes.
g. Teacher believes most pupils possess productive imagination.
h. Teacher believes most pupils are resourceful.
i. Teacher believes that students can behave themselves without constant supervision.
j. Teacher believes that most students are considerate of her wishes.
k. Teacher believes that her colleagues are willing to assume their share of the unpleasant tasks.

In summarizing these behaviors and attitudes, Gage (1968) argues that "teachers at this desirable end tend to behave approvingly, acceptantly, and supportively; they tend to speak well of their pupils, pupils in general, and people in general. They tend to like and trust rather than fear other people of all kinds." The reader must have noted a set of beliefs in the above categories. These beliefs, it is felt, are compatible with behaviors, extensive in scope, and dependable in action.

It may be pointed out here that conflict and commotion have been a constant companion of creative interaction and that every teacher gets a fair share of conflicts in the classroom. However, a teacher who (1) is blatantly nervous during face-to-face contact; (2) lacks a strong self-concept; (3) does not believe that children are capable of loving him and that he can get love from them; (4) is disconnected from his own desires, emotions, and inner experiences; (5) does not release his emotions; and (6) is not having contact with his inner-self, will find it extremely difficult to create a climate of warmth, affection, and acceptance.

3. **Indirectness**

Indirectness on the part of teachers has been found to yield positive results in many studies. In operational terms, indirectness means that the teacher behaves in the following ways:

a. Teacher permits pupils to discover underlying concepts and generalization for themselves.
b. Teacher gives students less rather than more direct guidance.
c. Teacher asks questions.
d. Teacher encourages pupils to become active, to seek for themselves, to use their own ideas, and to engage in some trial and error.
e. Teacher varies the degree of guidance.
f. Teacher is more alert to, concerned with, and makes greater use of statements made by students.
g. Teacher asks long, extended questions with greater fluency.
h. Teacher deals with ideas in detail.

Flanders' many studies on teacher effectiveness indicate that student achievement is significantly higher for indirect teachers.

4. **Expert Knowledge of Subject**

Another teaching concept that has been found to relate to student achievement is teachers' expert knowledge of subject. Other terms used to convey the meaning of the concept are cognitive structure, learning structure, logic tree, and organizers. This does not mean that the teacher is a storehouse of knowledge. Instead, it means that the teacher has a grasp or control of the cognitive organizations of the subject matter the teacher is trying to teach. Some of the teaching behaviors included are:

a. Teacher defines objectives.
b. Teacher analyzes learning tasks.
c. Teacher sequences subtasks into hierarchies according to the characteristics of the learning tasks.
d. Teacher details sequence of sub-behaviors.
e. Teacher matches subtasks with sub-behaviors.

In discussing results of his study, Worthen (1968) argues that teachers should be encouraged to develop skills in sequencing of learning tasks and suggests simulation as a viable technique to achieve this objective. Many learning theorists and researchers also support this view that the major requirement for learning and retaining verbal information is its presentation within an organized and meaningful context.

5.   Clarity

Ability to explain clearly has been found to be related to student achievement. Other words used to express the concept of clarity are lack of confusion in a lesson, coherence of the lesson, and intellectual effectiveness. Some of the behaviors included under this concept are:

a.   Teacher provides an overview of a lesson.
b.   Teacher summarizes a lesson.
c.   Teacher selects words for easy comprehension and minimal connotative possibility.
d.   Teacher checks the accuracy of the facts.
e.   Teacher arranges facts in a logical order to maintain an unbiased point of view.
f.   Teacher shows concern for grammatical clarity and correctness.
g.   Teacher adjusts his lesson to any feedback—positive or negative—that the teacher encounters.
h.   Teacher describes simple things simply.
i.   Teacher avoids the use of vague words.
j.   Teacher focuses attention on the main "things."
k.   Teacher considers the knowledge and background of students and uses words and terms that they can understand.

Through behaviors listed above, the teacher is able to substitute for the *unclear passage*, such as, "the English language can be utilized in such ways as to debilitate the listener's capacity to comprehend the speaker's intended significances. The abiding predilection among practitioners in variegated fields of specialized endeavor is to manifest their cerebrations in unnecessarily esoteric phraseology which obfuscates their formulations and renders them almost incomprehensible," a *clear passage*, such as, "English can be used to make things harder to understand. People in many areas of learning often use such weird language that few people can understand them" (Miltz, 1972).

6. Effective Communication

Ability to communicate effectively is a prerequisite to the teaching-learning process. We all know, of course, that it is not merely verbal expression but also tone of voice, attitude of body, the look in the eyes, etc., that makes for communication. The importance of non-verbal communication has been clearly brought out in Troilus and Cressida, in which Ulysses said of the Lady Cressida when she was brought to the Grecian camp and strangely disturbed that warrior: "There's language in her eye, her cheek, her lip/nay, her foot speaks. . . ." Freud also supported this view and believed that man is revealing himself ceaselessly, whether he intends doing so or not. "None of us," he is reported to have said, "can keep our secret: if our lips are silent, then we are chattering with our fingers or in some other way betraying ourselves." Effective communication means:

- a. Teacher listens carefully to his students.
- b. Teacher relates directly to every child's needs.
- c. Teacher provides classroom climate where the voice of the normally voiceless can be heard.
- d. Teacher provides significant information.
- e. Teacher verifies the correctness of the information received.
- f. Teacher provides prompt feedback.
- g. Teacher modifies his instruction after receiving feedback from students.
- h. Teacher projects ideas clearly.
- i. Teacher stimulates discussion.
- j. Teacher consciously avoids verbosity in expression.

7. Fluency and Flexibility

A teacher is expected to commerce with a variety of stimulus elements comprising the realities of a classroom. Each interaction in the classroom is unique and asks for a unique set of conditions for the attainment of desirable physical, emotional, social, and intellectual goals. This means that the teacher should provide a classroom environment with characteristics such as: (1) communication and interaction; (2) motivation and incentives for achievement; (3) availability of human models and examples of language, communication, and reasoning; and (4) opportunities for the understanding of the environment (Bloom, 1964).

A mimetic performance will not prove effective in providing quality experiences to meet individual needs of children. That fluency is related to student achievement has been supported by the Coleman (1966) report, and flexibility has long been considered a characteristic of effective teachers (Hamachek, 1969). These characteristics are also being advocated by Medley (1969) in his model for teacher education programs. The behaviors included in this category are:

   a.   Teacher uses variety of behaviors.
   b.   Teacher uses a large number of behaviors in a given time interval.
   c.   Teacher varies classroom activities.
   d.   Teacher uses variety of instructional materials.
   e.   Teacher uses variety of instructional techniques.
   f.   Teacher uses variety of reinforcements.
   g.   Teacher uses various types of feedback.

Studies on teacher fluency and flexibility strongly indicate that the above behaviors yield significant results.

8.   Motivation and Reinforcement

Any instructional model, to be effective, should not only be purely phenomenologically descriptive but also instrumental and motivational. However, as the saying goes, you cannot be a brother without having one. So a teacher will not be successful in motivating children for learning unless he is himself motivated. Some of the teacher behaviors included in the category are:

   a.   Teacher assesses each child on the motivational behaviors.
   b.   Teacher determines each learner's reward preference in advance of instruction, group discussion, or individual conference.
   c.   Teacher approves each learner's effort and accomplishment.

d.   Teacher cooperatively establishes instructional goals with each child.
e.   Teacher accepts ideas of pupil.
f.   Teacher uses ideas of pupil.
g.   Teacher pays attention to each learner.
h.   Teacher provides prompt feedback to each learner.
i.   Teacher provides individual, small group, and large group instructional experiences.
j.   Teacher manipulates classroom by introducing new, unfamiliar, and complex objects.
k.   Teacher provides model behavior in language, communication, and motivation.
l.   Teacher uses interest-centered activities to ensure that children encounter refreshing experiences and pursue independent work.
m.   Teacher uses individual conferences with each student regularly.
n.   Teacher encourages children to follow their particular individual interests.
o.   Teacher involves parents in the development of each child's language, pattern of achievement, motives for achievement, and personality structure.
p.   Teacher selects and develops a variety of verbal and nonverbal response skills to elicit desired pupil behavior.
q.   Teacher uses disapproval responses selectively.

The combination of these behaviors representing different forms of motivation and reinforcement has consistently yielded positive results.

9.   Questioning

The importance of questioning has been very well brought out by Rudyard Kipling in the following lines:

> I keep six honest serving men
> (They taught me all I knew);
> Their names are What and Why and When
> And How and Where and Who.

Most investigators who have studied teacher questions or teacher-student interchanges agree that questioning skills are very important for effective teaching. The behaviors included in this category are (Borg *et al.*, 1970; Groisser, 1964):

1. Teacher asks questions to clarify a concept or a principle.
2. Teacher asks questions to aid comparison between two related concepts or principles.
3. Teacher asks student opinion to stimulate critical thinking.
4. Teacher asks questions to redirect a learner to add something to the answers of other pupils.
5. Teacher pauses for three to five seconds after asking a question.
6. Teacher asks questions from nonvolunteers as well as volunteers.
7. Teacher asks questions that elicit a number of alternative answers.
8. Teacher uses question-stems like why, discuss, interpret, explain, evaluate, justify, and if.
9. Teacher asks prompting questions to help a student develop his answers.
10. Teacher asks refocusing questions to help a student to relate the student's answer to another topic.
11. Teacher avoids repeating his own questions.
12. Teacher avoids answering his own questions.
13. Teacher avoids repeating pupil's answers.

The development of better questioning skills, interestingly, is enhanced by the teacher's ability to be respectful of the questions children ask (Torrance, 1970).

10. Listening

The above nine higher-order concepts of teaching and their corresponding specific teacher behaviors will not result in student growth unless the teacher has the skill to listen to what the student is saying, and listen carefully. In fact, an effective teacher develops this skill to a degree that enables him to listen to the student when the student is silent.

Some of the behaviors included in this category are:

1. Teacher looks at the student.

2. Teacher concentrates on what the student is saying.
3. Teacher takes in every word said by the student.
4. Teacher asks the student to repeat the question.
5. Teacher repeats the question back to the student and asks the student if that is right.
6. Teacher rephrases the question and asks the student if that is right.
7. Teacher asks the student to clarify his basic assumption contained in the question.

Summary

These, then, are some of the teacher behaviors in the classroom which have resulted in pupil growth. These behaviors, therefore, are those extra things that describe teaching effectiveness. Teachers vary in exhibiting these behaviors in the classroom for many reasons. Among these are: the teacher's fixed goals, his attitude toward his students, his colleagues' attitude toward him, his professional education and experience. However, these competencies can be acquired by the teacher and can be included in a teacher education program with successful results if planning, conduct, and follow-up activities take into consideration the following points:

1. Competencies are ordered into a hierarchical sequence.
2. Each teacher's performance is assessed with respect to these competencies.
3. Competencies are divided into compatible, complementary, and competing categories for each teacher.
4. The program begins with assessing the competencies that a teacher may possess because knowledge of a person's existing competencies may be more important in predicting future behavior than any other information about him.
5. Expected competencies are defined and there is no delay in helping the teacher achieve satisfactory performance and in providing immediate feedback.
6. The connection between these teacher behaviors and pupil performance is validated.

In this paper an attempt has been made to describe in

behavioral terms several performances that have been found to promote pupil growth. It further suggests an outline for a teacher preparation program. The search for improvement of education of all our children demands that the quality of teaching should be improved. Can this be done? It is the contention of this paper that it is possible if the teacher education program stops offering experiences which tickle the muscles and capillaries but leave the dying tissue and the soul untouched.

References

Bloom, B.S. *Stability and Change in Human Characteristics*. New York: John Wiley and Sons, 1964.

Borg, W.R. *et al. Effective Questioning: Elementary Level, Teachers Handbook*. Beverly Hills, California: Macmillan Educational Services, 1970.

Coleman, J.S. *Equality of Educational Opportunity*. U.S. Department of Health, Education, and Welfare. Washington, D.C.: U.S. Government Printing Office, 1966.

Flanders, N.A. *Teacher Influence, Pupil Attitudes, and Achievement*. Co-operative Research Monograph No. 12, U.S. Department of Health, Education, and Welfare, Office of Education. Washington, D.C.: Government Printing Office, 1965.

Gage, N.L. "Can Science Contribute to the Art of Teaching?" *Phi Delta Kappan*, March, 1968.

Glaser, R. (Ed.). *Teaching Machines and Programmed Learning, II: Data and Directions*. Washington: Department of Audio Visual Instruction, N.E.A., 1965.

Groisser, P. *How to Use the Fine Art of Questioning*. New York: Teachers Practical Press, 1964.

Hamachek, D. "Characteristics of Good Teachers and Implications for Teacher Education," *Phi Delta Kappan*, Vol. L, No. 6, 1969.

Harootunian, B. "Research on Teaching Effectiveness," *The Researcher*, Vol. 9, No. 1, 1971.

Hughes, M.M. *A Research Report: Assessment of the Quality of*

Teaching in Elementary Schools. Salt Lake City: University of Utah, 1959.

Medley, D.M. "The Research Context and the Goals of Teacher Education," *Educational Comment*, 1969.

Miltz, R.J. *How to Explain: A Manual for Teachers.* Stanford, California: School of Education, Stanford University, 1972.

Popham, W.J. *The Teacher Empiricist.* Los Angeles: Aegeus Press, 1964.

Rosenshine, B. "Enthusiastic Teaching: A Research Review," *School Review*, 78, 1970.

Stephens, M.J. *The Process of Schooling.* New York: Holt, Rinehart, and Winston, 1967.

Torrance, E.P. *Encouraging Creativity in the Classroom.* Dubuque, Iowa: Wm. C. Brown Company, 1970.

Worthen, B.R. "A Study of Discovery and Expository Presentation: Implications for Teaching," *Journal of Teacher Education*, Volume XIX, Number 2 (Summer, 1968), pp. 223-242.

Section Three

TEACHER PREPARATION

Introduction to Section Three

Teacher Preparation

In Section One many crucial problems were cited which must be overcome before the evaluation of teacher effectiveness can be accomplished. In Section Two research-based evidence of teaching behaviors related to achievement of youngsters was presented. However, the achievement-related teaching behaviors specified in Section Two need further validation. In leading off this section, Donald M. Medley, in his article, *The Research Context and the Goals of Teacher Education*, claims that research has identified no pattern of teaching behavior which can be defined as effective teaching. He goes on to recommend that the function of teacher preparation programs should be to prepare each teacher to find out for himself what behaviors are effective for him. Medley's model for teacher preparation provides for development of experimental attitudes in teachers, a theoretical knowledge base, technical skills, and the ability to use feedback to analyze one's own teaching behavior and the behaviors of students.

Frances F. Fuller's article, *Concerns of Teachers: A Developmental Conceptualization*, points up the need for teacher educators to consider seriously teachers' concerns if preparation programs are to be geared to the needs of teachers. Fuller found that teachers' concerns are developmental and tend to move from a concern for self to a concern for children as early "survival" problems are solved or ameliorated. Fuller's article supports Medley's assertion that teacher preparation programs should be based, in part, on the predispositions of the persons who are being prepared for the teaching profession.

157

Ronald E. Hull, in his paper, *Effective Induction of Teachers: A Point of View*, builds on Fuller's conceptualization of teacher concerns by providing data that show that self-concerns are not necessarily unique to beginners; experienced teachers new to a school system or new to a particular set of expectations may also exhibit self-concerns. Hull contends that both pre-service and in-service teacher preparation programs should be systematized to the extent that teachers know what is expected of them and what to expect from others. The induction process is discussed in terms of planned intervention following a model for individualizing the treatment of teachers.

David E. Hunt's article, *A Conceptual Level Matching Model for Coordinating Learner Characteristics with Educational Approaches*, deals with a model which specifies the appropriate educational approach for accomplishing a particular objective for an individual learner. This article adds specificity to Medley's plea for a teacher preparation program that can identify which teacher behaviors have which effects on which pupils in which situations. Hunt's conceptual level (CL) matches model controls for the following clusters of variables: (1) short- and long-range educational objectives; (2) conceptual levels of teachers and pupils; and (3) educational approaches, and conception of the interactive process between person and environment. Empirical tests of the model have indicated, for example, that low CL students profit more by increasing environmental structure and vice versa.

Hunt acknowledges that adoption of the CL matching model will depend on teachers' acceptance of his proposed theory of matching and the extent to which teachers have decision-making prerogatives with regard to instruction of their students. It seems necessary that teacher educators must play a role in helping to develop in their students the predispositions to accept Hunt's ideas; and it is incumbent upon schools to support in-service teachers in their efforts to try systematic approaches to matching characteristics of teachers and learners.

In an attempt to end this section on a positive note, Don Hamachek's article, *Characteristics of Good Teachers and Implications for Teacher Educators*, is included. Hamachek contends that good teachers do exist and can be identified. For example, research findings indicate that good teachers are flexible, learner-centered, and have good self-concepts. Hamachek supports Hunt's ideas by asserting that teacher candidates need to be sensitized to the subtle complexities of personality structure; he supports Fuller's notion that instruction must be related to immediate needs and concerns of the teacher candidates; and he recommends that teacher preparation be grounded in a strong knowledge of subject matter, with special emphasis on communication skills.

9.

The Research Context
and the Goals of Teacher Education

Donald M. Medley

In preparing this paper on the research context I have not attempted any kind of a summary of research related to teacher education or to teacher effectiveness.

What I have tried to do, instead, is to put down some of my own current thinking on the subject. Most of my professional life has been spent doing, reading, or thinking about research in teacher education—and trying to make sense out of it. This paper will attempt to convey the results of this effort. It is, of course, impossible at this point in time for me to trace many of these notions back to the specific pieces of research out of which they grew, so I shall not try to do so. What I say may properly be regarded as nothing more than personal opinion, I hope; but opinion still.

The relationship that ought to exist between research and teacher education is quite clear. The plan or design of a program for a modern teacher education program should be based on the answers supplied by the research literature to three questions:

1. What are the behavioral skills a teacher must possess in order to be effective?
2. What are the characteristics a student must possess before he can acquire these skills?

Reprinted from *Educational Comment*: Toledo, The University of Toledo, College of Education, 1969, with permission of the author and the publisher. The author is Professor of Education, Bureau of Educational Research, University of Virginia.

3.   What are the training experiences which will help the student acquire the skills most efficiently?

Unfortunately, research has not yet produced useful answers to these questions. In particular, the failure to answer the first question has precluded any possibility of success in answering the other two.

This failure may be chiefly due to methodological defects which plague most of the studies. Research in learning has only recently begun to abandon an unsuccessful attempt to imitate medical research, as it becomes obvious that the similarity between physiological processes in men and mice which medical research has used to such advantage does not hold for the psychological processes which concern the classroom teacher. Research in methods of teaching has been even less successful in efforts to adapt the methods of classical physics and the law of the single variable to the fantastically complex phenomena of teaching and learning.

But there may be a more fundamental flaw underlying research of both types: an inappropriate model. Research in learning has by and large ignored the teacher; research in teaching has neglected individual differences among teachers. Recent research in the teaching-learning process (as it is called today) is beginning to recognize these differences, and may yet begin to develop the understanding of the nature of effective teaching we need as a basis for training teachers.

Recognition of individual differences among teachers, and all that it implies, requires a model for research in teaching radically different from that implicit in past research. And the teacher education program of the future also needs a new model if it is to keep pace with the new science of teaching as it develops. I shall now sketch in rough detail the principal features of such a model.

A Model for the Study of Teaching

The crucial distinction upon which this model is based is that between teacher effectiveness and other teacher characteristics. While the ultimate goal of a teacher education program has to do with teacher effectiveness, more immediate objectives have to do with other characteristics (especially behavior patterns or strategies), and it is in this domain that the program must operate.

Let us imagine a set of N dimensions describing N character-istics of teachers which are orthogonal—that is, uncorrelated. Assume that there exists a measure for each characteristic such that for any given teacher there is a point on each axis of the space corresponding to the degree to which that teacher possesses that characteristic. The N points locate a single point in the space representing all of the measured characteristics of that teacher. Two points that are close together will represent two teachers who are very much alike; too far apart will represent very different teachers. For simplicity in this discussion, let us assume that the characteristics represented by the axes are all behavior dimen-sions—dimensions describing how the teacher behaves while teaching in a population of pupils and situations in which he must work, while he is trying to achieve a certain set of objectives.

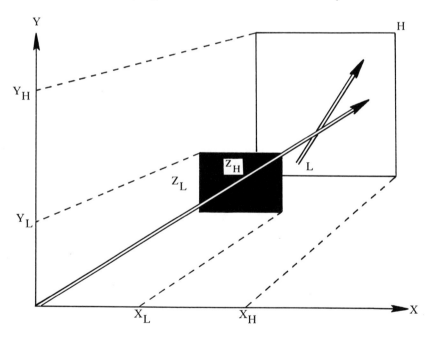

Figure 1

A Model for the Study of Teaching

Figure 1 is provided to assist the reader in visualizing such a behavior space. In the figure it is assumed that N = 3—that there are three dimensions of behavior in terms of which each teacher is to be described: X, Y, and Z. Two points have been plotted corresponding to two teachers. Point H represents a teacher whose behavior scores are X_H, Y_H, and Z_H; point L represents a teacher whose scores are X_L, Y_L, and Z_L.

Let us suppose that point H represents the pattern of behavior a teacher education program is designed to produce—represents the behavioral goals of the program. And let us suppose that point L represents the way a certain student behaves under the same circumstances. Then it is clear that what the training program must do is change the student's behavior so that it resembles "effective" behavior more closely—that is, to move L toward H.

By comparing X_L to X_H, Y_L to Y_H, and Z_L to Z_H, it would be possible to describe the needed changes in terms of the three known dimensions X, Y, and Z—to plan a strategy for achieving goal H. It might become apparent, for example, that changes on characteristic Y would produce more improvement than changes on the other two. If other students' behaviors were also plotted in the diagram of Figure 1, some of them might be closer to H or farther from it, and might even lie on the other side of H from L. Thus, it appears that, in order to reach the same point H, different students may need to change not only in varying degrees, but even in opposite directions. One teacher may, perhaps, need to go up on dimension Y while another needs to come down.

Let us now turn to the problem of what is meant by teacher effectiveness. Teacher effectiveness must be defined, not in terms of teacher behavior, but in terms of effects on pupils. A particular criterion of teacher effectiveness will specify the effects to be produced (objectives), a population of pupils upon whom they are to be produced, and a set of situations in which the effects are to be produced. There will be not one, but many different kinds of teacher effectiveness, then, and a particular teacher may be much more effective in one sense than in another.

Suppose that we agree for the present on one particular kind of effectiveness as the one we are trying to produce. Then it is theoretically possible to rank any set of teachers in order of effectiveness from highest to lowest. Suppose that we have done this, that teachers H and L are two of the teachers in our set or population of teachers, and that H is the most effective and L the least effective of the teachers in the population. This would justify our taking the pattern of behavior represented by point H as a specification of the behavioral objectives of our training program, and teacher H would be ready for graduation.

Teacher L, on the other hand, would need to change his behavior (as we have already suggested) and the line LH would indicate the direction of change.

The crucial question is, Where do the rest of the teachers in our population fall? Suppose we were to plot the position of another teacher, whose effectiveness was about halfway between those of teacher L and H. Where would his behavior be plotted? Would it lie on the Line LH somewhere near the center? Most theory and research in teacher effectiveness has tended to assume that it would lie on or near the center of the line LH; and that, in general, if all of a population of teachers were located in the space, they would tend to line up in order of their effectiveness. One implication of this that is important to us is the implication that any teacher who wishes to change his behavior in such a way as to increase his effectiveness (as defined) must change it to resemble that of teacher H more closely.

It would be very convenient both for research and for teacher education if all of the behavior patterns of all teachers did fall along line LH, with more effective teachers tending to be closer to H and less effective ones closer to L. The linear models used in research would be appropriate to such a situation; and the procedures needed for training different teachers would be similar, differing in the amount rather than kind of change needed.

I am afraid that the situation is probably very different. If all of the teachers' behavior patterns were plotted in the space, and a line then drawn from the "best" teacher (H) to the next-best, then to the third best, and so on, ending at the "poorest" (L), the line would not run straight from L to H but would zigzag all over the place. Research designed to inter-relate behavior and effectiveness would tend to yield low and conflicting correlations. Attempts to get all of a group of teachers to adopt the same pattern of "effective" behavior would produce relatively little average improvement; some teachers would even get worse. Does this sound familiar? Of course it does, because this is exactly what our experience has been.

Suppose that we plot only the points representing (say) the most effective ten percent of the teachers in the population, and leave the rest out. If the classical model were even approximately correct, we would expect these points to cluster in a relatively small region around point H. I suggest that we are most likely to find them clustering in two or more different regions of the space, with each region representing a behavior pattern that some teachers have found to be highly effective. These regions may be quite far from one another, representing quite different styles which are approximately equal in effectiveness.

If we now plot the remaining ninety percent of the teachers, chances are that each point will be relatively nearer to one effective region than to any other. This would suggest that we ought to identify quite different behavioral goals for different teachers selecting for each one the style nearest where he is as his goal. This would make it possible to produce greater increases in effectiveness with less change in behavior (and hence less effort) than would be required if a single set of behavioral goals were adopted for all students. Even when the goal of a teacher education program is to produce teachers all of whom are effective in the same sense, then, the behavioral goals for individual students may need to be quite different. Such a state of affairs also points to a different strategy for research in teacher effectiveness, based not on a search for a single optimal behavior pattern for producing maximum effectiveness, but on an attempt to discover several distinct teaching styles, each of which is just about as effective as any of the others.

We have so far considered only one criterion of effectiveness. If there are different kinds of effectiveness to be developed in a program (if we wish to produce teachers of different subjects, or teachers who will be effective with pupils of different sexes, ages, cultural backgrounds, etc.), there is no reason to expect that the same behavior patterns will be highest on all of the dimensions of effectiveness that interest us, although some of them may. The research question now becomes that of finding which teaching styles go with which effectiveness criteria.

If consideration is given to each student's present or natural behavior pattern, the kind of teacher he wishes to be, and the situations in which he may be employed, the problem becomes so complex that we may as well adopt as a working assumption the proposition that the behavioral goals of teacher education are an individual matter. The direction and amount of change that should be produced in each teacher will tend to be unique to him, and few or no generalizations can be made about what constitutes "improvement" in teacher behavior—at least in our present state of ignorance.

Perhaps the picture I have painted is too dark. Maybe there are not quite as many different types of teacher behavior all of which are equally effective as I have imagined. But I am sure this picture, pessimistic as it is, is closer to the truth than the simplistic model we have used in the past, the model which assumes that for any given definition of effectiveness there is one behavior pattern which is most effective for all teachers. Research has certainly not been able to identify any such pattern, and it has certainly tried.

Implications for Program Design

If we assume, then, that research does not provide any adequate basis for a prescriptive approach to teacher training, for a program designed to tell a teacher how he must behave to be effective with the class he will face in his first year on the job, what kind of training program can we design? If our objective is not to train teachers to behave in certain ways, what is it? I submit that the proper function of the "professional" component in a teacher education program is to prepare each teacher to find out for himself what behaviors are effective for him. We must offer teachers, not solutions to all of the instructional problems they will meet, but ways of solving these problems for themselves. We must produce teachers ready, willing, and able to do their own clinical research; teachers who will look upon teaching, not as a craft in the practice of which a teacher applies rules and recipes, but as a profession in which he is constantly solving new problems for which no recipe exists.

The model teacher education program must provide the teacher with four things:

1. An experimental attitude—a willingness to examine, evaluate, and modify his own teaching behavior throughout his career.

2. Theoretical knowledge—familiarity with all that past experience and research has discovered which might be useful to him.

3. Technical skill—control over methods, techniques, and media of instruction (including his own behavior), so that he can implement the theoretical knowledge he possesses.

4. Feedback techniques—ability to use objective methods for analyzing teacher behavior and assessing its outcomes, so that he can learn from his experiences.

Let us examine each of these objectives in somewhat greater detail.

Experimental Attitude. The present structure of teacher preparation and utilization tends to foster the idea that teacher competence is a point which most teachers reach at some time in their careers. Once a teacher reaches that point, his training is over. He may take a refresher course now and then to learn about recent innovations, but these are minor matters. Once a teacher has been awarded tenure, his competence is no longer supposed to be questioned, or to need upgrading. He has arrived.

The new teacher education program should produce a new kind of teacher, a teacher who looks upon his skill as something dynamic, something like a plant which dies when it stops growing. A teacher who looks upon teacher behaviors and effectiveness in terms of the model proposed above will not think that when he graduates from his pre-service course his training is over. He will go into his first teaching position with the expectation of learning at least as much during his first year in service as he has learned during each year of pre-service training. He will view his teaching certificate as a license to practice, rather than as a release from any obligation to learn. He will look upon the achievement of permanent tenure as a recognition of past progress and as admission to advanced study. He will be a true professional.

Theoretical Knowledge. Much of the content of didactic instruction in present-day teacher education can continue to function in the new program as a means to the achievement of this objective. But the attitude toward this material will be very different. Results of laboratory studies in learning theory, for example, may still be taught to teacher education students. But instead of presenting generalizations about classroom behavior extrapolated from these studies as established principles that teachers can depend on, such generalizations will be presented as hypotheses about classroom learning which the teacher may wish to try out as possible solutions to teaching problems he encounters. The teacher with a solid and comprehensive theoretical background may be expected to deal more effectively with novel problems that come up while he is teaching than a teacher who lacks such training, because he will have better ideas about what to try—will be more creative in his classroom behavior.

Technical Skill. When a teacher confronts a teaching problem and his theoretical training or past experience suggests a particular course of action, it is essential that he is able to implement it, whatever it may be. His training must, as far as is possible, help him learn to use all of the technological aids, teaching materials, and instructional methods in the modern teaching collection; it must also help him develop those skills commonly referred to as teaching skills—the ability to interact effectively with pupils, to manage a class, to explain, ask questions, conduct discussions, etc. These skills and techniques will be viewed as tools of the trade, all of which he knows how to operate and from which he can select at will the one he thinks will be most effective in a given instance.

Feedback Techniques. The teacher must also learn techniques for assessing what is happening to pupils—must know how to administer and interpret standardized tests and to build tests of his own, as well as how to use less formal procedures for observing pupils. He must be able to find out how effective he is from day to day and hour to hour. He must also be able to monitor his own behavior—to use some of the interaction analysis systems, for example—so that when his behavior is effective he will understand what he did well enough to be able to do it again when he wishes to do so.

It should be clear that all of these objectives are closely inter-related—that achievement of any one will affect and be affected by the achievement of the others. Possession of a full range of technical skills will free a teacher to try new things. A broad theoretical training will suggest more things to try. Ability to obtain objective and accurate feedback about what happens will enable the teacher to profit from such experiments. And all three will strengthen his willingness to experiment, will build the experimental attitude identified as the first objective of teacher education. And if and when research makes available to him new information about what is likely to work for him when he faces a particular problem, the teacher will be ready, even eager, to try it out.

Implications for Research and Evaluation

Nowhere is it more important to maintain the distinction between teacher behavior and teacher effectiveness than when considering the problem of evaluation. The ultimate objective of any teacher education program must be to produce effective teachers; and the program, therefore, must be measured in terms of what happens to pupils. The intermediate goal of any teacher education program must be to produce teachers with certain characteristics, and must be measured in terms of what teachers do. When we wish to evaluate a program, then, we must confront the question, "How effective are its graduates in the classroom?" When we wish to evaluate a student, we must ask, "What effect is our program having on his behavior?"

If a student achieves all of the goals of the program to a high degree—develops an experimental attitude, acquires a broad and rich knowledge of pedagogical theory, acquires adequate skill in both conducting learning experiences and in evaluating their effects—and then fails as a teacher, it is the program that has failed, not the student.

As a student passes through the program, there will be numerous occasions on which he will be evaluated, for diagnostic purposes, for measurement of progress, for feedback in super-vision. Many of these evaluations will and should be based on his behavior in laboratory, clinical, internship, and induction teaching situations, and will involve comparing what he does with what he is trying to do. To the extent that the teacher is able to control his own behavior, the evaluation will be positive. The effects his behavior has on the pupils with whom he is working are irrelevant to the evaluation of the teacher.

This does not mean, however, that data about his effects on pupils should not be collected. In each instance in which the behavior of a teacher is measured while he is trying to affect pupils, the effects on the pupils (and other relevant variables such as student characteristics and situational factors) should also be measured.

Such data should be collected, first of all, for feedback to the teacher, so that in addition to learning how successful he has been in implementing the behavior he has tried to exercise, he may also gain information about the effects this way of behaving has on pupils. Later on, when the teacher is on his own, he must continue to collect this kind of information, since the contribution of experience to his competence depends on its telling him something about the relationship between his behavior and its effects on pupils.

The same data will also serve another purpose. If the student's progress is to be evaluated, this should be, as we have seen, based on his own behavior. But the information obtained about its effects on pupils can be used to evaluate and improve the program of training. If students who are learning to exhibit the behaviors we recommend are achieving the effects on pupils they are supposed to achieve, our program is effective in some degree in achieving its ultimate goal of producing effective teachers. If students who are learning to exhibit these behaviors are not having the intended effects on pupils, the behavior does not do what it is supposed to do. Since the information relates specific behaviors to specific effects, it is diagnostic.

These same data may also serve a third important function, by providing research data of value to teacher education as a whole. The accumulation of data relating specific teacher behaviors to specific outcomes under measured conditions in various institutions over a period of time should build up a much needed stock of information. Gradually we would accumulate more and more knowledge about which teacher behaviors have which effects on which pupils in which situation. Such data would soon enable us to weed out from the theoretical content of the program those extrapolations which do not work, as well as shedding light on those which do, indicating which ones do have validity, for what purposes, and under what conditions.

It seems to me that this line of reasoning points to a research strategy quite different from anything we find in past or present teacher education programs. It appears that research, evaluation, and what might be called the teacher's own clinical experience can all merge into a single operation which has the potential of achieving the functions of all three—development of research knowledge, provision of continuous diagnostic feedback to the program, and facilitation of teacher self-improvement at both the pre-service and in-service levels—much more effectively than any present structure does or could possibly do.

No function performs itself, no operation is performed without an operator. If this process is to go on, someone must be responsible for it. Someone must manage the collection, collation, and dissemination of this information. This person would have to be a member of the program staff with close contact and rapport with faculty, students, and school personnel, and something more—not primarily a research type person, although he would need considerable competence in research methodology. He would be a key person in ensuring that all three functions met in their common goal of improving teaching, and in preventing any of the information being gathered from inappropriate use or interpretation.

One final suggestion. If a research enterprise of this nature is contemplated, early consideration should be given to the possibility of storing all of the information in a computer-based data bank with access through objectives, behaviors, pupil variables, and situations, so that ultimately it would be possible to query the system in a number of ways. A teacher might ask what behaviors had been found effective in achieving goal X with pupils of type Y in situation Z, for example, and receive a printout summarizing all experience relevant to that problem reported to date. A teacher educator might request information related to the effectiveness of a particular strategy for training teachers, or for the most effective strategy for a particular purpose.

Concluding Remarks

If I had to sum up the relationship between research and teacher education in one sentence, I would say that the teacher educator should ask, not what research can do for teacher education, but what teacher education can do for research. Past research has developed so little knowledge of the nature of effective teaching that I have had to propose a model for teacher education which does not assume the existence of any such knowledge at all.

The program for training teachers based on the model I have described above is designed primarily to prepare each graduate to discover for himself what style of strategy is effective for him in his own situation.

I have also suggested that a feedback system be incorporated in the program that will use the experiences of teachers trained in it to develop, bit by bit, the understanding of the teaching-learning process which research has so far failed to provide. As such knowledge accumulates, the amount of help the program can give its students in their search for effectiveness should increase, and it is in this process that all our hope of ever developing a viable theory of teaching lies.

Once more I say that teacher education should not look to research in teaching for help in training teachers; on the contrary, research must look to teacher education for help in developing a science of teacher behavior as a by-product of the process of teacher education.

10.

Concerns of Teachers:
A Developmental Conceptualization

Frances F. Fuller

The motivation of the learner is generally conceded to influence his learning. To be useful, however, this principle requires specification of the goals of particular learners in particular situations. As McKeachie (1963, p. 1119) says about undergraduates:

> We know that student learning and memory are closely tied to motivation. Students usually learn what they want to learn but often have great difficulty learning material which does not interest them. Most of us have to recognize that not all students are deeply interested in everything we want to teach them. One primary problem, then, is motivating students. Usually the learning psychologist stops with this point, but to be useful the principle of motivation needs to be accom-

This research was begun in the Mental Health in Teacher Education Project NIMH Grant No. 2N6635 and continued under USOE Grant No. OE 3-10-032 in the Personality, Teacher Education and Teaching Behavior Project and USOE Grant No. OE 6-10-108 of the Research and Development Center for Teacher Education, Co-directors Robert F. Peck and Oliver H. Bown. The author wishes to acknowledge the contributions to this study of O.H. Bown, Geneva H. Pilgrim, Meda M. White, and Beulah Newlove and the assistance of Mildred Bunch, Jane O'Brien, Carol Case, and Judith Garrard.

Reprinted from the AERA *Journal*, Vol. 6, No. 2, March, 1969, with permission of the author and the publisher. The author is Associate Professor and Research Coordinator, Research and Development Center for Teacher Education, University of Texas.

panied by information about dependable motives of college students.

Of all the sectors of undergraduate education, teacher preparation is probably in greatest need of such information. Education courses are admittedly not regarded as the most interesting on the campus. In some quarters they are even held in contempt. They "take" less well than educators would wish and attrition is high. In general, the opinion that many education courses are not relevant to the needs of teachers is so common in the academic community, in legislatures, and among the public at large that it requires little documentation.

Two explanations might be given for this state of affairs. One is that education courses are worthless. As the layman puts it, those who can, do; those who can't, teach; those who can't teach, teach teachers.

A second possibility is that beginning education majors are not prepared to benefit from education courses as they are now taught. Like other students, they learn what they want to learn but have difficulty learning what does not interest them. Education courses may be answering quite well questions students are not asking.

A phenomenon relevant to this point was observed in a pilot study of teacher attitudes toward preparation. Of 100 education students questioned by the author in confidential hour-long depth interviews, ninety-seven spoke disparagingly of a particular introductory education course. The ninety-seven were all typical undergraduates: young and without teaching experience. The other three were articulately enthusiastic about the same course. Interestingly, the three enthusiasts were all middle-aged men and women with considerable teaching or similar experience.

Are typically inexperienced undergraduates not yet ready to benefit from a conventional teacher preparation program? What are they ready to learn? What does concern them? Can we discover what McKeachie calls "dependable motives," i.e., regularities in the interests of beginning education students, regularities which might furnish guides to educators in choosing course content and experiences for teacher preparation programs?

The purpose of this study was to examine intensively the

developing concerns of small groups of prospective teachers and to reexamine the findings of other investigators in the hope of discovering what teachers are concerned about and whether their concerns can be conceptualized in some useful way.

Concerns of Beginning Teachers

There has been considerable speculation about teachers' concerns and problems (Ahlering, 1963; Deiulio, 1961; Schunk, 1959 are examples). Recently, pleas have been made for intensive clinical descriptions of concerns of both undergraduates (Mitra and Khatri, 1965) and teachers (Newman, 1965).

Surveys of teachers' problems have been reported but some restrict what the teachers can report. For example, teachers choose from a list of alternatives selected by instructors or supervising teachers (Triplett, 1967). The MTAI or STPS is used to discover whether measured attitudes or preferences change over the period of student teaching (Campbell, 1967) or are related to effectiveness defined in terms of ratings by various supervising teachers (Kracht and Casey, 1968) or to teaching behavior (Frankiewicz and Merrifield, 1967). Student teachers' classroom activities (Alterman, 1965), self-concepts (Lantz, 1964) or discomfort (Sorenson and Halpert, 1968) have been surveyed. Six published studies have examined young teachers' perceived problems without severely restricting the alternatives among which the teachers could choose.

New teachers in England complained in "extensive correspondence" about difficulties in maintaining discipline, about inadequate equipment, social background of schools in which they taught, about their own unwise job placement, and about the depressing effects of neighborhood areas and aggressive attitudes of parents toward teachers (Phillips, 1932). More recently, new British teachers were most concerned about class control and evaluations by their inspectors (Gabriel, 1957).

Female elementary education majors in the United States responding to three-sentence completion stems expressed most concern with discipline and with being liked by their pupils, both before and after student teaching. More were concerned about discipline after student teaching than before (Travers *et al.*, 1952).

Thompson administered a thirty-five-item checklist to 125 student teachers near the end of student teaching. Their most frequent concerns were the expectations of their critic teachers, their own subject-matter adequacy, evaluation of their lesson plans, pupil reaction to them, desired standards of teacher conduct, inability to answer pupil questions, and discipline (Thompson, 1963).

Using Thompson's questionnaire, Robinson and Berry queried an additional 193 elementary and secondary student teachers. They expressed most concern about the frequency of visits and observation of the college supervisor and about being graded themselves and giving grades to their pupils (Robinson and Berry, 1965).

Of ninety home economics students in North Dakota surveyed before student teaching, three-quarters were most concerned about knowing enough to teach the units and how they would be evaluated. All had great or some concern about what the supervising teacher would be like (Erickson and Ruud, 1967).

To summarize the data as they are reported by these investigators, what we know is that beginning teachers are concerned about class control, about their own content adequacy, about the situations in which they teach, and about evaluations by their supervisors, by their pupils, and of their pupils by themselves.

The consistency of these findings is remarkable in the light of the different populations surveyed. The consistency lies not only in the similarity of concerns expressed but in the absence of concern about topics which are usually included in education courses: instructional design, methods of presenting subject matter, assessment of pupil learning, dynamics of child behavior, etc.

This discrepancy between what teachers say they need and what is supplied them warrants a closer look. Perhaps the procedures used still restricted the responses subjects could make. Perhaps more frequent observations are needed, rather than just one- or two-time samples. Perhaps concern with methods, assessment, and other topics was already being resolved in on-going course work. Possibly new teachers, intensely concerned about evaluation, are reluctant to admit problems in areas they are "supposed" to know.

In order to take these possibilities into account, the concerns of small groups of student teachers were studied intensively as these occurred over the student-teaching semester. Then other groups were surveyed. Finally, other investigations were reanalyzed and interpreted in light of these findings.

First Study: Counseling Seminars

Procedure

A student-teaching supervisor agreed to substitute group counseling sessions for the conventional weekly student teaching seminar. One counseling psychologist met for two hours each week with six young student teachers during the student-teaching semester. The supervisor was not present at any of these sessions. Student teachers were guaranteed confidentiality and were told they could discuss anything they wanted to talk about. All sessions were tape-recorded and typescripts were made of the recordings.

The same procedure was repeated the following semester with a second group of eight student teachers, this time co-counseled by two counseling psychologists who checked one another to be sure that opportunities for expression were not restricted.

Each statement in the typescripts of these two groups was classified according to its main topic. The topic categories used were derived inductively from the typescripts. Two judges categorized the statements and resolved differences by conference until agreement was reached on every statement.

A third group of seven student teachers was similarly counseled and tape-recorded during a third semester but statements were not categorized.

Results

Frequencies of statements by topic during successive weeks of the semester for the two categorized groups combined are shown in Table 1, where the topic most frequently discussed each week is asterisked (*). As can be seen there, concern with the parameters of the new school situation and with discipline were, in an absolute sense, the most frequently mentioned topics during

Table 1

Frequencies of Student Teachers' Statements by Topic of Concern
at Eleven Time Intervals During Student Teaching
(N = 14 Student Teachers)

Time Intervals

		Topic of Concern					
Chronological order of seminars	Supervising teachers, pupils' parents, and school principals	School situation†	Subject matter and grading of pupils	Discipline	Seminar, re-search project, group members	Attitudes toward self	Pupils, pupil learning, and methods
Week # 1	86*	13	53	10	66	20	54
2	40	167*	45	0	65	26	29
3	100	90	133*	0	37	46	32
4	16	80	46	128*	33	12	71
5	17	54	117	174*	16	37	78
6	17	32	82	108*	6	2	103
7	25	57	21	21	9	30	254*
8	20	28	38	0	45	97	209*
9	18	68	122*	76	10	80	31
10	24	3	58	1	10	80	160*
Week # 11	19	2	9	0	19	0	186*

*The most frequent concern each week
†Includes school plant, facilities, rules, policies

early weeks. Concern with pupils and pupil learning was more frequent during later weeks. This pattern characterized not only combined frequencies but each group separately.

Both the frequencies of the topics discussed and the clinical impression gained from listening to tapes of all three seminars suggested a more parsimonious division than categorization by topics.

On the one hand was concern with self, i.e., concern with self-protection and self-adequacy: with class control, subject-matter adequacy, finding a place in the power structure of the school, and understanding expectations of supervisors, principal, and parents.

On the other hand was concern with pupils: with their learning, their progress, and with ways in which the teacher could implement this progress.

When the data in Table 1 are dichotomized into concern with self, broadly defined, and concern with pupils, also broadly defined (Table 2), student teachers were, during the first three

Table 2

Proportions of Self-Centered and Pupil-Centered Concern Statements During Early, Middle and Late Student Teaching

	Nature of Concerns			
	Self-Centered			
Period in Semester	My Performance*	Discipline	Pupil-Centered	Total Statements
Early	86.24	0.01	13.65	100.00
Sessions 1, 2, 3	(N=727)	(N=1)	(N=115)	(N=843)
Middle	41.05	36.51	22.44	100.00
Sessions 4, 5, 6	(N=461)	(N=410)	(N=252)	(N=1123)
Late	35.31	6.76	57.93	100.00
Sessions 7-11	(N=512)	(N=98)	(N=840)	(N=1450)

*"My Performance" includes master teachers, pupils, parents, school principals, school situation, subject-matter adequacy, and grading.

weeks of the semester concerned mostly with themselves. They continued to be self-concerned during most of the semester, shifting to more concern with pupils toward the end of their student teaching.

One possible explanation of these data is that student teachers changed topics merely because they became bored with a topic or had nothing more to say about it. This seems unlikely since some subjects continued avid discussion of self-concerns to the end of the semester. Nevertheless, the need to continue talking (in the group situation) about something might have accounted for some of the change observed. In addition, fourteen subjects is a small sample and all fourteen taught in the same school system and were supervised similarly. Consequently, concerns might have been related to the specific situation and hence atypical. Also, frequencies used were frequencies of statements, so that talkative students could have contributed disproportionately. Because of these possibilities, the concerns of other groups of student teachers were surveyed in a different way.

Second Study: Written Concerns Statements
Procedure

Twenty-nine different student teachers, supervised by four different supervisors, were asked at the beginning of informal luncheons followed by discussion with a counseling psychologist to write "what you are concerned about now." The groups were surveyed at approximately two-week intervals so that some responses were secured near the beginning of the semester and some near the end of the semester.

Responses were classified into three categories: (1) Where do I stand? How adequate am I? How do others think I am doing? (2) Problem behavior of pupils. Class control. Why do they do that? (3) Are pupils learning? How does what I do affect their gain?

Results

Of these twenty-nine subjects, twenty-two expressed concerns classified mainly as (1); six expressed concerns in both (1) and (2); one expressed concern in (2) only. None expressed concerns classified as (3). In short, they were all concerned with self-adequacy and/or class control. None was concerned primarily with what pupils were learning. The overlap between (1) and (2) and the lack of overlap between (1) and (3) or (2) and (3) supports the posited dichotomy between concern with self and concern with pupils.

Regrouped Data of Other Investigators
Early Concerns

We then defined early concerns as the perceived problems of student teachers or beginning in-service teachers. Six surveys of early concerns so defined have been reported and were reviewed above, those of Phillips (1932), Travers *et al.* (1952), Gabriel (1957), Thompson (1963), Robinson and Berry (1965) and Erickson and Ruud (1967).

When we dichotomize these studies into those reporting principal concerns which we classify as concern with self and those reporting principal concerns which we classify as concern with pupils, we find all six studies reporting early concerns to be concern with self and none reporting early concerns to be concern with pupils.

Recently York (1967; 1968) has made available to us some additional unpublished data gathered from first year in-service teachers in Indiana and Texas. Among 113 Indiana teachers, the most frequently mentioned problem was discipline. When these teachers were asked to specify one single area of greatest concern, discipline was named by thirty-six percent and subject-matter adequacy by twenty-two percent. Only thirteen percent named, as their single major concern, problems of pupil learning or methods of adapting subject matter to individual pupils.

When we dichotomize York's Indiana data into concern with self-adequacy (discipline, own content adequacy, and personal adjustment problems), we find seventy-eight percent concerned with self and twenty-two percent concerned with pupil learning (planning, pupil problems, adapting subject matter to pupils) or without problems. It is even possible that seventy-eight percent is too low a figure. Pupil problems, which were classified here as concern with pupils, may well have included acting out or discipline problems and challenges to the teacher's authority.

First year teachers in Texas agreed with those in Indiana. In a survey of 107 first year in-service teachers in Texas (York, 1968), problems relating to self-adequacy (discipline, budgeting time, conferences with parents, the teacher's own poor health, motivation, knowledge of resources, knowing how to use equipment, etc.) were mentioned twice as often as problems in methods of teaching, understanding pupils, etc. This was true even though some problems, difficult to classify, were eliminated which might have reflected concern with self-adequacy (coping with the first few days of school, recordkeeping).

Three points seem worthy of special note when we consider all ten of these studies: six published studies, two unpublished surveys, and the two studies reported here. One is their obvious consistency with one another despite the fact that diverse populations were surveyed over a period of thirty-six years. This consistency is further supported by a review of the literature on anxiety in early student teaching (Petrusich, 1967) concluding that student-teacher anxiety is due to fear of inability to gain control of classes and fear of inability to gain pupils' emotional support.

The similarities in findings seem not to be due to expectancies of investigators. Many of them apparently worked independently of one another and some seem not to have known about the data of the others. Neither were we, in 1963, when the first of these seminars was conducted, familiar with the work of any of the others, since the seminars were undertaken initially to help therapists understand teachers rather than to survey teachers' concerns.

The second point worthy of note is that no study supports the proposition that beginning teachers are concerned with instructional design, methods of presenting subject matter, assessment of pupil learning, or with tailoring content to individual pupils, the areas often presented before student teaching in education courses.

Third, the findings about beginning in-service teachers (those of Phillips, Gabriel, and York) are similar to those about pre-service teachers (Travers, Thompson, Robinson and Berry, Erickson and Ruud). Both pre-service and new in-service teachers had principal concerns we would classify as concerns with self. This similarity seems to support findings (Erickson and Ruud, 1967; Travers *et al.*, 1952) that concerns and perceived problems change little during student teaching.

However, it might be argued that everyone is always concerned with himself and that teachers, experienced as well as inexperienced, are no different from the rest of us. The question arises: Do these self-concerns persist? Do teachers continue to be preoccupied throughout their teaching life with problems of self-adequacy? To answer this question, we turn to studies of concerns and problems of experienced teachers and teachers termed superior.

Late Concerns

If we define late concerns as perceived problems or worries of experienced teachers, late concerns are reported in two studies.

Gabriel (1957) surveyed both the problems and satisfactions of experienced teachers in England and contrasted their problems and satisfactions with those of beginning teachers. When we regroup his data (Table 3), we find the experienced teachers significantly less often concerned with maintaining discipline and with criticism from inspectors.

Experienced teachers were concerned more often with the slow progress of pupils. Experienced teachers found satisfaction more often from success of former pupils while inexperienced teachers found satisfaction more often from holidays and praise from inspectors.

Jackson (1968) observed and interviewed fifty experienced American teachers termed superior. His primarily clinical study seems to indicate that more experienced teachers are concerned about pupil progress. Jackson's superior teachers not only expressed such concerns almost exclusively, but in some instances they spontaneously recalled a decrease in concern with discipline and self-adequacy during their years of teaching. Some, however, were not concerned about evaluation because they refused to allow evaluators in their classes, in some cases maintaining that they would resign if forced to endure them!

Table 3

Concerns of Experienced vs. Inexperienced Teachers in England

	Who Is More Concerned?	p
Problems:		
Criticism from superiors	Inexperienced	.01
Maintaining discipline	Inexperienced	.01
Slow progress of pupils	Experienced	.05
Satisfactions:		
Praise from inspectors	Inexperienced	.01
Holidays	Inexperienced	.01
Success of former pupils	Experienced	.01

Source: Adapted from John Gabriel's *An Analysis of the Emotional Problems of the Teacher in the Classroom* (London & New Zealand: Angus and Robertson, Ltd., 1957), pp. 197-199.

Early vs. Late Concerns

When early and late concerns are defined in terms of extreme groups, as in Gabriel's sample, early concerns seem clearly self-concerns and late concerns seem clearly about pupils.

When early and late concerns are defined in terms of pre- and post-student teachers' concerns, early and late concerns are not so clearly distinguishable. As noted earlier, two studies, those of Travers *et al.* and of Erickson and Ruud, contrasted pre- and post-student teachers' concerns and found little change over the student-teaching semester. Student teachers had self-concerns both before and after student teaching. In our counseling seminars, however, some changes were observed. Late in student teaching, student teachers expressed more concern about pupils. Why the discrepancy between the counseling seminar study and the other two studies, when all report concerns before (or at the beginning of) and after (or at the end of) student teaching?

There were several differences in the data-gathering procedures which may account for different findings. First is the almost microscopic examination of the concerns of the seminar student teachers. Second, eleven time samples were taken there as contrasted with two time samples in the other studies. Third, counseling seminar student teachers were not restricted in what they could report and the measure used was the frequency of statements in a group rather than the number of individuals who reported a concern, as was true in other studies. (Numbers of individuals reporting concerns did not seem appropriate as a measure both because of the small number of subjects and because the interaction probably contaminated statements.) So it is possible that if, in other studies, all possible concerns had been elicited and many time samples taken, as was done in the counseling seminars, some changes might have been found by other investigators over the student-teaching period. It is also possible, of course, that the counseling seminar or some related experience of these counseled subjects fostered these changes. For example, articulate student teachers might have led others into discussion of concerns about pupils.

It is our clinical impression that concerns can change over preparation. There are other possibilities, of course. Perhaps concerns do not change. Teachers who retain early concerns may drop out of teaching. Perhaps Gabriel's sample (as well as Jackson's) contained only "superior" experienced teachers and that "inferior" experienced teachers would report concerns similar to those of beginning teachers. There are no good data to help choose among these possibilities. However, some tentative evidence indicates that concerns *can* change during preparation even if they do not often do so (Dilley, 1953; Fuller, Peck, Bown, Menaker and White, 1968).

Conceptualizing Concerns

The evidence seems to support a developmental conceptualization of teacher concerns. We posit three phases of concern: a pre-teaching phase, an early teaching phase, and a late teaching phase.

Pre-teaching Phase: Non-concern

So far, the time span considered here has been that between first actual contact with pupils in classrooms (student teaching) and experience on the job. This span is truncated since it does not include the pre-teaching period. Most education majors, however, take courses before they have had any actual contact as teachers with pupils.

Information about concerns during this pre-teaching phase may actually be of more interest to many teacher educators than information about concerns during student teaching. First, actual teaching, though stressful (Sorenson and Halpert, 1968) is generally reported to be of more interest and benefit than other experiences offered in teacher education programs (Bruner, 1968; Hodenfield, 1961). Lack of interest is a problem before, rather than during, student teaching. Unfortunately, no studies seem to have been reported about concerns of education students during the years before they have had actual contact with teaching.

We tried to conceptualize teaching-related concerns during these years and at first seemed essentially unable to do so. In the course of the pilot study mentioned earlier, the author counseled individually, and in groups, forty-one sophomore and junior education majors before they had had any actual contact with teaching. Although these students had problems, their spontaneously reported problems were those usually encountered in counseling adolescents. These students rarely had specific concerns related to teaching itself. The teaching-related concerns they did express were usually amorphous and vague: anticipation or apprehension. Most often they did not know what to be concerned about. They thought of teaching in terms of their own experiences as pupils and as college students. What concerns they did spontaneously express about their coming student teaching were based mostly on hearsay: discipline problems, getting a good grade or wangling an assignment to a favored supervisor. We concluded that findings from surveys of pre-teaching concerns would be related to the manner in which the question was stated. If asked about problems, they reported problems with roommates, academic failure, etc. If asked about teaching concerns, they either parroted, somewhat unconvincingly, rumors they had heard, or else their responses were vague and difficult to classify. This pre-teaching period seemed to be a period of non-concern with the specifics of teaching, or at least a period of relatively low involvement in teaching.

Early Teaching Phase: Concern with Self

Covert Concerns: Where Do I Stand? When teaching starts, teachers ask themselves, "Where do I stand?" As the student teachers in the seminars asked, "Is it going to be my class or the teacher's class?" "Does she tell me what to do? Or can I try things myself?" "If I see a child misbehaving in the hall, do I handle it, ignore it, or tell someone else?"

They try to estimate how much support will be forthcoming from the school principal and supervisors in a great variety of situations; to build working relationships with school personnel; to determine the limits of their acceptance as professional persons in halls, cafeterias, teachers' lounge, and principal's office.

This phase seemed unique among all the others because expressions about it occurred only during confidential contacts. During those contacts and among student teachers themselves, such concerns were discussed endlessly. But these concerns were rarely expressed in either written statements or in routine interviews unless directly elicited. Our clinical impression from counseling sessions and from confidential depth exit interviews at graduation is that answering the question "Where do I stand?" involves questions like "What is the hidden agenda?" and judgments about those in authority. These judgments they were extremely reluctant to express.

As a result, they seemed, overtly, to be concerned with teaching pupils and coping with the class. Covertly, however, they were trying to discover the parameters of the school situation. It seemed to us that teachers who continued to be uncertain about these parameters were "stuck." Their concern about where they stood might abate even if they discovered that they were not wanted or that they had little authority. What did get them "stuck" was continuing in a state of uncertainty.

Overt Concerns: How Adequate Am I? The concern student teachers feel about class control is no secret. It is a blatant, persistent concern of most beginning teachers.

Ability to control the class, however, is apparently just part of a larger concern of the new teacher with his adequacy in the classroom. This larger concern involves abilities to understand subject matter, to know the answers, to say "I don't know," to have the freedom to fail on occasion, to anticipate problems, to mobilize resources and to make changes when failures recur. It also involves the ability to cope with evaluation: the willingness to listen for evaluation and to partial out the biases of evaluators.

To some extent, these concerns are overt. But the intensity of concern with self-adequacy (and evaluation) is so great that it is easily underestimated. Many times, a student in counseling discussed at considerable length what a supervisor might have meant by some instructions but would not ask the supervisor for clarification. Before one seminar, the supervisor had stopped by briefly to make an assignment. There were only routine questions from the student teachers about the assignment. When the supervisor left, pandemonium broke loose. "What did he mean?" "Someone run after him." Someone started out the door. "Wait a minute! Maybe we can figure this out."

In the studies reviewed, concerns with class control, content adequacy, and supervisor evaluation often occurred together. Perhaps all are assessments of the teacher's adequacy, by the class and by the supervisor. Taken together they are a massive concern of beginning teachers.

Late Concerns: Concern with Pupils

So little data are available about concerns of experienced teachers that any formulations about them are necessarily tentative. When concerns are "mature", i.e., characteristic of experienced superior teachers, concerns seem to focus on pupil gain and self-evaluation as opposed to personal gain and evaluations by others. The specific concerns we have observed are concern about ability to understand pupils' capacities, to specify objectives for them, to assess their gain, to partial out one's own contribution to pupils' difficulties and gain and to evaluate oneself in terms of pupil gain.

Concluding Remarks

A three-phase developmental conceptualization of teachers' concerns has been posited. Such a sequence is in accord with Bijou's (1968) view that development after childhood is better conceptualized in terms of subdivisions of empirically defined social interactions than in terms of age, environmental events, or other such constructs. As he points out, statements about such subdivisions might be expected to accelerate the formulation of empirical laws with increasingly longer chains. The conceptualization of teacher development offered here is just a mediating statement, of course, but one which might eventually contribute to some longer chain. At the same time, it is not inconsistent with more ultimate statements about development over the life cycle like those of Maslow (1954) and Erickson (1956), and about teaching like those of Combs (1965), and others (ASCD, 1962).

Educators with other viewpoints might be persuaded by frequent comments of student teachers to the effect that knowing where they stand and having the class under control is their "food and drink." If you do not have that, they say, you cannot begin to think about teaching the class.

The data reviewed can of course be subsumed in other terms: learning, threat, stress, self-concept, situational novelty, etc. The self-other dichotomy posited here is merely the most parsimonious division which seems to us to account for all our observations. In any case, the apparent convergence in findings about concerns raises many questions.

Implications for Research

First, are questions about the sequence itself. Is it correct and complete? Are there phases even "lower" and "higher" than those suggested here? What are the specific tasks and competencies involved in different concerns phases?

Second, is concern phase a function of the person, of the situation, or of both? If concerns are related to characteristics of the person and/or the situation, what are these characteristics? Must situations, for example, be interpersonal, stressful, and novel?

Third, do individuals as well as groups go through these phases? So far the findings come only from data about groups. Can some individuals skip a phase, be in more than one phase at a time, regress to an earlier phase? If an experienced teacher in a new situation does regress to an earlier phase, will he go through the early phase more quickly than an inexperienced teacher?

Fourth, what generalization to other groups is warranted? Would the phases observed here also be found among college professors, school administrators, and persons in non-teaching situations?

Fifth, are concerns really related to teaching behavior, teaching competency, or pupil learning? This is an important, still unresolved, question. No one seems to have had the temerity to survey the concerns of experienced *inferior* teachers. Even if concerns are not related to outcome, controlling for concerns may help untangle conflicting results about teacher personality and teaching behavior.

There are also questions about measurement and research design. Is it possible to develop a structured scorable concerns test which rules out social desirability as an explanation for responses? Is it possible to avoid retest effects? For example, subjects may have a tendency to avoid repeating concerns on successive testing.

There are other questions related to teacher education. Do students become more interested and involved when course content has been selected according to surveyed concerns than when content is selected without regard to concerns?

Are concerns manipulable? Can changes toward concern with pupils be encouraged by treatment? Two kinds of procedures appear to be promising. First are procedures which arouse teaching-related concerns. Perhaps very brief actual teaching can arouse such concerns. Newlove (1966) reports arousal of teaching-related concerns after only fifteen minutes of teaching a public school class. Education students may need to teach before enrolling in even a first education course.

Promising also are procedures which resolve early concerns in the hope that when these early concerns are resolved, later, more mature, concerns will appear. Individual counseling may be such a procedure and its effects on concerns are being studied at this center. Procedures which can be demonstrated to resolve self-concerns and excite pupil concerns seem clearly desirable.

We are attempting in current studies to test the hypothesis that later concerns will appear when early concerns are resolved. After concern with pupils appears, then instructional design, psychology, and other education courses may seem more relevant.

If this is so, and the evidence seems strong that it is, teacher education may yet harness the enthusiasm of young teachers.

In any case, teaching against the tide is unlikely to increase interest in education courses. Teaching with the tide is at least easier on both the instructor and the teacher in preparation than breasting the waves.

References

Ahlering, I. "Reactions by Student Teachers," *Clearing House*, February, 1963, pp. 337-340.

Alterman, R.D. "Using Student Teachers' Diaries to Develop an Evaluative Instrument for Teacher Education Programs," *Journal of Educational Research*, April, 1965, pp. 369-372.

Association for Supervision and Curriculum Development. *Perceiving, Behaving, Becoming*. Washington, D.C., 1962.

Bijou, S.W. "Ages, Stages and the Naturalization of Human Development." *American Psychologist*, June, 1968, pp. 419-427.

Bruner, J.S. *A Symposium on the Training of Teachers for Elementary Schools*. IDEA, Box 446, Melbourne, Florida, 1968.

Campbell, D.E. "Dimensional Attitude Changes of Student Teachers." *Journal of Educational Research*, December, 1967, pp. 160-162.

Combs, A.W. *The Professional Education of Teachers*. Boston: Allyn and Bacon, 1965.

Deiulio, A.M. "Problems of Student Teachers," *American Teacher*, December, 1961, pp. 9-10.

Dilley, N.E. "Group Counseling for Student Teachers," *Educational Administration and Supervision*, April, 1953, pp. 193-200.

Erickson, E.H. "The Problem of Ego Identity," *Journal of the American Psychoanalytic Assn.*, January, 1956, pp. 56-121.

Erickson, J.K. and J.B. Ruud. "Concerns of Home Economics Students Preceding Their Student Teaching Experiences," *Journal of Home Economics*, November, 1967, pp. 732-734.

Frankiewicz, R.G. and P.R. Merrifield. "Student Teacher Preferences as Predictors of Their Teaching Behavior." Paper presented at American Educational Research Association meetings, 1967.

Fuller, F.F., R.F. Peck, O.H. Bown, S.L. Menaker, and M.M. White. *Effects of Personalized Feedback During Teacher Preparation on Teacher Personality and Teaching Behavior.* United States Office of Education Grant No. 3-10-032 (PTETB Project), The University of Texas, Research & Development Center, Austin, Texas, 1968.

Gabriel, J. *An Analysis of the Emotional Problems of the Teacher in the Classroom.* London: Angus and Robertson, 1957.

Hodenfield, G.K. *The Education of Teachers.* Englewood Cliffs, New Jersey: Prentice-Hall, 1961.

Jackson, P.W. *Life in Classrooms.* New York: Holt, Rinehart, and Winston, 1968.

Kracht, C.R. and I.P. Casey. "Attitudes, Anxieties, and Student Teaching Performance," *Peabody Journal of Education,* January, 1968, pp. 214-217.

Lantz, D.L. "Changes in Student Teachers' Concepts of Self and Others," *Journal of Teacher Education,* June, 1964, pp. 200-203.

Maslow, A. *Motivation and Personality.* New York: Harper, 1954.

McKeachie, W.J. "Research on Teaching at the College and University Level." In N.L. Gage (Ed.) *Handbook of Research on Teaching.* Chicago: Rand McNally, 1963, pp. 1118-1172.

Mitra, S.K. and A.A. Khatri. "Understanding College Students' Problems," *Indian Psychological Review,* November, 1965, pp. 2-16.

Newlove, B. *The 15 Minute Hour.* Austin, Texas: The University of Texas, 1966. (Mimeo.)

Newman, R.G. "Where We Fail Our Teachers." Paper presented at Orthopsychiatric Association meeting, 1965.

Petrusich, M.M. "Separation Anxiety as a Factor in the Student Teaching Experience," *Peabody Journal of Education,* May, 1967, pp. 353-456.

Phillips, M. "Some Problems of Adjustment in the Early Years of a Teacher's Life," *British Journal of Educational Psychology,* November, 1932, pp. 237-256.

Robinson, E. and C.A. Berry. *An Investigation of Certain Variables Related to Student Anxieties Before and During Student Teaching.* Grambling, Louisiana: Grambling College, 1965. (Mimeo.)

Schunk, B. "Understanding the Needs of the Student Teachers." In *The Supervising Teachers' Yearbook. 38th Yearbook of the Association for Student Teaching,* 1959, pp. 1-50.

Sorenson, G. and R. Halpert. "Stress in Student Teaching," *California Journal of Educational Research,* January, 1968, pp. 28-33.

Thompson, M.L. "Identifying Anxieties Experienced by Student Teachers," *Journal of Teacher Education,* December, 1963, pp. 435-439.

Travers, R.M.W., W. Rabinowitz and E. Nemovicher. "The Anxieties of a Group of Student Teachers," *Educational Administration and Supervision,* October, 1952, pp. 368-375.

Triplett, De W. "Student Teachers Rank Their Needs," *Michigan Educational Journal,* November, 1967, pp. 13-14.

York, J.L. "Relationships Between Problems of Beginning Elementary Teachers, Their Personal Characteristics, and Their Preferences for In-service Education." Unpublished Ph.D. thesis, Bloomington, Indiana: Indiana University, 1967.

York, J.L. *Problems of Beginning Teachers.* Austin, Texas: Research and Development Center for Teacher Education, The University of Texas, 1968. (Mimeo.)

11.

Effective Induction of Teachers: A Point of View

Ronald E. Hull

To date, induction into teaching has been studied and reported (NCTEPS, 1966; Bouchard and Hull, 1970) primarily in terms of problems of beginning teachers, with the idea that once these "problems" are identified, training institutions can help teachers adjust to their difficulties, respond appropriately to expectations of their role-set, and ultimately fit into a particular school system. The goal of induction, thus, has been to provide experiences (usually in *pre-service* instructional settings, i.e., methods courses and student teaching) which will allow the neophyte teacher to function as a full-fledged professional. Beginning teachers contend, however, that their education courses do not prepare them for the realities of the classroom. Furthermore, there are indications that *systematic in-service* induction programs are practically non-existent in many schools (Bouchard and Hull, 1970).

Typically, beginning teachers find that they are expected to adapt their behavior to the expectations of both training institution and school officials during their student-teaching experience. Also, they are expected to take over full teaching responsibilities upon their arrival on the job. Unfortunately, they are expected to accomplish these tasks without much systematic help from either the training institution or the school.

The concept of induction presented in this paper differs from

This paper was written for this book at the special request of the editors. The author is Associate Professor, State University College, Fredonia, New York.

the fortuitous approach which now exists in most teacher education institutions and schools. The writer contends that a more effective and pervasive concept of induction is needed if induction programs are to result in the development of instructional effectiveness.* It is asserted that induction programs should have the following characteristics: (1) induction should be adaptive in nature, i.e., the program should be sensitive to the needs of the inductee rather than being geared to molding the inductee to fit the system; (2) the idea of induction should be extended to include not only beginning teachers, but teachers new to a school system, and teachers who are involved in innovative instructional programs; (3) induction procedures should be individualized—there is some evidence that group-oriented induction procedures are ineffective (Bouchard and Hull, 1970); and (4) induction should be viewed in terms of planned intervention as opposed to the "natural" socialization process that takes place when an employee enters an organization.

To carry out the type of induction activities that will result in improvement of instruction, these activities must be practical and relevant to the immediate needs of each teacher. Fuller's findings (1969) indicate that relevance can be approached if the concerns of teachers are considered seriously. Further, her data demonstrate that concerns are developmental and change over time. Once a lower level concern, e.g., gaining classroom control, has been satisfied, the teacher can become concerned with higher level needs, e.g., concern for children's learning. This self-concern/student-concern continuum proves to be very useful in determining the types of induction activities that are relevant to teachers.

Fuller (1969) has delineated three phases of teacher concerns: the pre-service phase (time span between the student-teaching experience and on-the-job experience); the early teaching phase (early teaching years); and late concerns (those concerns evidenced by experienced teachers). The pre-service phase is characterized by "non-concern." These students have not had

---

*Some procedures for developing instructional effectiveness are discussed in detail by John E. Bicknell in Section Four of this book.

enough experience and/or information about teaching to really know about what to be concerned. They usually think of teaching in vague terms and often recall their own school experiences as students. The early teaching phase is characterized by *self-concerns* which are often expressed as feelings of inadequacy as teachers face new and unexpected situations in their relations with colleagues, superiors, students, parents, and the community. These self-concerns are expressed in terms of "Where do I stand?" or "How adequate am I?" After teachers have developed a measure of security in terms of ameliorating or satisfying self-concerns, they are able to direct their energies toward satisfying the needs of students. Experienced, superior, "mature" teachers seem to be able to focus their energies on attending to individual differences of pupils, improving their evaluation techniques, and on trying out new ideas and innovative modes of instruction.

Recent studies (Goldbas *et al.*, 1973; Hull and Driscoll, 1972; Mohan, Hull, and Petrie, 1972; and Rezende, 1972) tend to support and extend the concept of the developmental nature of teacher concerns. Rezende (1972) used the Teacher Concerns Statement (TCS) (Fuller and Case, 1971) to detect the concerns of juniors who had no student-teaching experience; seniors who were involved in student teaching; and in-service teachers. Generally, the concerns of these Ss did tend to change from self-concern to concern for students as they became more experienced in the classroom. However, one exception to the pattern was found. The sample of pre-service teachers scored higher on the TCS (more concern for students) than did the student teachers on both the pre- and the post-test. Although the pre-service sample expressed general and theoretical concerns, these statements tended to fall on the "pupil-concern" end of the continuum. Rezende (1972) generalized that these pupil-concerns may be the result of an idealistic view of teaching which may exist until the inductee has actually had teaching experience.

Teachers' energies are often dissipated in self-concern when they are not able to resolve conflict. More specifically, student teachers are often caught in conflicting situations because they are in the process of passing through the boundaries* of two organizations—the training institution and the school. The research on role-conflict within and between organizational structures has been summarized by Katz and Kahn (1967, p. 192):

> In general, positions contained deep within the organizational structure were relatively conflict-free; positions located near the skin or boundary of the organization were likely to be conflict-ridden. Thus jobs involving labor negotiations, purchasing, selling, or otherwise representing the organization to the public were subject to greater stress. Living near an intraorganizational boundary—for example, serving as liaison between departments—revealed many of the same effects but to a lesser degree.

The studies cited below may illustrate the type of conflict and ambiguity that inductees often experience.

Hull and Driscoll (1972) found that student teachers who were forced to choose between going on strike with their college classmates or continuing their student-teaching duties (thus fulfilling a commitment to cooperating teachers, principals, and college supervisors) almost without exception chose to continue their student teaching. A considerable number, however, resented certain "pressure" tactics used by both college supervisors and cooperating school personnel to "keep them in line." Uncertainty concerning the severity of the negative sanctions also tended to cause them to feel that it was necessary for them to continue their student-teaching duties. The salient point in this study in terms of induction was the amount of pressure exerted by both school people and college supervisors to insure conformity to expectations. It seems that some students, especially the few who supported the strike on moral principles, were forced to compromise their beliefs because the price for acting in accord with their beliefs was simply too high. Only one of the 151 student

---

*For further discussion of organizational boundary permeability and the role-conflict that often accompanies boundary positions, the reader may refer to Robert Katz and Daniel Kahn. *The Social Psychology of Organizations*, New York: John Wiley and Sons, Inc., 1967, pp. 60-62, 122.

teachers was willing to risk failing student teaching and the possibility of not graduating with his class.

Mohan, Hull, and Petrie (1972) examined the concerns of in-service teachers enrolled in a summer workshop on individualized instruction. Their findings showed that the sample of experienced teachers were concerned about: (1) how to individualize instruction; (2) attaining knowledge about various systems of individualization; (3) ways to record effectively pupil progress in an individualized setting; and (4) ways of effectively grouping children for individualized instruction. However, they were also concerned about lack of cooperation and support of administration with regard to implementing individualized instruction programs. This concern for · support of administration is a self-concern which falls into Fuller and Case's (1971) category, "Where do I stand?"

Follow-up in-service training and monitoring of the development of a sub-group of the summer workshop participants indicated that the "Where do I stand?" concern regarding administrative support persisted as the group continued to study and work toward implementation of an individualized program. This concern subsided, at least temporarily, when the staff was assured by the superintendent and the board of education that their innovative program would be supported by providing necessary resources. Even with these assurances, a few teachers expressed self-concerns regarding implementation of the program. These data suggest that concerns of experienced teachers may change from concern for pupils to concern for self when they are faced with new and unfamiliar instructional goals, expectations, and situations. In some instances their concerns were not unlike the concerns of beginning teachers.

Another area of conflict or ambiguity which plagues both the student teacher and the in-service teacher is evaluation of their teaching performance. Goldbas *et al.* (1973) found that expectations of teaching performance as designated by a Student Teacher Evaluation Form did not relate significantly to grades, recommendations, or success in getting a teaching position the year after graduation. Inasmuch as these criteria did not relate to formal evaluation criteria, e.g., lesson plans or scholastic background, the researchers concluded that teachers must be hired on some other criteria. It was averred that student teaching "success" is probably a function of adapting to the personality of the cooperating teacher and the college supervisor. When specified competencies are ignored, the inductee is left with ambiguity as to what is really expected. In any event, clear communication of expectations of the inductees seemed to be lacking among the sample visited.

In analyzing and studying the concerns of teachers, the writer has found that concerns are generated by lack of trust, role-conflict and ambiguity, lack of skills and competencies, and perceived constraints. Lack of trust seems to stem from incomplete communication patterns between the inductee and those "significant others" who are part of the inductee's role-set. When the communication patterns are incomplete, inductees are forced to "play the game" by intuition. They seek to "psych out" organizational expectations. Too often the inductee is traumatized in the process; thus, he is reduced to a survival level of concern and it is often difficult for him to meet the needs of children.

When the beginning teacher enters the classroom or when the experienced teacher embarks upon some innovative teaching procedure, he tends to ask, "Am I adequate to the task?" "Will I be able to fulfill the expectations of self and others?" Induction programs must therefore be competency oriented. The feeling of being well prepared to carry out a well-defined task will invariably quell self-concern and will allow the inductee to direct energy to the task of facilitating the learning of youngsters.

Research on perceptions of role (Foskett, 1966) indicates that teachers may perceive constraints that do not exist. When constraints are perceived, they are real—to the teachers. These perceived constraints preclude feelings of self-actualization in teaching. What teachers are asking is, "Can I have a unique identity?" "Can I use my talents in ways which will bring about new integrations?" Here the norm of the school may be broken. Merton (1967) contends that innovative behavior is tantamount to deviant behavior. Therefore, the innovative teacher is likely to be punished by "significant others" if innovation is not part of the normative structure. Perceived constraints are often used by inductees and others to ameliorate this conflict. An indicator of the extent to which change is resisted is clearly spelled out by the sociologist Wilbert E. Moore (1963, p. 68):

> Until challenged, "the way it has always been done" is the right way, and no degree of emphasis on rationality is likely to prevent conflict between tradition and its upholders and rational innovation and its partisans.

Considering the above words of wisdom, is it any wonder that experienced teachers revert to self-concern when they try to do things differently? The remainder of this paper will focus on recommendations which are posed in light of the data presented above.

Individualizing Teacher Induction

Inasmuch as the conceptualization of teacher concerns clearly indicates that teachers' needs vary with time, knowledge, experience, goals, and situations, it seems necessary that induction procedures must be tailored to individuals. Again, it is pointed out that group-oriented induction procedures have often been ineffective (Bouchard and Hull, 1970).

An effective induction program must be based on needs of inductees, whether they are beginning teachers, teachers new to a particular school system, or teachers who are embarking upon an innovative program. Information on concerns of teachers, ages of students being taught, subject area(s) being taught, perceptions of relationships with colleagues, administrators, and parents, and specific situational information must be used to specify general objectives of the induction program and specific objectives for individuals. A variety of techniques may be used to pre-assess the inductee's needs. For example, inductees may be asked to respond to the Teacher Concerns Statement or other techniques, i.e., interviews, which have proved effective in detecting concerns.*

Once the information is analyzed, objectives can be formulated. General objectives of the program may be stated in broad

---

*Frances F. Fuller, the Research and Development Center for Teacher Education, University of Texas at Austin, has informed the editors that a quick-scoring instrument is being developed to supplant the Teacher Concerns Statement.

terms. For instance, assessment of the needs of a group of in-service teachers who were enrolled in a workshop on individualized instruction revealed that the teachers were seeking a common understanding and definition of "individualized instruction." In this case, it was determined that a common frame of reference could be established by having all participants read selected materials which provided a logically consistent knowledge base on the concept of individualization of instruction and learning. The objective was stated in these terms: To establish a knowledge of various components of individualized instruction and their intended uses in the teaching-learning process. Attainment of this objective was determined through cognitive measures.

Specific objectives for individuals and small groups should be stated in behavioral terms or in terms that would make it possible to measure attainment of the objectives. For example, pre-assessment data may indicate that one or more teachers want (or need) to learn a certain skill, such as, skill in the use of "Encouragement." In this event, the behavioral objective for that particular sub-group may be stated: Given the protocol materials on "Encouragement" (Rector, Hull, and Mohan, 1972), each teacher will be able to identify at eighty percent mastery level three levels of encouragement on a written test and will be able to use three levels of encouragement in an audio or videotape minilesson. The Encouragement Protocols are self-contained and can be used individually by teachers; thus, one may progress through the materials and may attain mastery at his own rate. The Encouragement Protocol materials have the evaluation criteria built in; thus, teachers can check their own progress and set their own goals for skill achievement.

Pre-assessment data may indicate that one or more of the teachers are having difficulty motivating certain children. This is often a concern of beginning teachers and also it is mentioned by experienced teachers on occasion. In this situation, the objective may be stated: Given the materials and instruction on the use of goal-setting procedures (Wisconsin R and D Center, 1973) the teacher will conduct a series of goal-setting lessons with a child from her class until she has mastered the goal-setting model with 100 percent accuracy. These goal-setting sessions can be arranged on an individual basis, and each teacher may work at her own rate to attain mastery.

Evaluation of the effective induction program must be in terms of the two levels of objectives mentioned above: general objectives of the program and specific objectives for individuals and/or small groups of teachers.

Through the approach discussed above, induction becomes a process of planned intervention by which needs, interests, and capabilities of inductees are ascertained; objectives are formulated on the basis of solid pre-assessment data; relevant activities are planned and carried out based on explicit objectives; and evaluations of the induction procedures—grounded in measurable behavioral outcomes. Figure 1 illustrates graphically the individualized induction model upon which this discussion has been based.

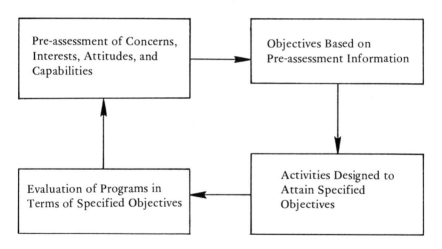

Figure 1

Recommendations

The following recommendations are offered as a guide for a planned, systematic induction program:

1. Planning the induction program must involve representatives from various groups; for example, inductees, school administrators, college supervisors, and/or con-

sultants. Such participation has been found to be a significant factor in the success of a program.

2.   Relations between inductees and those significant others in the organization(s) must be characterized by clear, explicit communications so there will be no doubt in the mind of the inductee as to what the expectations are. Expectations of the inductee must be taken seriously by teacher trainers.

3.   To minimize organizational boundary conflict, the objectives of the two organizations (college and school) must be congruent with respect to treatment of inductees.

4.   Induction programs must be intervention oriented, i.e., definite, explicit steps must be taken using a model like the one presented above to attend systematically to concerns of inductees. Normative structures of teaching must be tested: not all constraints are real.

5.   Competencies of inductees must be made explicit. Once a problem has been identified and recognized by both the inductee and the teacher trainers, definite steps for skills development must be specified.

6.   Evaluation of induction programs must be grounded in measurable objectives.

In summary, the writer has attempted to present a framework through which neophyte teachers, teachers new to a school system, and experienced teachers who are beginning to try new and innovative teaching practices may be helped through early, and often frustrating, stages of development. Studies of concerns of teachers were discussed because research shows that attention to immediate and developing concerns of teachers can provide a sound basis upon which to develop a relevant induction program. An individualized induction model was offered as the individualizing facet of the induction program. Finally, recommendations were listed as a rough guide for insuring that objectives of the induction program will be attained.

References

Bouchard, J.B. and R.E. Hull. *A Pilot Study of Problems and*

Practices in the Induction of Beginning Teachers. Fredonia, New York: Teacher Education Research Center, State University College, Fredonia, New York, 1970.

Foskett, J.M. *The Normative World of the Elementary School Teacher*. Eugene, Oregon: The Center for the Advanced Study of Educational Administration, University of Oregon, 1966.

Fuller, F.F. "Concerns of Teachers: A Developmental Conceptualization," *American Educational Research Journal*, 1969, pp. 207-226.

Fuller, F.F. and C. Case. *A Manual for Scoring the Teacher Concerns Statement*. Austin, Texas: Research and Development Center for Teacher Education, The University of Texas at Austin, 1971.

Hull, R.E. and R.L. Driscoll. "Student Strike: An Educational Career Decision for Student Teachers," *Journal of Teacher Education*, 1972, pp. 355-357.

Katz, D. and R. Kahn. *The Social Psychology of Organizations*. New York: John Wiley and Sons, 1967.

Merton, R.K. *Social Theory and Social Structure*. New York: The Free Press, 1967.

Mohan, M., R.E. Hull, and T.A. Petrie. *Concerns of Teachers in a Workshop on Individualized Instruction*. Fredonia, New York: Teacher Education Research Center, State University College, Fredonia, New York, 1972.

Moore, W.E. *Social Change*. Englewood Cliffs, New Jersey: Prentice-Hall, 1963.

National Commission on Teacher Education and Professional Standards. *The Real World of the Beginning Teacher*. Washington, D.C.: National Education Association of the United States, 1966.

Rector, D., R.E. Hull, and M. Mohan. *A Field Test of the Effectiveness of One of the Utah State University Protocol Training Materials, in an In-service Workshop Setting*. Fredonia, New York: Teacher Education Research Center, State University College, Fredonia, New York, 1972.

Rezende, H. "A Study of Teachers' Concerns." Unpublished manuscript. Available from the Teacher Education Research

Center, State University College, Fredonia, New York, 1972.
Wisconsin Research and Development Center for Cognitive Learn-
    ing. *Individually Guided Motivation*. Madison, Wisconsin:
    Wisconsin Research and Development Center for Cognitive
    Learning, University of Wisconsin, Madison, 1973.

12.

A Conceptual Level Matching Model
for Coordinating Learner Characteristics
with Educational Approaches

David E. Hunt

*"I suppose alert teachers have always been intuitively aware
of the fact that, when they change their method of teaching,
certain children who had appeared to be slow learners or even
non-learners became outstanding achievers and some of their
former star learners became slow learners. They have also learned
that when they change the nature of the test used for assessing
achievement, such as from a multiple-choice test to one requiring
creative applications of knowledge and decision-making, the star
learners may change position in class ranking markedly"*
(Torrance, 1965, p. 253).

Without worrying for the moment about how many teachers
are in fact aware of the differential effects of various educational
approaches or the differential consequences of measuring educational achievement, let us consider the implications of Torrance's
statements in terms of our major assumption: If a psychological
principle is to be useful for educational decision-making, it should
take account of both differential effectiveness of educational
approaches upon various learners, and the differential results from
using various measures of indexing educational accomplishment.

To consider the differential effectiveness of an educational
approach (or any other form of environmental influence) is not
simply to point out a few persons to whom the principle does not

Reprinted from *Interchange*, Vol. 1, No. 3, 1970, with permission of the
author and the publisher. The author is Professor at The Ontario Institute for
Studies in Education, Toronto, Canada.

apply, nor is it to consider the individual differences as unwanted error variance. To take the differential approach seriously means asking different questions and generating principles in a different form. Rather than ask whether one educational approach is generally better than another, one asks, "Given this kind of person, which of these approaches is more effective for a given objective?"

The classic statement of the differential, or interactive, approach was made by Lewin (1935) in the formula, $B = f(P,E)$, or Behavior is a combined function of the Person and the Environment. At first glance, this formulation may seem a pedantic restatement of the obvious. However, when translated into educational terms, i.e., the accomplishment of an educational objective depends upon the effect of the educational approach on the individual learner, one realizes that educational problems are rarely viewed in differential terms.

In his 1957 Presidential address to the American Psychological Association, Cronbach (1957) concluded with the following recommendation:

"It is not enough for each discipline to borrow from the other. Correlational psychology studies only variance among organisms; experimental psychology studies only variance among treatments. A united discipline will study both of these, but it will also be concerned with the otherwise neglected interactions between organismic and treatment variables. *Our job is to invent constructs and to form a network of laws which permits prediction.* From observations we must infer a psychological description of the situation and of the present state of the organism. Our laws should permit us to predict, from this description, the behavior of organism-in-situation" (pp. 681-682, italics mine).

Despite the logical appeal of Cronbach's suggestion for an interactive approach, the development of constructs that coordinate person-environment effects has proceeded slowly. Perhaps one reason is, although the general nature of such a coordinated approach is quite straightforward, that the specific research strategies developing such principles are much less clear. Cronbach has more recently (1967) stated the interactive formulation specifically for education by suggesting an "Aptitude-Treatment-Interaction" (ATI) model in which one searches for combinations of learner aptitude and educational treatment that will produce differential effects. Cronbach and Snow (1968, p. 9) have suggested three sources of hypotheses in the ATI approach: "(1) derived from review of literature, (2) derived from aptitude variables of particular importance for theories of cognitive and personality development, and (3) comparisons of controversial instructional methods."

The Conceptual Level (CL) matching model to be described here has emerged from a theory of cognitive and personality development, Conceptual Systems Theory (Harvey, Hunt, and Schroder, 1961). Similar in rationale to the ATI approach, the matching model aims to set forth principles that specify those approaches most likely to facilitate achieving certain objectives for different kinds of persons. In educational terms, the ultimate form of a matching model is a set of "if . . . then . . ." conditional statements specifying that educational approach most likely to accomplish a particular objective for an individual learner.

Before the matching model and empirical evidence derived from it are described, the personality dimension on which it is based, Conceptual Level, is described and its construct validity and characteristics summarized.

Conceptual Level
Theoretical Background

In its initial form, the Conceptual Systems approach (Harvey, Hunt, and Schroder, 1961) viewed personality development as an interactive function of the person's level of personality development (or stage) and the environmental conditions he encountered. Optimal development was assumed to occur when the environmental conditions facilitated the "conceptual work" necessary for the person's conceptual growth. When the environmental conditions were not optimal, then some form of arrestation was assumed to occur. The dimension of conceptual development was identified by a series of hierarchically ordered stages numbered from I to IV, and it was assumed that a person must go through the fixed sequence. Since persons at higher stages were more abstract and more capable of tolerating stress, a higher level of conceptual development was regarded as more desirable, at least when the person was required to cope with, or adapt to, a changing environment.

It is important to note that the 1961 position was intended as a *provisional* statement to generate empirical investigations that would either support, or lead to revisions of, this initial position. Not surprisingly, therefore, the initial position has undergone considerable revision as each of the original three authors has worked in various domains and made conceptual and methodological revisions that have led to derivative theories (Harvey, 1967; Hunt, 1966a; Schroder, Driver, and Streufert, 1967). The present derivative—the Conceptual Level matching model—can be better understood if seen in a perspective of the original Conceptual Systems viewpoint and its derivatives.

In the original 1961 statement, Conceptual Systems (or stages) were defined partly in terms of motivational orientations: Stage I, unilateral dependence; Stage II, negative independence; Stage III, conditional dependence and mutuality; and Stage IV, interdependence. These hypothesized stage-specific characteristics led to the assumption that a person could be classified into one of the four stages or systems on the basis of his primary motivational concern. When a motivationally based definition is used, measurement is likely to be based on the *content* of a person's response, with each person being classified into one of the four relatively discontinuous system categories on the basis of system-specific content. Conceptual systems were also defined partly in terms of *structure*, and we hoped by so doing to coordinate the otherwise discrete features of motivation and structure through a single personality construct. When a structurally based definition is used, measurement is likely to be based on structural referents such as differentiation, discrimination, and integration, and the person classified on a dimension of conceptual complexity. Although systems were *assumed* to vary in both motivation and structure, there was no supporting evidence for this assumption.

A major difference among the Conceptual Systems derivatives, therefore, is their relative emphasis on motivation (or content) as opposed to conceptual complexity (or structure).

During the past decade, for example, Harvey (1967) and his colleagues have emphasized the motivation or system-specific content characteristics; have used content-oriented measures (both objective and free response) for classifying persons into one of the four system categories; and have investigated system-specific hypotheses (not always hierarchically ordered) in several areas including attitude change. By contrast, Schroder and his colleagues (1967) have viewed personality organization as varying on a continuously distributed dimension of integrative complexity (defined in terms of differentiation, discrimination, and integration); have measured integrative complexity by coding free responses in terms of complexity to provide the basis for assigning each person a score on the integrative complexity dimension; and have investigated the differential responses of persons varying in complexity to variations in environmental complexity.

It should be noted that the present distinction among the three authors is not intended to place more value or desirability on one derivative or another, but rather to set them each in clear perspective. Unless these distinctions are made clear, and the derivative theories updated, other investigators, assuming that the earlier provisional statement is still accepted, may design investigations that use the measures from one derivative to test hypotheses in another, e.g., using one of Harvey's content-based measures to test a hypothesis in information processing according to some of Schroder's structural notions.

The third derivative position that uses Conceptual Level as the basic personality dimension is one that I have been developing, and is summarized in the remainder of this section. One of the first revisions made in developing the Conceptual Level derivative was to note the occurrence of a form of conceptual organization not anticipated earlier; because this pattern represented the lowest point on the CL dimension, it was initially referred to as a "Sub I stage" (Hunt, 1966a) and, more recently, is considered in continuous terms as very low in CL. Next, on the basis of cross-sectional investigations in the twelve- to eighteen-years age range, the motivational orientation hypothesized to characterize the hypothetically "superior" Stage III persons (mutuality and affiliation) did not occur more frequently in older than younger children as might have been expected. Further, persons with Stage IV characteristics were essentially non-existent. Therefore, the CL derivative extended the dimension lower (a step that in turn led to a reconsideration and redefinition of the "negative independence" in Stage II, with this high CL group being reconceptualized as more conceptually complex and independent), and seriously questioned the usefulness of the motivationally based system-specific characteristics of Stage III and Stage IV. In sum, the CL derivative views personality organization on a continuous dimension, with very general anchor points at what we have referred to earlier as Sub I stage, Stage I, and Stage II, which are hierarchically ordered. Most of our work described here is based on persons in the twelve- to eighteen-years age range so that the reservations expressed about the usefulness or occurrence of patterns about Stage II should be considered in terms of the samples studied and the methods used, i.e., it is possible that higher levels may occur in older samples.

Though the principles of construct validity clearly emphasize that such procedures involve validating both the method for indexing the construct and the construct, this unavoidable fusion of method and construct has frequently been overlooked. In the present work, all of the results related to the CL construct were based on the Paragraph Completion Method, unless noted otherwise.

Measurement of CL

Paragraph Completion Method

One of the initial assumptions for CL variation was a developmental rationale in which various levels of conceptual development were conceived in a succession of hierarchically ordered stages (Hunt, 1966a). The lowest level of conceptual development (Sub I stage) is characterized by very poor organization, egocentricity, and immaturity. At the next level (Stage I), the characteristics are categorical thinking, use of a fixed rule structure, and reliance on external standards. At the high level (Stage II), the characteristics are a capacity for generating new concepts, conditional thinking, and greater reliance on internal standards. This developmental rationale assumed that, given optimal training conditions, every person would increase in CL, progressing from the poorly organized, very low level to the next more structured level, and then to the higher level of greater conceptual complexity. A developmental theory, however, requires longitudinal evidence that supports the orderly succession of stages hypothesized by the theory, and the evidence must also demonstrate not only that each stage follows the prescribed sequence, but that every person passes through each stage. The developmental rational in the CL model is an assumption with virtually no longitudinal support; therefore, it should be regarded as a helpful metaphor that may or may not turn out to be validated. However, one can arrive at a very similar set of hierarchically arranged referents through a contemporaneous rationale based entirely on conceptual complexity, i.e., greater differentiation, discrimination, and integration. In this sense the CL dimension (and its method of measurement) are very similar to the integrative complexity derivative used by Schroder *et al.* (1967).

The method for measuring CL was developed to index a person's position on the continuous CL dimension rather than to follow the developmental stage notion exclusively and devise methods to classify each person into one or another of these discontinuous categories. It may be useful for some research or decision-making purposes to use the person's position on the CL dimension to classify him into a particular group, e.g., high CL, but it is important to emphasize that such classification is based on similarity of conceptual orientation, and does not imply that these persons are all in the same "stage."

To index CL, we have used a method that requires the person to do some "conceptual work" by reacting to a stimulus likely to require some "cognitive work" in his response. Specifically, the Paragraph Completion Method consists of six topics, to each of which the person responds with three or four sentences indicating his own personal reactions to the topic. The topics are: "What I think about rules . . ."; "When I am criticized . . ."; "What I think about parents . . ."; "When someone disagrees with me . . ."; "When I am not sure . . ."; and "When I am told what to do. . . ."

Each of the six responses is a unit to be coded according to the scoring manual (Hunt, Lapin, Liberman, McManus, Post, Sabalis, Sweet, and Victor, 1968). The manual provides the basis for assigning a number from 0 to 3 to each response by specifying generic referents for each of these numbers and by presenting topic-specifying examples for each of the scores. The metric scoring is similar to the earlier stage metaphor in that a score of 0 is similar to the Sub I characteristics; 1 to Stage 1; 2 to a transitional stage; and 3 to Stage II. Also, the CL scores are quite similar to the scores used for indexing integrative complexity (Schroder *et al.*, 1967, Appendix 2).

Generic referents for a score of 0 are: very undifferentiated response, overgeneralized exclusion of any negative input, lack of affective control, etc. Generic referents for a score of 1 are: categorical judgments, overgeneralized and unqualified acceptance of single rule, recourse to external standards, etc. Generic referents for a score of 2 are: some form of conditional evaluation, beginning self-delineation, expression of alternatives, etc. Generic referents for a score of 3 are: taking two viewpoints into account simultaneously, coordination of evaluation of situation with differential response, and clear indications of self-delineation and internal standards. In using the manual, the judge is encouraged to maintain a set that disregards content as such in order to infer the nature of the "program" or underlying conceptual structure that might generate such a response. In some cases, where there is insufficient information, the "unscorable" category is used.

A person's CL index is calculated as a composite of his six scores. Two procedures for aggregating scores have been used: (1) a simple average of all scorable responses, and (2) the average of the highest three scores. Schroder *et al.* (1967) originally proposed this latter procedure for aggregating scores, and it is based on a rationale not unlike that of the Binet "ceiling" (i.e., if a person scores on one or two occasions at a higher level, then this score must be an accurate referent of his underlying structure) and also because there is some general demand characteristic to give lower level responses if one becomes bored or disinterested with the task. Most of the results described in the next section are based on this second procedure for indexing CL.

With trained raters, the inter-rater reliability is .80 to .85. In many of the studies reported, two judges have scored all protocols in order to sharpen precision, but it is hoped that as the manual is improved, two will not be necessary.

Correlates, Characteristics, and Construct Validity of CL

The following summary is based on CL as indexed by the Paragraph Completion Method and, with only an occasional exception, using the manual of Hunt *et al.* (1968).

Relation to intelligence. As Table 1 indicates, there is a relation between CL and intelligence, and this relation, though significant with the fairly large samples, is of a relatively low order. Table 1 gives only a sample, but it represents the usual finding: in groups fairly heterogeneous on intelligence, the relation is usually in the .20's, while for more intellectually homogeneous groups, e.g., college students, the relation is typically positive but not significant. The major implication of this relation is the importance of controlling or assessing the effects of intelligence in designing studies to investigate CL effects.

Relation to age of school grade level. Since CL is presumably related to development, the low correlations with chronological age (CA) are initially surprising. When the relation of CL to age is investigated by cross-sectional analysis, the mean scores show a fairly orderly, though slight, pattern of increase from age twelve to sixteen: 1.28, 1.36, 1.44, 1.51, and 1.47, respectively (Hunt, 1964). Of more significance are the only available longitudinal results on CL (Hunt, 1968b), which reported scores for a group of seventy-two boys over a four-year period. At initial testing the boys were in Grades 6-8, and their mean CL score was 1.36; four years later when they were in Grades 10-12, the mean score for the total group showed a significant increase ($p < .01$) to 1.54. The most likely reason for the fairly low relation to CA in these three sets of results (correlational, cross sectional, and longitudinal) is probably that no one of these studies included measures of environmental effects. It would be necessary to conduct a longitudinal investigation that included measures of the environment experienced in order to verify developmental hypotheses of an interactive nature. On the basis of these results, it appears that during the twelve- to sixteen-years age range there are relatively

Table 1

Correlates and Characteristics of Conceptual Level

Related Variable	N	School Grade	Results	Source
Intelligence				
California Test of Mental Maturity	206	7-9	r=.09	Hunt, 1965
Lorge-Thorndike	175	8-12[a]	r-.24**	Cross, 1966
Canadian Academic Aptitude Test	175	11	r=.15*	McLachlan, 1969
Vocabulary	1550	9-12	r=.29**	Hunt and Hardt, 1967
Vocabulary	830	9-12	r=.27**	Hunt, Hardt, and Victor, 1968
Scholastic Aptitude Test (verbal)	160	College	r=.10	Pohl and Pervin, 1968
Age	207	7-9	r=.08	Hunt, 1965
Age	175	8-12[a]	r=.07	Cross,1966
School Grade	830	9-12	r=.17**	Hunt, Hardt, and Victor, 1968
Social Class				
Lower	277	7-9	Middle higher	Hunt and Dopyera, 1966
Middle	692	7-9	than lower	
Sex				
Girls	481	7-9	Girls higher	Hunt and Dopyera, 1966
Boys	488	7-9	than boys	
Academic Achievement				
GPA	830	9-12	r-.17**	Hunt, Hardt, and Victor, 1968
GPA (with SAT partialed out)	150	College	r=.16*	Pohl and Pervin, 1968
Personality Measures				
Kohlberg Moral Maturity Scale	120	9-13	r=.40**	Sullivan, McCullough, and Stager, 1970
Loevinger Scale of Ego Development	120	9-13	r=.34**	Sullivan, McCullough, and Stager, 1970
Future Orientation	1550	9-12	r=.26**	Hunt and Hardt, 1967
Alienation	1550	9-12	r=.21**	Hunt and Hardt, 1967
Internal Control	1550	9-12	r=.12**	Hunt and Hardt, 1967

[a]Boys only
*p<.05
**p<.01

orderly, though not very large, increments for persons in general.

Relation to social class. More important than the not surprising middle class superiority in CL indicated in Table 1 (and it should be noted that the lower class sample was about 90 percent Black) was the additional finding that the lower class sample showed *greater* variability in CL than did the middle class sample. Proportionately more middle class students are at the low (CL = 1) level while proportionately more lower class students are at the very low level, and, surprisingly, the lower class sample contained a slightly greater proportion (almost all female) at high CL. As we have noted elsewhere (Hunt, 1966b; Hunt and Dopyera, 1966), these results urge caution in treating lower class students as a monolithic entity.

Sex differences. The female superiority was noted for both the middle and lower class samples, but, as implied above, was much more striking for the lower class sample in which the girls were much higher in mean CL than were the boys. Although results are likely to vary slightly from one sample to another, the results of most of our investigations suggest that at the high school level, the sex difference in CL is likely to have disappeared. However, as with intelligence, we have regarded it as important, wherever possible, to include sex in the design to investigate whether the same pattern of CL effects hold for both sexes.

Relation to academic achievement. As Table 1 indicates, CL is generally, though not strongly, related to academic achievement. The more interesting results appear when one considers the content area and method for indexing achievement. The correlation between CL and Grade Point Average (GPA) with the effect of SAT partialled out, for twenty-eight Engineering students, was -.56 (p<.01) while the CL-GPA correlation for twenty-two Social Science students was .44 (p<.05), and for sixty Humanities students r=.38 (p<.05) (Pohl and Pervin, 1968). These differential results indicate that the overall correlation of .16 in Table 1 showed quite different patterns depending upon the nature of the subject matter: in the case of Engineering, which presumably requires a more conventional orientation of memorization, CL is inversely related to achievement, while in Social Science and Humanities, which presumably require more critical thinking, analysis, and generation of alternatives, the correlation is positive.

In addition, when achievement was indexed by an objective multiple-choice task, Claunch (1964) found no difference in students varying in CL but matched on SAT; however, when achievement was indexed by a more complex criterion (an essay examination requiring students to compare and contrast), the high CL group performed significantly better ($p<.05$) than the low CL group. The implication of these results for designing investigations of CL effects is to underline the importance of indexing achievement at different levels on the taxonomy.

Relation to social desirability. Campbell (1960) has suggested, among other additional criteria for construct validity, information on the susceptibility of the measure to social desirability or "fake good" instructions. When the Paragraph Completion Method was administered under "fake good" instructions, the mean CL scores decreased significantly ($p<.05$) when compared with the same group's performance under standard instructions (Hunt, 1962). These results were interpreted to mean that the "fake good" set induces persons to respond with many responses scored 1, e.g., reliance on authority, categorical judgments, etc. This interpretation is supported by results of another investigation in which the scores on the Children's Social Desirability (CSD) Scale (Crandall, Crandall, and Katkovsky, 1965) were compared for three groups of students varying in CL. Mean CSD score for the very low group was 17.35, for the low (CL = 1) group 23.80, and for the high group 16.53 (Hunt, 1965). This curvilinear pattern suggests that what is referred to as a "social desirability" tendency, whether induced or dispositionally present, is very similar to a CL score of 1. It is interesting to recall the strong tendency of the middle class junior high school sample, when compared to the lower class sample, to score 1.

Relation to parental training conditions. Cross (1966) has studied the parental training conditions associated with boys varying in CL. The major portion of the investigation consisted of defining two groups of boys, individually matched for IQ and CA, but varying in CL; the mean of the high CL group (N = 27) was 2.0 while the mean of the low CL group (N = 27) was 1.1. Both parents of all fifty-four boys were individually interviewed with a specially designed schedule, and their responses coded for degree of interdependence (scale ranged from very interdependent and reflective to very unilateral and autocratic). When the scores of the mothers, fathers, and combined parents of the two CL groups were compared, the parents of the high CL group were significantly higher in interdependence in all three comparisons. In a correlation analysis with a larger sample (N = 175) Cross found that a boy's CL was significantly correlated (r = .23, p.<.01) with parental non-authoritarianism as indexed by the Parental Attitude Research Instrument. Although these results cannot be interpreted to represent longitudinal causal influence, they are in keeping with the hypothesized parental antecedents of persons varying in CL.

Relation to delinquency. The incidence of both observed and reported delinquency was found to be higher in the very low CL group of boys than in the group with higher CL scores (Hunt and Hardt, 1965), a finding that agrees with the hypothesized lack of organization and assimilation of norms for persons scoring 0 on CL.

Relation to other measures of developmental maturity. Sullivan, McCullough, and Stager (1970) investigated the relations among CL, Kohlberg's Moral Maturity scale (1964), and Loevinger's Ego Development scale (1966) in three different age groups: twelve, fourteen, and seventeen. The correlations in Table 1 have partialled out the effect of age, and indicate a substantial relation of CL to level of both moral and ego development.

Two investigations (France, 1968; Hunt and McManus, 1968) have investigated the relation between CL and the Interpersonal Maturity Level originally described by Sullivan, Grant, and Grant (1957). Although there were very general relations, the degree of correspondence was not high.

Relation to other personality measures. As Table 1 indicates, CL is significantly related to Future Orientation (Strodtbeck, 1958), Non-alienation (Srole, 1956), and to Internal Control (Rotter, 1966), though this latter relation is not as high as one might expect from the hypothetical descriptions of CL and Internal Control. These relations were replicated in another sample of 830 students by correlations of .26, .17, and .13, respectively

(Hunt, Hardt, and Victor, 1968). For persons at the college level, CL has been found to be inversely related to Dogmatism and Authoritarianism (Schroder *et al.*, 1967).

Conceptual Level Matching Model

The CL model is now considered according to the meta-theoretical framework suggested elsewhere (Hunt, 1970) for considering matching models. It consists of the following aspects: (1) desired change, (2) conception of the person, (3) conception of the environment, and (4) conception of the interactive process between person and environment. In Lewinian terms, the four aspects are B, P, E, and P-E interaction, respectively. In educational terms, these four aspects are educational objectives, learner characteristics, educational approaches, and theory of instruction, respectively.

Desired Change (Educational Objectives)

When the CL matching model is applied in education, the desired objectives can be initially conceived in terms of the two widely used taxonomies, cognitive (Bloom, 1956) and affective (Krathwohl, Bloom, and Masia, 1964). Matching predictions will vary according to the particular objectives. For example, it seems likely that for such objectives as recall and memorization (cf. Claunch, 1964), CL-treatment interactions are unlikely, while for more complex objectives, interactions may be expected. Although very little is known about the relation between cognitive and affective outcomes, it seems important to include both whenever possible in order to learn more about their inter-relation and their differential susceptibility to matching.

A major dimension of variation in objectives (Hunt, 1970) is that of phenotypic vs. genotypic. Phenotypic objectives are defined as short-term changes in behavior that are unlikely to generalize either over space (to other content areas) or time (resist extinction). Genotypic goals, on the other hand, or what Schroder has called "process" goals, involve more enduring structural reorganization. Genotypic objectives are exemplified by problem-solving strategies, learning sets, etc. A major reason why genotypic objectives have not been more widely adopted is that they are much more difficult to measure. It may also be, as some have recently suggested, that they are very difficult, if not impossible, to attain, but it seems clear that we cannot approach the question until adequate indices of genotypic educational objectives are available.

Conception of the Person (Learner Characteristics)

Personal variation is considered on the CL dimension, which is thought to represent conceptual complexity and the other characteristics previously summarized. Specific person-environment hypotheses are developed based on the person's position on the CL dimension, i.e., given a person with specified level of information-processing capacity, what educational approach is likely to be most effective?

A person's CL may be considered as either cause or effect. In the matching model and the work derived from it, we have considered learner CL as the "cause," or what we describe later as an "accessibility channel," i.e., CL in this sense is thought of as a fairly stable characteristic. However, this view should not indicate that, for certain purposes, it may not be important to treat CL as "effect," i.e., to attempt to increase learner CL through deliberative educational intervention. Cronbach and Snow (1969) have referred to this paradox in relation to aptitude as follows: "Work on personality will have continually to contend with the technical and philosophical problems that arise from the fact that 'aptitude' may be a predictor, an intervening variable arising from the treatment and affecting further response to the treatment, or a significant 'final' outcome" (p. 192).

To consider only the learner's cognitive orientation in planning the most effective form of educational approach is to oversimplify the situation considerably. We have begun with this single dimension, however, with the belief that it will put us in a better position to extend the number of learner characteristics considered, e.g., to motivational orientation and value orientation. We describe this extension of the model in a later section.

Conception of the Environment (Educational Approaches)

The generic dimension of the educational environment in the

CL matching model is *degree of structure*, which is similar to what Schroder *et al.* (1967) refer to as environmental complexity. The specification of educational approach in matching model terms requires that the approach meet criteria of both theoretical adequacy and, at least to some extent, pedagogical reasonableness. In order to design investigations, it is necessary to consider simultaneously the source described by Cronbach and Snow (1968) as "comparisons of controversial instructional methods" along with the theoretical relation of such methods to learner characteristics.

Degree of structure may take the form of variations in rule-example sequencing in which example-only would be regarded as low structure while rule-example would be regarded as high structure. It may also be represented by variations from the low structure of a discovery approach to the high structure of a lecture approach, from independent study to highly organized study, and from student-centered approaches to teacher-centered approaches.

This use of multiple referents for a generic environmental dimension (degree of structure) is similar to the definition of environmental complexity (Schroder *et al.*, 1967), which used multiple referents of information load, informational diversity, rate of information change, noxity, and eucity (amount of reward). Whether the advantages of such a general definition outweigh the possible disadvantages of overlooking important differences among the referents must be continually evaluated. Specifically, to group together such otherwise diverse educational approaches as discovery learning, example-first order in rule-example presentation, and student-centered approaches because of their assumed low degree of structure provides potential generality, but also may mask important differences; therefore, the need exists for continually reevaluating the generality assumption.

Conception of the Interactive Process
(Theory of Instruction)

Learner CL characteristics determine the basic matching predictions. In specifying predictions at this initial phase, we consider two points on the CL dimension—low CL defined as scores in the range from 1.0 to 1.4 and high CL defined as scores ranging above 1.8. Students lower in CL (below 1.0) are not presently considered because relatively few such students are encountered in the secondary schools where we are working.

Given the characteristics of low CL learners—categorical, dependent on external standards, and not capable of generating their own concepts—the prediction follows that they will profit more from educational approaches providing a high degree of structure. Given the characteristics of high CL learners—capable of generating new concepts, having a greater degree of internal standards, and being capable of taking on different perspectives— either they should profit more from approaches that are low in structure, or degree of structure may not affect their performance. Thus, the heart of the CL matching model is generally inverse relation between CL and degree of structure: *low CL learners profiting more from high structure and high CL learners profiting more from low structure, or, in some cases, being less affected by variations in structure.*

In his recent discussion of heuristics for devising ATI hypotheses, Snow (1969) provided a metatheoretical basis for viewing the present hypotheses. He suggested two models for thinking about ATI hypotheses (which are not necessarily mutually exclusive): a compensatory model and a preferential model. He described the compensatory model as follows: "Here we might argue that the treatments should compensate for each learner's deficiency by providing the mode of representation that the learner cannot provide for himself" (p. 15). "The preceding discussion leads toward a general conception of instructional treatments as prosthetic devices for particular aptitude groups. A treatment that proves especially appropriate for a person deficient in some particular aptitude may be functioning as an 'artificial' aptitude. It contains the information processing functions that the learner cannot provide for himself" (p. 21).

The hypothesized relation between low CL learners and high structure is clearly an example of the compensatory model. Perhaps the reason for hedging the general matching prescription for high CL learners can be understood by considering Snow's preferential model in which "the treatments are designed to captilize on the apparent strengths and preferences of each kind of learner" (p. 15).

If only compensatory factors were at work, then one would expect only ordinal interactions between CL and variations in structure, i.e., high CL learners would do well under both conditions while low CL learners would do well only under high structure (see Figure 1 for an example). The compensatory model, however, provides no basis for understanding the occurrence of disordinal or "crossover" interactions.

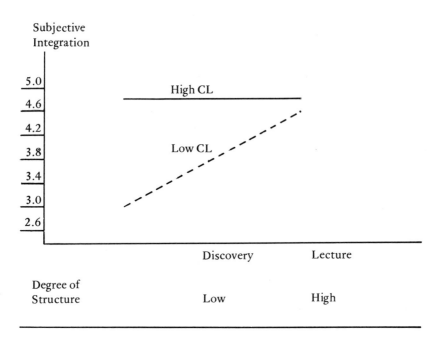

Figure 1

Subjective Integration as a Function of Discovery vs. Lecture and Learner CL (after McLachlan, 1969)

Why should a high CL learner perform more poorly than a low CL learner in a treatment when he presumably possesses the requisite information-processing capacities for performance? (See Figure 2 for a qualified example.) One possible answer comes from Snow's preferential model: on this basis, one would understand the high CL decrement in performance as reflecting interference

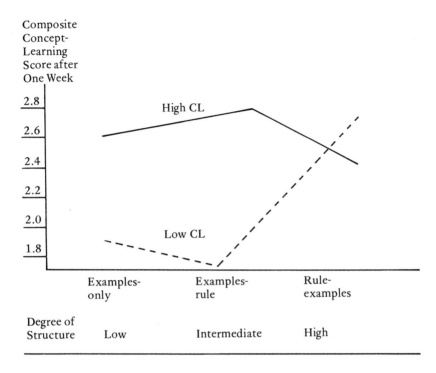

Figure 2

*Concept-Learning as a Function of Rule-example Order
and Learner CL (after Tomlinson, 1969)*

with the learner's preference or attitude. Thus the high CL learner
with a capacity for generating his own solutions might resent a
high structure treatment, and his performance might worsen
accordingly.

It should be clear that we do not regard the compensatory
and preferential models as providing highly precise means for
reaching *a priori* hypotheses; rather, they are ways of thinking
about the person-environment interactions. They are, as Snow
observed, provisional holding terms until newer, more comprehensive integrations can be generated.

In the discussion of empirical evidence for the CL matching
model, it will be noted in some cases we expected disordinal

interactions and in other cases we hedged the prediction for high CL learners because we did not know to what extent preferential factors would operate.

Specific Tasks (Subject Matter)

It would be naive to conclude without at least mentioning task specificity—the role of skill level and its relation to content. Without minimizing the importance of the relation between learner skill level and content, we have thus far designed novel materials and tasks for the matching studies in order to minimize this factor. As we proceed it is unquestionably necessary to coordinate elements of subject matter into the definition of degree of structure.

Empirical Support
for Conceptual Level Matching Model

The first study employing the CL matching model (Hunt, 1966a) provided evidence of a qualitative, impressionistic nature. Classroom groups, homogeneous on CL, were formed—a very low (Sub 1) group, a low CL (Stage I) group, and a high (Stage II) group—without the nature of the groups being known to their teachers. The teachers reported that the very low group profited most from a high degree of structure, e.g., concrete examples, clearly outlined assignments, no discussion; the low CL group profited most from moderate structure, e.g., debates, group competition; and the high CL group seemed to perform best with a low degree of structure, e.g., independent study, self-selected projects, etc.

Another source of construct validity was obtained from the national evaluation of Project Upward Bound (pre-college enrichment program for culturally disadvantaged American high school students). When students' gains in attitude and motivation during the summer were considered for possible differential effects, the pattern was exactly as expected from the model: when the majority of students in a program were low in CL, they gained more when the program approach was structured than when the approach was flexible; when the majority of the students in a program were high in CL, they showed the opposite pattern—

greater gains with a flexible approach than with a structured approach. It was also noted that differences in approach affected the high CL students less than the low CL students.

Using the matching model, McLachlan (1969) investigated the interactive effects of learner CL and variations in structure represented by a discovery (low structure) vs. lecture (high structure) approach. Equal numbers of low and high CL students, matched on ability, were assigned to each of the two conditions. The content of the presentation consisted of a specifically designed set of visual materials aimed at acquainting the student with the Picasso painting, "Guernica." Students in both conditions were shown the same pictorial materials, a slide containing the entire picture, and a series of component parts of the picture on separate slides. Students in the lecture condition heard a short "lecturette" on the meaning of each component slide, while students in the discovery condition viewed each slide for a comparable amount of time, but were instructed to work out for themselves what the picture meant. Afterward, students were asked to give their own idea of the central meaning of the picture, how the parts fit together into this meaning (subjective integration), and measures of recall and attitude recorded. Figure 1 indicates the pattern of results for subjective integration. Results indicated an ordinal interaction with the low CL students performing significantly better (p<.05) with high structure (lecture) than with low structure (discovery). Since no differences were noted for the high CL students, this pattern illustrates the compensatory model suggested by Snow.

In a companion study, Tomlinson (1969) used the matching model rationale to investigate the differential effects of rule-example order as a function of learner CL. Groups of low and high CL students were assigned equally to three treatment conditions thought to vary in degree of structure: (1) low structure, in which the examples were presented first and the rule was presented some time later; (2) intermediate structure, in which the examples were presented first followed almost immediately by the rule; and (3) high structure, in which the rule was presented before the examples. The rule, or principle, was Festinger's concept of "cognitive dissonance," and the examples were included in a brief excerpt from a story about two college boys. Students' concept-learning was indexed by multiple criteria: definition of concept, recall of examples, and production of new examples. Figure 2 presents the composite scores one week after the treatment condition (IQ effects were removed from the scores by linear regression).

Analysis of Figure 2 results indicated a highly significant CL treatment effect, and the expected pattern was borne out when comparing the mean scores. Under conditions of low and intermediate structure, the low CL groups were significantly lower ($p < .05$) than the high CL groups in these same conditions, and the low CL groups under low and intermediate structure were also significantly lower ($p < .05$) than the low CL group under high structure. Although there was a tendency toward disordinal interaction, the difference between CL groups in the high structure condition was not significant. Nonetheless, this tendency toward a high CL "decrement" illustrates the principle in the preferential model suggested by Snow.

Finally, a study by Tuckman (1968) should be noted, although he used an objective test for indexing CL (Interpersonal Topical Inventory) rather than the Paragraph Completion Method. Investigating the interactive effects of learner CL with degree of structure represented by non-directive teachers vs. directive teachers, he followed the CL matching model rationale to predict matching effects for low CL students with directive teachers and for high CL students with non-directive teachers. When the measures of teacher preference, satisfaction, and course grade were analyzed, he found that the primary results occurred in one "mismatched" cell. Compared to the other three combinations, the high CL students who experienced directive teachers rated these teachers lower and were less satisfied with them, thus providing an even clearer illustration of the preferential model.

Most of the studies just described have investigated the effect of high vs. low CL with either extreme—group or median—split designs. A study by Noy (1970) was designed to investigate CL effects by using randomized blocks design, with CL continuously distributed through the blocks so that a more precise estimate of the points on the CL distribution where maximum interactions occur will be possible.

Extension of the Model:
"Accessibility Channels"

Although the results we have reviewed in relation to the CL matching model are encouraging, it is also obvious that other learner characteristics need to be considered. The model has therefore been extended (Hunt, 1968a) to include other possible person-environment combinations, and in this extended model the student is viewed in terms of "accessibility channels."

Taking account of "accessibility channels" is almost unavoidable when working with a physically handicapped student. Though less apparent, it seems equally important to consider any student in terms of channels of accessibility so that the form of educational approach can be most appropriately "tuned in" to the student. The CL matching model gives an example of how the accessibility channel, the learner's cognitive orientation, can be used to "tune in" by modulating the structure of the presentation. The model in Table 2 extends this rationale to other orientations. Table 2 deals only with the coordination between the form of educational approach and the "accessibility channel," and is not concerned with the relation between learner's skill level and the content of the presentation.

Table 2 presents the general nature of the relation, but in order to be useful for designing investigations or contributing to educational decisions, these general relations must be translated into more specific forms comparable to the low CL-high structure prescription in the CL matching model. When matching motivational orientation with form of feedback and reward, the hypothesis would be that learners with self-directed orientations are more likely to profit from intrinsic reward and self-anchored feedback while learners with more socially based (affiliative) orientation are more likely to profit from extrinsic reward and normative feedback. When matching value orientation with value content of the presentation, the central hypothesis would be that learners are more likely to profit from a presentation that is within the "latitude of acceptance" of their current value orientation, and less likely to profit from a presentation either identical to their present stand, or outside their "latitude of acceptance." Finally, when matching sensory orientation and modality of presentation, the quite obvious hypothesis is that when learners have a preferred modality, e.g., visual or auditory, they will profit more from a presentation in that modality. The rationale for these matching hypotheses is amplified in Hunt (1968b).

Table 2

Model for Coordinating Learner
Characteristics with Educational Approaches

Accessibility channels	Form of presentation
1. Cognitive orientation	Structure of presentation
2. Motivational orientation	Form of feedback and reward
3. Value orientation	Value context of presentation
4. Sensory orientation	Modality of presentation

Investigations are planned that will attempt not only to test these hypotheses as we have done with the CL matching model, but also to consider the possible role of more than one accessibility channel in response to a treatment variation. Table 2 may be thought of as providing the basis for investigations to determine whether, for example, CL is, in fact, more important than motivational orientation in determining differential response to structure of presentation; conversely, does motivational orientation provide a better differential predictor of reaction to form of feedback and reward than cognitive orientation? Since we have reported only positive evidence, it should be noted that there is some evidence that bears on this last question, but not as predicted in the Table 2 model. Stuempfig and Maehr (1970) reported differential CL effects upon reaction to feedback (personal vs. impersonal): While high CL students showed no variation between feedback conditions, low CL students performed better with personal rather than impersonal feedback. (No measure of motivational orientation was available.) Therefore, there is clearly a need to circumscribe those areas in which CL will provide differential reactions and those conditions that will be susceptible to other orientations; Table 2 should serve as a useful guide in collecting such information.

As the proposed accessibility channels are found to be functionally related to students' differential susceptibility to different educational approaches, such results have important implications for the school psychologist. He is often accused of gathering information about students that has nothing to do with the decisions teachers and educational planners must make. The model in Table 2 suggests that if the school psychologist could provide a profile of a student in terms of accessibility channels, such information might be quite helpful.

Finally, an obvious comment regarding construct validity of personality measures may be noted. Although it has frequently been implied, the importance of the degree to which a personality construct will predict differential response to different forms of environmental effect has not received sufficient emphasis. Although there can be danger in limiting ourselves to only pragmatic criteria, it seems nonetheless worthwhile to suggest that when a measure of personality is described, one of the most valuable bits of information is the degree to which a person's variation on the measure gives some predictive power as to his differential reaction to different environmental effects.

Concluding Comments

Having described CL and summarized its construct validity, derived the rationale for the CL matching model and provided some evidence for its construct validity, and indicated some directions for extending the matching model, we are left with the question of what effect these principles can and should have in actual decisions and planning in educational settings.

Of course, the prime consideration is whether the principle is sufficiently well established to attempt implementation, and such validity should not be ignored. However, at the risk of seeming cynical, it seems unlikely that the validity of an educationally relevant psychological principle will have very much to do with whether or not it is accepted in educational practice. Validity of a principle is probably a necessary, but certainly not a sufficient, condition to insure its adoption.

Assuming that the matching principle is sufficiently well established, it seems probable that one of the major determinants of its acceptability will be the degree to which it is congruent with the "implicit matching principles" that teachers have in their heads (alluded to by Torrance in the initial quotation). If one accepts this formulation, then the task of implementing a matching model should begin with an investigation of what "theory of matching" the educational decision-maker is now using, because from what we know of attitude change and adoption of new procedures, the suggested matching prescriptions should not be too far out of line with those held by the person who will be implementing the prescription. Such problems of implementation will require concepts and strategies at least as comprehensive as those set forth in this paper on matching. Although this is not the place to begin this large task, it seems important at least to point out this rather neglected area of understanding.

One final complicating feature in the possible adoption of matching principles into the schools comes from the increasing tendency for student-determined options and courses. How does a matching model operate in a situation where the students themselves decide the "prescriptions"? It would seem that work will be necessary in exploring ways in which matching information can be provided to students in constructive, non-threatening ways so that it can serve as a guide in helping students arrive at effective decisions.

References

Bloom, B.S. (Ed.) *Taxonomy of Educational Objectives. Handbook I: Cognitive Domain.* New York: McKay, 1956.

Campbell, D.T. "Recommendations for APO Test Standards Regarding Construct, Trait, or Discriminant Validity," *American Psychologist*, 15, 1960, pp. 546-553.

Claunch, N. "Cognitive and Motivational Characteristics Associated with Concrete and Abstract Levels of Conceptual Complexity." Unpublished doctoral dissertation, Princeton University, 1964.

Crandall, V., V.J. Crandall, and W. Katkovsky. "A Children's

Social Desirability of Response Questionnaire," *Journal of Consulting Psychology*, 29, 1965, pp. 27-36.

Cronbach, L.J. "The Two Disciplines of Scientific Psychology," *American Psychologist*, 12, 1957, pp. 671-684.

Cronbach, L.J. How Can Instruction be Adapted to Individual Differences? In R.M. Gagné (Ed.), *Learning and Individual Differences*. Columbus, Ohio: Merrill, 1967, pp. 23-44.

Cronbach, L.J. and R.E. Snow. *Project on Individual Differences in Learning Ability as a Function of Instructional Variables*. Annual Report No. 2, 1968, School of Education, Stanford University, U.S. Office of Education.

Cronbach, L.J. and R.E. Snow. *Individual Differences in Learning Ability as a Function of Instructional Variables*. Final Report, 1969, School of Education, Stanford University, U.S. Office of Education.

Cross, H.J. "The Relation of Parental Training Conditions to Conceptual Level in Adolescent Boys," *Journal of Personality*, 34, 1966, pp. 348-365.

France, S.A. "A Comparison of Integration Level Theory and Conceptual Systems Theory Using a Delinquent Population." Unpublished master's thesis, Syracuse University, 1968.

Harvey, O.J. "Conceptual Systems and Attitude Change." In C.W. Sherif and M. Sherif (Eds.) *Attitude, Ego-involvement, and Change*. New York: John Wiley and Sons, 1967, pp. 201-226.

Harvey, O.J., D.E. Hunt, and H.M. Schroder. *Conceptual Systems and Personality Organization*. New York: John Wiley and Sons, 1961.

Hunt, D.E. *Personality Patterns of Adolescent Boys*. Progress Report, 1962, National Institute of Mental Health.

Hunt, D.E. *Personality Patterns of Adolescent Boys*. Progress Report, 1964, National Institute of Mental Health.

Hunt, D.E. *Indicators of Development Change in Lower Class Children*. Report, 1965, U.S. Office of Education.

Hunt, D.E. "A Conceptual Systems Change Model and Its Application to Education." In O.J. Harvey (Ed.) *Experience, Structure, and Adaptability*. New York: Springer, 1966a, pp. 277-302.

Hunt, D.E. "Adolescence: Cultural Deprivation, Poverty, and the

Dropout," *Review of Educational Research*, 36, 1966b, pp. 463-473.

Hunt, D.E. "Differential Training in Teacher Education and Its Implications for Increasing Flexibility in Teaching." In B.R. Joyce (Ed.) *Teacher as Innovator*. Washington, D.C.: U.S. Office of Education, 1968a, pp. 59-77.

Hunt, D.E. "Longitudinal Analysis of Conceptual Level Scores." Unpublished manuscript, Syracuse University, 1968b.

Hunt, D.E. "Matching Models and Moral Training." In C. Beck, B. Crittenden, and E.V. Sullivan (Eds.) *Moral Education*. Toronto: University of Toronto Press, 1970.

Hunt, D.E. and J. Dopyera. "Personality Variation in Lower-class Children," *Journal of Psychology*, 62, 1966, pp. 47-54.

Hunt, D.E. and R.H. Hardt. "Developmental Stage, Delinquency, and Differential Treatment," *Journal of Research in Crime and Delinquency*, 2, 1965, pp. 20-31.

Hunt, D.E. and R.H. Hardt. *Characterization of 1966 Summer Upward Bound Program*. Syracuse University Youth Development Center, 1967.

Hunt, D.E., R.H. Hardt, and J. Victor. *Characterization of Upward Bound: Summer and Academic Year 1967-1968*. Syracuse University Youth Development Center, 1968.

Hunt, D.E., S.Lapin, B. Liberman, J. McManus, R. Post, R. Sabalis, S. Sweet, and J.B. Victor. "Manual for Coding Paragraph Completion Responses for Adolescents." Unpublished manuscript, Syracuse University Youth Development Center, 1968.

Hunt, D.E. and J.M. McManus. *Preliminary Investigation of Boys Known to Probation*. Final Report, January 1968, Office of Law Enforcement Assistance.

Kohlberg, L. "Development of Moral Character and Moral Ideology." In M.L. Hoffman and L.W. Hoffman (Eds.) *Review of Child Development Research*. New York: Russell Sage Foundation, Vol. 1, 1964, pp. 383-431.

Krathwohl, D., B.S. Bloom, and B.B. Masia. *Taxonomy of Educational Objectives. Handbook II: Affective Domain*. New York: McKay, 1964.

Lewin, K. *Dynamic Theory of Personality*. New York: McGraw-

Hill, 1935.

Loevinger, J. "The Meaning and Measurement of Ego Development," *American Psychologist*, 21, 1966, pp. 195-206.

McLachlan, J.F.C. "Individual Differences and Teaching Methods in Student Interpretation of Modern Art." Unpublished master's thesis, University of Toronto, 1969.

Noy, J.E. "An Examination of the Utilization of a Data Bank Storage and Retrieval System on Biographical Data for Students of Differing Conceptual Level." Unpublished master's thesis, University of Toronto, 1970.

Pohl, R.L. and L.A. Pervin. "Academic Performance as a Function of Task Requirements and Cognitive Style," *Psychological Reports*, 22, 1968, pp. 1017-1020.

Rotter, J.B. "Generalized Expectancies for Internal versus External Control of Reinforcement," *Psychological Monographs*, 80, 1966 (1, Whole No. 609).

Schroder, H.M., M.J. Driver, and S. Streufert. *Human Information Processing*. New York: Holt, Rinehart, and Winston, 1967.

Snow, R.E. "Research on Media and Attitudes." Paper presented at Conference on Research on Instructional Media, Indiana University, Bloomington, June, 1969.

Srole, L. "Integration and Certain Corollaries," *American Sociological Review*, 21, 1956, pp. 709-716.

Strodtbeck, F.L. "Family Interaction, Values and Achievement." In D.C. McClelland, A.L. Baldwin, V. Bronfenbrenner, and F.L. Strodtbeck (Eds.) *Talent and Society*. New York: Van Nostrand, 1958, pp. 137-194.

Stuempfig, D.W. and M.L. Maehr. "Effects of Conceptual Structure and Social Quality of Feedback on Persistence," *Child Development*, 1970.

Sullivan, C.E., M.Q. Grant, and J. Grant. "The Development of Interpersonal Maturity: Application to Delinquency," *Psychiatry*, 20, 1957, pp. 373-385.

Sullivan, E.V., G. McCullough, and M. Stager. "A Developmental Study of the Relation Between Conceptual, Ego, and Moral Development," *Child Development*, 41, 1970, pp. 399-412.

Tomlinson, P.D. "Differential Effectiveness of Three Teaching Strategies for Students of Varying Conceptual Levels."

Unpublished master's thesis, University of Toronto, 1969.

Torrance, E.P. "Different Ways of Learning for Different Kinds of Children." In E.P. Torrance and R.D. Stom (Eds.) *Mental Health and Achievement: Increasing Potential and Reducing School Dropout*. New York: John Wiley and Sons, 1965, pp. 253-262.

Tuckman, B.W. *A Study of the Effectiveness of Directive vs. Non-directive Vocational Teachers as a Function of Student Characteristics and Course Format*. Final Report, 1968, U.S. Office of Education.

13.

Characteristics of Good Teachers
and Implications for Teacher Educators

Don Hamachek

It is, I think, a sad commentary about our educational system that it keeps announcing both publicly and privately that "good" and "poor" teachers cannot be distinguished one from the other. Probably no issue in education has been so voluminously researched as has teacher effectiveness and considerations which enhance or restrict this effectiveness. Nonetheless, we still read that we cannot tell the good guys from the bad guys. For example, Biddle and Ellena (1964) in their book, *Contemporary Research on Teacher Effectiveness*, begin by stating that "the problem of teacher effectiveness is so complex that no one today knows what *The Competent Teacher* is." I think we *do* know what the competent—or effective, or good, or whatever you care to call him—teacher is, and in the remainder of this paper I will be as specific as possible in citing *why* I think we know, along with implications for our teacher education programs.

What the Research Says

By and large, most research efforts aimed at investigating teacher effectiveness have attempted to probe one or more of the following dimensions of teacher personality and behavior: (1) personal characteristics; (2) instructional procedures and inter-action styles; (3) perceptions of self; and (4) perceptions of others.

Reprinted from *Phi Delta Kappan*, Vol. L, No. 6, February, 1969, with permission of the author and the publisher. The author is Associate Professor of Education at Michigan State University.

Because of space limits, this is by no means an exhaustive review of the research related to the problem, but it is, I think, representative of the kind and variety of research findings linked to questions of teacher effectiveness.

Personal Characteristics of Good Versus Poor Teachers

We would probably agree that it is quite possible to have two teachers of equal intelligence, training, and grasp of subject matter who nevertheless differ considerably in the results they achieve with students. Part of the difference can be accounted for by the effect of a teacher's personality on the learners. To what kinds of personality do students respond?

Hart (1934) conducted a study based upon the opinions of 3,725 high school seniors concerning best-liked and least-liked teachers and found a total of forty-three different reasons for "liking Teacher A best" and thirty different reasons for "liking Teacher Z least." Not surprisingly, over fifty-one percent of the students said that they liked best those teachers who were "helpful in school work, who explained lessons and assignments clearly, and who used examples in teaching." Also, better than forty percent responded favorably to teachers with a "sense of humor." Those teachers assessed most negatively were "unable to explain clearly, were partial to brighter students, and had superior, aloof, overbearing attitudes." In addition, over fifty percent of the respondents mentioned behaviors such as "too cross, crabby, grouchy, and sarcastic" as reasons for disliking many teachers. Interestingly enough, mastery of subject matter, which is vital but badly overemphasized by specialists, ranked sixteenth on both lists. Somehow students seem willing to take more or less for granted that a teacher "knows" his material. What seems to make a difference is the teacher's personal style in *communicating* what he knows. Studies by Witty (1947) and Bousfield (1940) tend to support these conclusions at both the high school *and* college level.

Having desirable personal qualities is one thing, but what are the results of rigorous tests of whether the teacher's having them makes any difference in the performance of students?

Cogan (1958) found that warm, considerate teachers got an

unusual amount of original poetry and art from their high school students. Reed (1962) found that teachers higher in a capacity for warmth favorably affected their pupils' interests in science. Using scores from achievement tests as their criterion measure, Heil, Powell, and Feifer (1960) compared various teacher-pupil personality combinations and found that the well-integrated (healthy, well-rounded, flexible) teachers were most effective with *all* types of students. Spaulding (1963) found that the self-concepts of elementary school children were apt to be higher and more positive in classrooms in which the teacher was "socially integrative" and "learner supportive."

In essence, I think the evidence is quite clear when it comes to sorting out good or effective from bad or ineffective teachers on the basis of personal characteristics. Effective teachers appear to be those who are, shall we say, "human" in the fullest sense of the word. They have a sense of humor, are fair, empathetic, more democratic than autocratic, and apparently are more able to relate easily and naturally to students on either a one-to-one or group basis. Their classrooms seem to reflect miniature enterprise operations in the sense that they are more open, spontaneous, and adaptable to change. Ineffective teachers apparently lack a sense of humor, grow impatient easily, use cutting, ego-reducing comments in class, are less well integrated, are inclined to be somewhat authoritarian, and are generally less sensitive to the needs of their students. Indeed, research related to authoritarianism suggests that the bureaucratic conduct and rigid overtones of the ineffective teacher's classroom are desperate measures to support the weak pillars of his own personality structure.

Instructional Procedures and Interaction Styles of Good Versus Poor Teachers

If there really are polar extremes such as "good" or "poor" teachers, then we can reasonably assume that these teachers differ not only in personal characteristics but in the way they conduct themselves in the classroom.

Flanders (1960) found that classrooms in which achievement and attitudes were superior were likely to be conducted by teachers who did not blindly pursue a single behavioral-instructional path to the exclusion of other possibilities. In other words, the more successful teachers were better able to range along a continuum of interaction styles which varied from fairly active, dominative support on the one hand to a more reflective, discriminating support on the other. Interestingly, those teachers who were *not* successful were the very ones who were inclined to use the same interaction styles in a more or less rigid fashion.

Barr (1929) discovered that not only did poor teachers make more assignments than good teachers but, almost without exception, they made some sort of textbook assignment as part of their unyielding daily procedure. The majority of good teachers used more outside books and problem-project assignments. When the text was assigned, they were more likely to supplement it with topics questions, or other references.

Research findings related to interaction styles variously called "learner-centered" or "teacher-centered" point to similar conclusions. In general, it appears that the amount of cognitive gain is largely unaffected by the autocratic or democratic tendencies of the instructor. However, when affective gains are considered, the results are somewhat different. For example, Stern (1963) reviewed thirty-four studies comparing non-directive with directive instruction and concluded:

> Regardless of whether the investigator was concerned with attitudes toward the cultural out group, toward other participants in the class, or toward the self, the results generally have indicated that non-directive instruction facilitates a shift in a more favorable, acceptant direction.

When it comes to classroom behavior, interaction patterns, and teacher styles, good or effective teachers seem to reflect more of the following behaviors:

1. Willingness to be flexible, to be direct or indirect as the situation demands.
2. Ability to perceive the world from the student's point of view.
3. Ability to "personalize" their teaching.
4. Willingness to experiment, to try out new things.
5. Skill in asking questions (as opposed to seeing self as a

kind of answering service).

6. Knowledge of subject matter and related areas.
7. Provision of well-established examination procedures.
8. Provision of definite study helps.
9. Reflection of an appreciative attitude (evidenced by nods, comments, smiles, etc.).
10. Use of conversational manner in teaching—informal, easy style.

Self-Perceptions of Good Versus Poor Teachers

We probably do not have to go any further than our own personal life experiences to know that the way we see, regard, and feel about ourselves has an enormous impact on both our private and public lives. How about good and poor teachers? How do they see themselves?

Ryans (1960) found that there are, indeed, differences between the self-related reports of teachers with high emotional stability and those with low emotional stability. For example, the more emotionally stable teachers (1) more frequently named self-confidence and cheerfulness as dominant traits in themselves; (2) said they liked active contact with other people; (3) expressed interest in hobbies and handicrafts; and (4) reported their childhoods to be happy experiences.

On the other hand, teachers with lower emotional maturity scores (1) had unhappy memories of childhood; (2) seemed *not* to prefer contact with others; (3) were more directive and authoritarian; and (4) expressed less self-confidence.

We can be even more specific. Combs (1965) in his book, *The Professional Education of Teachers*, cites several studies which reached similar conclusions about the way good teachers typically see themselves, as follows:

1. Good teachers see themselves as identified with people rather than withdrawn, removed, apart from, or alienated from others.

2. Good teachers feel basically adequate rather than inadequate. They do not see themselves as generally unable to cope with problems.

3. Good teachers feel trustworthy rather than untrustworthy.

They see themselves as reliable, dependable individuals with the potential for coping with events as they happen.

4. Good teachers see themselves as wanted rather than unwanted. They see themselves as likable and attractive (in a personal, not a physical sense) as opposed to feeling ignored and rejected.

5. Good teachers see themselves as worthy rather than unworthy. They see themselves as people of consequence, dignity, and integrity as opposed to feeling they matter little, can be overlooked, and discounted.

In the broadest sense of the word, good teachers are more likely to see themselves as good people. Their self-perceptions are, for the most part, positive, tinged with an air of optimism and colored with tones of healthy self-acceptance. I dare say that self-perceptions of good teachers are not unlike the self-perceptions of any basically healthy person, whether he be a good bricklayer, a good manager, a good doctor, a good lawyer, a good experimental psychologist, or you name it. Clinical evidence has told us time and again that *any* person is more apt to be happier, more productive, and more effective when he is able to see himself as fundamentally and basically "enough."

Perceptions of Others by Good Versus Poor Teachers

Research is showing us that not only do good and poor teachers view themselves differently, there are also some characteristic differences in the way they perceive others. For example, Ryans (1960) reported several studies which have produced findings that are in agreement when it comes to sorting out the differences between how good and poor teachers view others. He found, among other things, that outstandingly "good" teachers rated significantly higher than notably "poor" teachers in at least five different ways with respect to how they viewed others. The good teachers had (1) more favorable opinions of students; (2) more favorable opinions of democratic classroom behavior; (3) more favorable opinions of administrators and colleagues; (4) a greater expressed liking for personal contacts with other people; and (5) more favorable estimates of other people generally. That is, they expressed the belief that very few students are difficult behavior problems, that very few people are influenced in their opinions and attitudes toward others by feelings of jealousy, and that most teachers are willing to assume their full share of extra duties outside of school.

Interestingly, the characteristics that distinguished the "lowly assessed" teacher group suggested that the relatively "ineffective" teacher is self-centered, anxious, and restricted. One is left with the distinct impression that poor or ineffective teachers have more than the usual number of paranoid defenses.

It comes as no surprise that how we perceive others is highly dependent on how we perceive ourselves. If a potential teacher (or anyone else, for that matter) likes himself, trusts himself, and has confidence in himself, he is likely to see others in somewhat this same light. Research is beginning to tell us what common sense has always told us; namely, people grow, flourish, and develop much more easily when in relationship with someone who projects an inherent trust and belief in their capacity to become what they have the potential to become.

It seems to me that we can sketch at least five interrelated generalizations from what research is telling us about how good teachers differ from poor teachers when it comes to how they perceive others.

1. They seem to have generally more positive views of others—students, colleagues, and administrators.

2. They do not seem to be as prone to view others as critical, attacking people with ulterior motives; rather they are seen as potentially friendly and worthy in their own right.

3. They have a more favorable view of democratic classroom procedures.

4. They seem to have the ability and capacity to see things as they seem to others, i.e., the ability to see things from the other person's point of view.

5. They do not seem to see students as persons "you do things to" but rather as individuals capable of doing for themselves once they feel trusted, respected, and valued.

Who, Then, Is a Good Teacher?

1. A good teacher is a good person. Simple and true. A good

teacher rather likes life, is reasonably at peace with himself, has a sense of humor, and enjoys other people. If I interpret the research correctly, what it says is that there is no one best better-than-all-others type of teacher. Nonetheless, there are clearly distinguishable "good" and "poor" teachers. Among other things, a good teacher is good because he does not seem to be dominated by a narcissistic self which demands a spotlight, or a neurotic need for power and authority, or a host of anxieties and tremblings which reduce him from the master of his class to its mechanic.

2. The good teacher is flexible. By far the single most repeated adjective used to describe good teachers is "flexibility." Either implicitly or explicitly (most often the latter), this characteristic emerges time and again over all others when good teaching is discussed in the research. In other words, the good teacher does not seem to be overwhelmed by a single point of view or approach to the point of intellectual myopia. A good teacher knows that he cannot be just one sort of person and use just one kind of approach if he intends to meet the multiple needs of his students. Good teachers are, in a sense, "total" teachers. That is, they seem able to be what they have to be to meet the demands of the moment. They seem able to move with the shifting tides of their own needs, the student's, and do what has to be done to handle the situation. A total teacher can be firm when necessary (say "no" and mean it) or permissive (say "why not try it your way?" and mean that, too) when appropriate. It depends on many things, and good teachers seem to know the difference.

The Need for "Total" Teachers

There probably is not an educational psychology course taught which does not, in some way, deal with the highly complex area of individual differences. Even the most unsophisticated undergraduate is aware that people differ in readiness and capacity to handle academic learning. For the most part, our educational technology (audio-visual aids, programmed texts, teaching machines, etc.) is making significant advances designed to assist teachers in coping with intellectual differences among students. We have been making strides in the direction of offering flexible programs and curricula, but we are somewhat remiss when it comes to preparing flexible, "total" teachers. Just as there are intellectual differences among students, there are also personality and self-concept differences which can have just as much impact on achievement. If this is true, then perhaps we need to do more about preparing teachers who are sensitive to the nature of these differences and who are able to take them into account as they plan for their classes.

The point here is that what is important for one student is not important to another. This is one reason why cookbook formulas for good teachers are of so little value and why teaching is inevitably something of an art. The choice of instructional methods makes a big difference for certain kinds of pupils, and a search for the "best" way to teach can succeed only when learners' intellectual *and* personality differences are taken into account. Available evidence does not support the belief that successful teaching is possible only through the use of some specific methodology. A reasonable inference from existing data is that methods which provide for adaptation to individual differences, encourage student initiative, and stimulate individual and group participation are superior to methods which do not. In order for things of this sort to happen, perhaps what we need first of all are flexible, "total" teachers who are capable of planning around people as they are around ideas.

Implications for Teacher Education

Research is teaching us many things about the differences between good and poor teachers, and I see at least four related implications for teacher education programs.

1. If it is true that good teachers are good because they view teaching as primarily a human process involving human relationships and human meanings, then this may imply that we should spend at least as much time exposing and sensitizing teacher candidates to the subtle complexities of personality structure as we do to introducing them to the structure of knowledge itself. Does this mean personality development, group dynamics, basic counseling processes, sensitivity training, and techniques such as life-space interviewing and encounter grouping?

2. If it is true that good teachers have a positive view of themselves and others, then this may suggest that we provide more opportunities for teacher candidates to acquire more positive self-other perceptions. Self-concept research tells us that how one feels about himself is learned. If it is learned, it is teachable. Too often, those of us in teacher education are dominated by a concern for long-term goals, while a student is fundamentally motivated by short-term goals. Forecasting what a student will need to know six months or two years from now, we operate on the assumption that he, too, perceives such goals meaningful. It seems logical enough, but unfortunately it does not work out too well in practice. Hence much of what we may do with our teacher candidates is non-self-related—that is, to the student it does not seem connected with his own life, time, and needs. Rather than talk about group processes in the abstract, why can we not first assist students to a deeper understanding of their own roles in groups in which they already participate? Rather than simply theorize and cite research evidence related to individual differences, why not also encourage students to analyze the individual differences which exist in *this* class at *this* time and then allow them to express and discuss what these differences mean at a more personal level? If one values the self-concept idea at all, then there are literally endless ways to encourage more positive self-other perceptions through teaching strategies aimed at personalizing what goes on in a classroom. Indeed, Jersild (1955) has demonstrated that when "teachers face themselves," they feel more adequate as individuals and function more effectively as teachers.

3. If it is true that good teachers are well informed, then it is clear that we must neither negate nor relax our efforts to provide them with as rich an intellectual background as is possible. Teachers are usually knowledgeable people, and knowledge inculcation is the aspect of preparation with which teacher education has traditionally been most successful. Nonetheless, teachers rarely fail because of lack of knowledge. They fail more often because they are unable to communicate what they know so that it makes a difference to their students. Which brings us to our final implication for teacher-education programs.

4. If it is true that good teachers are able to communicate

what they know in a manner that makes sense to their students, then we must assist our teacher candidates both through example and appropriate experiences to the most effective ways of doing this. Communication is not just a process of presenting information. It is also a function of discovery and the development of personal meanings. I wonder what would happen to our expectations of the teacher's role if we viewed him less as dispenser, answerer, coercer, and provoker and more as stimulator, questioner, challenger, and puzzler. With the former, the emphasis is on "giving to," while with the latter the focus is on "guiding to." In developing ability to hold and keep attention, not to mention techniques of encouraging people to adopt the reflective, thoughtful mood, I wonder what the departments of speech, theater, and drama on our college and university campuses could teach us? We expose our students to theories of learning and personality; perhaps what we need to do now is develop some "theories of presentation" with the help of those who know this field best.

This paper has attempted to point out that even though there is no single best or worst kind of teacher, there are clearly distinguishable characteristics associated with "good" and "bad" teachers. There is no one *best* kind of teaching because there is no *one kind* of student. Nonetheless, there seems to be enough evidence to suggest that whether the criteria for good teaching is on the basis of student and/or peer evaluations or in terms of student achievement gains, there are characteristics between both which overlap consistently. That is, the good teacher is able to influence both student feeling and achievement in positive ways.

Research is teaching us many things about the differences between good and bad teachers and there are many ways we can put these research findings into our teacher-education programs.

Good teachers do exist and can be identified. Perhaps the next most fruitful vineyard for research is in the classrooms of good teachers so we can determine, by whatever tools we have, just what makes them good in the first place.

References and Suggested Readings

Barr, A.S. *Characteristic Differences in the Teaching Performance of Good and Poor Teachers of the Social Studies.* Bloomington, Illinois: The Public School Publishing Co., 1929.

Biddle, B.J. and W.J. Ellena. *Contemporary Research on Teacher Effectiveness.* New York: Holt, Rinehart, and Winston, 1964.

Bousfield, W.A. "Student's Rating on Qualities Considered Desirable in College Professors," *School and Society*, February, 1940, pp. 253-256.

Cogan, M.L. "The Behavior of Teachers and the Productive Behavior of Their Pupils," *Journal of Experimental Education*, December, 1958, pp. 89-124.

Combs, A.W. *The Professional Education of Teachers.* Boston: Allyn and Bacon, 1965, pp. 70-71.

Flanders, N.A. *Teacher Influence, Pupil Attitudes and Achievement: Studies in Interaction Analysis.* University of Minnesota, U.S. Office of Education Cooperative Research Project No. 397, 1960.

Hart, W.F. *Teachers and Teaching.* New York: Macmillan, 1934, pp. 131-132.

Heil, L.M., M. Powell, and I. Feifer. *Characteristics of Teacher Behavior Related to the Achievement of Children in Several Elementary Grades.* Washington, D.C.: Office of Education, Cooperative Research Branch, 1960.

Jersild, A.T. *When Teachers Face Themselves.* New York: Bureau of Publications, Teachers College, Columbia University, 1955.

Reed, H.B. "Implications for Science Education of a Teacher Competence Research," *Science Education*, December, 1962, pp. 473-486.

Ryans, D.G. "Prediction of Teacher Effectiveness." In *Encyclopedia of Educational Research*, 3rd Ed. New York: Macmillan, 1960, pp. 1486-1490.

Spaulding, R. "Achievement, Creativity, and Self-Concept Correlates of Teacher-Pupil Transactions in Elementary Schools." University of Illinois, U.S. Office of Education Cooperative Research Project No. 1352, 1963.

Stern, G.C. "Measuring Non-cognitive Variables in Research on Teaching." In N.L. Gage (Ed.) *Handbook of Research on Teaching.* Chicago: Rand McNally, 1963.

Witty, P. "An Analysis of the Personality Traits of the Effective Teacher," *Journal of Educational Research*, May, 1947, pp. 662-671.

Section Four

EVALUATION OF INSTRUCTIONAL EFFECTIVENESS

Introduction to Section Four

Evaluation of Instructional Effectiveness

The papers included in this section represent current thinking on evaluation of instruction. Barak Rosenshine, in his paper, *Evaluation of Classroom Instruction*, reviews available instruments, suggests modifications for local use, describes four uses of evaluation of instruction, and notes several difficulties that may arise in the use of instruments and in the interpretation of results. In order to make accurate judgments regarding the worth and merit of classroom transactions, he concludes that there are three major needs to be fulfilled. These needs are: greater specification of teaching strategies to be used with instructional materials, improved observational instruments that attend to the context of the interactions and describe classroom interactions in more appropriate units than frequency events, and student outcome measures.

In his paper, *The Instructional Effectiveness Quotient*, J.E. Bicknell first defines instructional effectiveness and then proceeds to suggest a useful procedure for measuring this effectiveness. Various ways of analyzing data and making use of information are also discussed.

In his paper, *Performance Tests of Teaching Proficiency: Rationale, Development, and Validation*, W. James Popham proposes that the objective of the assessment of teaching effectiveness should be to measure the extent to which a teacher has accomplished the prespecified objectives. The merits of this approach to the assessment of teaching effectiveness were validated and are described. This paper offers a novel approach, and the results offer a challenge to teacher educators.

14.

Evaluation of Classroom Instruction

Barak Rosenshine

In this review, an attempt is made to describe available instruments for the observation of classroom instruction and to suggest modifications for local evaluation of instruction. Four potential uses of these instruments are described and examples are given of each: assessing variability in classroom behavior, assessing whether the teacher's performance agrees with specified criteria, describing classroom interaction, and determining relationships between observed classroom behavior and outcome measures. Finally, several difficulties in the use of observational instruments and in the interpretation of the results are noted. Major emphasis is given to the evaluation of instruction within specific curriculum projects, that is, programs in which the instructional materials were developed by special groups such as the Biological Sciences Curriculum Study. The term *curriculum* refers to the instructional materials and the suggestions for their use; the term *instruction* or *instructional program* refers to the interaction among teachers and students as the materials are used.

Drs. Norma Furst, Temple University, Lillian Katz and Terry Denny, University of Illinois, served as consultants to Dr. Rosenshine on the preparation of this chapter. Mrs. Robin Nelson, Temple University, provided valuable bibliographic assistance. This review was supported by a Temple University Summer Faculty Research Award to the author.

Reprinted from *Review of Educational Research*, Vol. 40, No. 2, April, 1970, with permission of the author and the publisher. The author is Associate Professor of Educational Psychology at the University of Illinois.

The Need for Data on Instruction

Classroom instruction is usually measured indirectly in the evaluation of instructional programs. Data obtained from direct observation of classroom interaction are seldom collected and analyzed. For example, among hundreds of research and evaluation reports at the ERIC Clearinghouse on Early Childhood Education, Katz (1969b) found only ten observational studies reported since 1960. Of nine reports comparing pre-school programs, only one (Katz, 1969a) included data on classroom interaction. Similarly, in a review of curriculum evaluation in science, Welch (1969) discussed the evaluation activity in forty-six science projects (Lockard, 1968); apparently only the reports on Harvard Project Physics contained information on classroom interaction.

The lack of information on classroom interaction hinders evaluation of a single curriculum or different curricula because without this information one tends to assume that all classrooms using the same curriculum materials constitute a homogeneous "treatment variable." Such an assumption is questionable because teachers may vary widely in what activities they select and how they implement them. In studies where teacher behavior in special curricula was compared with the behavior of teachers in "traditional instruction" (to be discussed below), there often was significant variation in the behavior of teachers within each group. Although the number of classrooms observed in these studies is small, the results are consistent enough to cause serious doubts about whether all classrooms using the same curriculum constitute a single treatment variable.

The futility of treating a curriculum as a single variable is illustrated in the Head Start Impact (Cicirelli, 1969). In this study a group labeled "Head Start Children" was compared with control children on a number of achievement, behavioral, and attitudinal variables. Most of the post-tests showed no significant differences between the two groups when the children were in the second grade. But is there a single treatment that can be labeled "Head Start"? In their study of thirty-eight teachers in a single summer Head Start program, Conners and Eisenberg (1966) found significant differences in class mean IQ gains over the summer. In addition, there were significant differences in several of the observed behaviors of the teachers of the high-, middle-, and low-achieving classes. These differences suggest that within a single Head Start program the students were exposed to different treatments. If these differences are ignored in the analysis, and if something labeled "Head Start" is compared to something labeled "control," then the comparison is being made between the effect of one vague complex of variables and the effect of another vague complex (Travers, 1969).

Classroom Observational Instruments

Instruments for the observation of instruction are currently divided into category systems and rating systems. This division is based on the amount of inference required of the observer or of the person reading the research report. Inference here refers to the process intervening between the objective data seen or heard and to the coding of those data on an observational instrument. Category systems are classified as low-inference measures because the items focus upon specific, denotable, relatively objective behaviors such as "teacher repetition of student ideas," or "teacher asks evaluative question" and because these events are recorded as frequency counts. Ratings systems are classified as high-inference measures because they lack such specificity. Items on rating instruments such as "clarity of presentation," "enthusiasm," or "helpful toward students" require that an observer infer these constructs from a series of events. In addition, an observer must infer the frequency of such behavior in order to record whether it occurred "consistently," "sometimes," or "never," or whatever set of gradations are used in the scale of an observation instrument. To a reader, the statement that a teacher repeated students' answers seven percent of the time is much more specific than the statement that a teacher was sometimes helpful toward students.

These distinctions between category systems and rating systems are gross because the instruments which have been developed for the observation of classroom behavior vary greatly in both the specificity of the behaviors to be observed and in the manner of recording the frequency of the behavior. For example, the item "teacher use of ridicule or threatening behavior" appears to be a low-inference item, even though it was used as part of a rating system (Solomon, Bezdek, and Rosenberg, 1963); the item "teacher use of student ideas" (Flanders, 1965) can be classified as requiring higher inference for interpretation because a variety of behaviors is subsumed under this category. In current usage, category systems contain fewer high-inference behaviors because frequency counts are used to record instances of a behavior. Behavioral constructs such as "enthusiasm," "understanding," or "clarity" (Solomon, Bezdek, and Rosenberg, 1963) have not been used as items in category systems because they need to be broken up into specific behaviors before the frequency of these events can be counted. The development of such specific behaviors is a difficult task.

Rating systems also vary widely in the scales used to record behavior. For example, when a teacher's "clarity" is scored on a five-point scale ranging from "consistently" to "seldom," the scale is apparently being used to estimate frequency. But on some instruments, clarity is evaluated on five-point scales ranging from "superior" to "unacceptable" or from "clear" to "unclear." Depending upon the words given to each point on the scale, a person who received the top rating on a scale used to rate clarity might be described as consistently clear, clear ninety percent of the time, rated No. 1 in clarity, outstandingly clear, or superior in clarity. These differences in scale markings make it difficult to determine if rating scales are being used to judge the value or estimate the frequency of a behavior. Perhaps many investigators dislike the use of rating systems because words such as superior and unacceptable appear on some scales. In such cases, it is rather simple to convert the scale markings so they are estimates of frequency. Because of this problem, it would be useful to determine whether the connotation of different scale markings affect ratings, and whether any differences which might occur are systematic or random.

Category systems have become very popular in descriptive educational research and in teacher training because they offer greater low-inference specificity and because an "objective" count of a teacher's encouraging statements to students appears easier for a teacher to accept than a "subjective" rating of his warmth. The major disadvantages of category systems are the cost of using observers and the difficulty of specifying behaviors before they can be included in a category system.

Rating systems offer greater flexibility than category systems because they can include high-inference variables. Rating systems can also be less expensive if the students in the classrooms are used as observers. For example, by using unpaid students as observers, the investigators in Harvard Project Physics (Anderson, Walberg, and Welch, 1969) were able to obtain information on the classroom climate of more than 150 classrooms without any payment to observers. The disadvantages of using rating systems are summarized by Mouly (1969); they include the halo effect, the error of central tendency, generosity or leniency error, and the lack of a common referent for scoring calibrations such as "excellent" or "seldom." Another disadvantage, noted by Gage (1969), is that high-inference items are difficult to translate into specific behaviors. This suggests that evaluative reports based on high-inference measures may offer few specific suggestions for improving an instructional program. An evaluative report which suggests that teachers need to improve their clarity and organ-ization, without giving the low-inference correlates of such behaviors, may amount to little more than suggesting that the teachers be "good and virtuous."

Category Systems
Reviews and Anthologies
Several recent articles have included reviews and critiques on the development and use of category systems (Amidon and Simon, 1965; Biddle, 1967; Biddle and Adams, 1967; Campbell, 1968; Gage, 1969; Lawrence, 1966). In each of these articles, the authors cite a number of category systems and provide a general introduction to research in this area. Three more comprehensive articles are Bellack (1968), Furst (1971), and Nuthall (1968). There are at least four books of readings which contain reprints of original reports on the development and use of category systems (Amidon and Hough, 1967; Hyman, 1968; Nelson, 1969; Raths, Pancella, and Van Ness, 1967). The volume by Amidon and Hough

contains a number of studies on the application of Interaction Analysis to the training of teachers; the volume edited by Hyman contains eleven articles which present the descriptive results obtained when the category systems were used to observe teaching.

The most comprehensive reference on observational category systems is the anthology, *Mirrors for Behavior* (Simon and Boyer, editors), which describes eighty systems.

Far more than eighty observational category systems have been developed. I can specify forty systems which are not cited by Simon and Boyer; no estimate can be made of the additional category systems which could be located. For example, eleven category systems cited in this review were not included in the eighty selected by Simon and Boyer (see Bloom and Wilensky, 1967; Conners and Eisenberg, 1966; De Landsheere, 1969; Evans, 1969; Fortune, 1967; Katz 1969a; Morsh, 1956; Solomon, Bezdek, and Rosenberg, 1963; Spaulding, 1965; Vickery, 1968; Zahorik, 1969).

Types and Examples of Observational Category Systems

There is no simple way to classify the variety of existing category systems which have been developed for the observation of classroom behavior. Some reviewers have classified them as primarily "affective," "cognitive," or as representing a combination of these dimensions (Amidon and Simon, 1965; Bellack, 1968; Simon and Boyer, 1967a, 1967b). Although such terms may be useful for classifying the major variables in an observational category system, one could also classify a category system by the number of "factors" which it contains.

Most category systems are one-factor systems in which each behavior is coded only in terms of its frequency. The variables in the factor can be affective, cognitive, or both. One-factor systems have been developed which are primarily affective (e.g., Flanders, 1965), primarily cognitive (e.g., Davis and Tinsley, 1967), or which focus on teacher feedback (Zahorik, 1968). There is no limit to the number of variables which can be included in a one-factor system. Systems have been developed with as few as four variables (Bloom and Wilensky, 1967) or as many as eighty variables (De Landsheere, 1969). The major advantages of one-factor systems are the ease of coding and the ease with which they can be modified for use by other investigators.

One-factor systems seem to offer only gross measures, which may obscure other important classroom variables. These systems do not provide for specifying the content, activity, level of conceptualization, or topic of teacher or student behavior. For example, two teachers may be teaching the same BSCS unit and be coded as having identical percents of various types of question, yet one teacher may be discussing the use of the microscope and another may be discussing the decoration of the bulletin board. Similarly, teacher praise regarding student knowledge may be a different variable from praise of student persistence. Student persistence itself can differ in context; in one class the students may be attempting persistently to sound out new words, and in another classroom students may be making Halloween decorations persistently.

The need for more comprehensive information on classroom interaction led to the development of new systems, and two approaches were used: the addition of "factors" in the analysis of variance factorial design sense, and the division of categories by subscripting the variables within a category.

The clearest example of a factorial category system is the Topic Classification System developed by Gallagher and his associates (Gallagher, 1968) in which each "topic" of classroom interaction is classified three ways: according to emphasis upon skill or content, the level of conceptualization (e.g., data, generalization), and the logical style used by the teacher (e.g., description, explanation, expansion). Openshaw and Cyphert (1966) developed a four-factor system in which each "encounter" is categorized according to the origin of the encounter, the target, the mode (e.g., speaking, reading, writing), and the purpose of the behavior. This last factor is subdivided into five categories, each one containing three to eight subcategories.

Zahorik (1969) reported on the use of a three-factor system in which types of teacher feedback (Zahorik, 1968) were also classified according to the type of venture (Smith *et al.*, 1964) in which they were used and whether the feedback occurred within or at the end of the venture. This system allows an investigator to explore the effect of different types of feedback during different types of cognitive ventures. Zahorik's system appears to have strong potential value because it represents the factorial combination of two highly developed category systems.

An ingenious and unique two-factor system was developed by Denny (*Educational Product Report*, 1969). The two factors were: the type of question asked by teacher or student, and the activity on which the question focused (e.g., teaching lecture, class report, test, or quiz). The factor on activities may be very useful because (a) it is easy to add to one-factor systems such as those developed by Flanders and his students, (b) it may provide important information on the context of an event, and (c) it can be modified easily to fit the special activities of different programs and subject areas. An activities factor developed for a reading program would be quite different from one developed for math, but an observational report which included activity variables might provide important information on the content and activities of a lesson.

In the category system used by Spaulding (1965), teacher behaviors are classified according to their (a) major type, (b) source of authority, (c) number of class members included, (d) amount of attention the class gives to the statement, (e) tone of voice, (f) technique used, and (g) topic. This category system is not clearly factorial because the options for classifying technique and topic differ according to the major behavior. For example, there is a topic for disapproval regarding "violation of rules," but violation of rules does not appear under topics of approval. The result is an extremely comprehensive category system, but one which is very long and requires tape recordings for coding.

Other investigators expanded category systems by "subscripting" larger categories. Thus, Amidon, Amidon, and Rosenshine (1969) developed the Expanded Interaction Analysis System by adding from two to four subscripts to each of the ten categories developed by Flanders (1965). This subscripting was accomplished by adding variables from other category systems such as those of Gallagher and Aschner (1963) and Hughes (1959). For example, the original category "teacher asks questions" was subscripted to specify four types of question, and the category "teacher gives directions" was subscripted to specify cognitive directions and managerial directions. De Landsheere (1969) developed a nine-category system containing from four to eight subscripts for each category. For example, the category "positive feedback" was subscripted to specify (a) stereotyped approval, (b) repetition of student response, (c) giving reasons for approval, and (d) other forms of positive feedback. An interesting compromise was developed by Parakh (1968) in which seventeen categories were used, but only five contained subscripts.

General and Specific Category Systems

Almost all of the category systems are general systems: they are designed for use in all instructional situations. Some investigators demonstrated the general usefulness of their systems by applying them to more than one subject area (see Flanders, 1965; Gallagher, 1968). Those systems developed for special subject areas contain little to distinguish them from the general category systems. For example, of the twenty-three categories and subcategories in the Biology Teacher Behavior Inventory (Balzar, 1969; Evans, 1969), only two categories are specific to science, and none is specific to biology; of the twenty-six categories and subcategories developed by Parakh (1967-68; 1968), there is only one category related to science: the subscript "gives or asks for information about the nature of science"; the OSCAR R (Medley and Smith, 1968) that was developed specially for observing reading instruction has only two categories unique to reading. With little modification, any of the category systems examined for this review could be applied to another subject area. Even the system developed by Wright and Proctor (1961) for the observation of mathematics lessons could be applied to any situation in which the focus is upon deductive and inductive reasoning.

Rating Systems

In preparing this review, I found no anthologies of rating forms for observing teaching, no body of descriptive research resulting from the use of these instruments, and no reviews of research. This lack of attention to rating forms is regrettable because recent research using fairly specific items with rating forms has yielded promising results. An estimate of the predictability of rating systems may be obtained by studying the results of seven investigations in which teacher behavior was described using category systems and rating scales. In all the studies some items in each system were related significantly to the adjusted criterion score or discriminated significantly among teachers grouped according to student achievement. However, in six of the studies (or sets of studies) the bi-variate correlations or F-ratios were higher for specific rated behaviors (rating systems) than they were for specific counted behaviors (category systems) (Fortune, 1967; Gage *et al.*, 1968; Morsh, 1956; Morsh, Burgess, and Smith, 1955; Solomon *et al.*, 1963; Wallen, 1966; Wallen and Wodtke, 1963). The raters were classroom students or observers. Measures of inter-rater reliability were comparable to those obtained using category systems. The above results are too varied to attempt to synthesize the findings, but they suggest that ratings are a useful source of information about an instructional program.

Perhaps one advantage of rating systems is that an observer is able to consider clues from a variety of sources before he makes his judgment. Even though the low-inference correlates of "clarity" are presently unknown, ratings on variables referring to the clarity of the teacher's presentation were related significantly to student achievement in all studies in which such a variable was used (Belgard, Rosenshine, and Gage, 1968; Fortune, 1967; Fortune, Gage, and Shutes, 1966; Solomon, Bezdek, and Rosenberg, 1963; Wallen, 1966). The results on "clarity" are particularly robust because the investigators used different observational instruments. Furthermore, some investigators used student ratings, some used observer ratings, and the student ratings were given before the criterion test in some studies and after the test in others.

Rating Forms in Curriculum Evaluation

The studies cited above in which rating scales were used were focused on traditional instruction; they were not studies of the use of instructional packages such as a science program. Only two sets of studies were found in which rating scales were used to describe specific instructional packages: the studies of Harvard Project Physics (Welch, 1969) and the studies of the School Mathematics Study Group materials (Torrance and Parent, 1966).

Rating scales in which the students responded to specific items on a four- or five-point scale (ranging from "strongly agree" to "strongly disagree") were used in both sets of studies. The Learning Environment Inventory (Walberg and Anderson, 1967) was used in the evaluation of Harvard Project Physics. This inventory consists of fourteen scales, each containing seven items. The scales on Diversity and Difficulty were designed specifically to evaluate the physics project, and the remaining scales were justified on the basis of research in social psychology and the results of previous research using a slightly different instrument (Anderson, 1968, pp. 20-44).

The Learning Environment Inventory, or an earlier version of it, was used in a number of multivariate studies conducted to determine the relationship between the students' perceptions of the class environment and class learning (Anderson and Walberg, 1968; Walberg, 1969a, 1969b), individual learning (Walberg and Anderson, 1968b; Anderson, 1968), student pre-test scores (Walberg and Anderson, 1968a), and teacher personality measures (Walberg, 1968). The inventory was also used to determine if classes in different courses perceived the environment differently (Anderson, Walberg, and Welch, 1969). Significant relationships between the rating scale scores and the criterion variable(s) were found in each study.

An SMSG Student Attitude Inventory was developed as part of the study of School Mathematics Study Group instruction (Torrance and Parent, 1966). The inventory contained sixty-four items which focused on (a) whether the teacher encouraged various types of cognitive activities, (b) the amount of help offered by the school, (c) the clarity and organization of the textbook, and (d) the ability and activities of the class. Those classes in the upper third (as measured by post-test scores adjusted for pre-test achievement) had significantly higher scores than classes in the lower third on fifty-eight of the sixty-four items and on all four scales.

Checklists of activities have also been used to describe

instruction. During the first year of study by Torrance and Parent (1966) the teachers completed a checklist immediately after eight lessons each month. The teacher checklists contained thirty-one highly specific teacher activities (e.g., "gave alternative solution to problem") and twenty-eight specific student activities. A single check indicated that the activity occurred at least once during the lesson; a double check was entered for continuous activity or one which occurred three or more times. At the end of the first year the students completed a checklist on twenty-three specific activities (e.g., "asked questions because of learning difficulties," "thought of an unusual but correct solution to a problem"). The frequency estimate was on a six-point scale ranging from "never" to "every class period." Although the checklists had items similar to those used in the rating scale described above, and although a lower-inference scale was used, almost none of the items discriminated between the upper third and lower third of the classes.

In four studies of elementary reading (Harris and Serwer, 1966; Harris *et al.*, 1968) the teachers completed logs on five consecutive teaching days each month for five months. The teachers estimated the number of minutes spent each day on different reading activities (e.g., sight word drill) and on different supportive activities (e.g., art work with reading). The results were used to compare the amounts of time spent by teachers using different reading approaches and to correlate time spent in various activities with measures of student growth. As in previous studies, there was much variation within each teaching approach in the amount of time teachers reported spending on various reading and supportive activities.

The above results on the use of rating systems do not imply that rating systems should replace category systems. The optimum strategy for research and description may be to use both systems. Rating systems would be used to probe for unknown complexes of variables that appear to be significant correlates of outcome variables; category systems may be used to help identify the specific components of the significant items. In addition, rating forms and category systems which are specific to the instructional program may be developed.

Uses of Observational Systems

Four major uses of observational systems for the evaluation of instruction are discussed in this section: (a) assessing the variability of classroom behavior either within or between instructional programs, (b) assessing the agreement between classroom behavior and certain instructional criteria, (c) describing what occurred in the implementation of the instructional materials, and (d) determining relationships between classroom behavior and instructional outcomes. The four areas overlap, and many of the studies which are cited fit more than one use. The lack of conceptual clarity is a reflection of the problems inherent in any new undertaking.

Variability in Special Curriculum Programs

Program evaluators are particularly interested in studies in which the behaviors of teachers within a special curriculum were compared, or in which comparisons were made between the behaviors of teachers in a special curriculum and the behaviors of teachers using the "traditional" program. Such studies may be useful for ascertaining whether there is sufficient congruence in classroom behavior to hypothesize that an instructional program is a homogeneous variable, or that two instructional programs are indeed different instructional programs. Only a few studies of either of these types were found, and the generalizability of the results is limited by the small number of teachers observed and the disparity of category systems used to encode the behaviors. Therefore, the findings discussed below might better be treated as hypotheses for further study.

Gallagher (1966, 1968) recorded the discussion sections of six BSCS teachers while each was presenting identical material. He coded the discussions using his Topic Category System and found significant differences among the teachers in the number of topics on goals (content vs. style) and on conceptual level (data, concept, and generalization). There were no significant differences among classes on the number of topics coded according to cognitive style (e.g., description, explanation, evaluation, and expansion), but there were significant differences among classes in the percentage of teacher talk devoted to the cognitive styles of description, explanation, and expansion.

The reports of other investigators also demonstrate the variability of teacher behavior within a specific curriculum, although the statistical significance of the differences was not reported. Such trends are evident from reports of investigators who used category systems (Parakh, 1967-1968, 1968) and teacher log reports (Harris and Serwer, 1966; Harris *et al.*, 1968).

Other investigators used different category systems to compare the behavior in traditional classrooms to the observed behavior in classrooms in which special instructional materials were used. Although a large number of comparisons was made, very few differences were statistically significant (Evans, 1969; Furst and Honigman, 1969; Hunter, 1969; Vickery, 1968). I conclude that such results occurred because there was greater variation in student or teacher behavior within these curricula than among the curricula.

In two of the above studies (Hunter, 1969; Vickery, 1968) student use of laboratory material was a major focus of the special instructional program. The category systems developed for classroom observation included items on student use of materials and on teacher verbal behavior. In Hunter's study, there was significantly more talk among students while they used the materials, but no significant differences on verbal behaviors such as types of teacher questions or types of student response to the teacher. In Vickery's study, teachers using the experimental materials spent significantly more time interacting with individuals in laboratory-centered behaviors, but there were no significant differences among the teacher groups in the amount of indirect or direct teacher talk as measured by the Interaction Analysis categories.

The results obtained by Hunter and by Vickery may be related to the training program. In both studies the in-service program for introducing the teachers to the new curriculum stressed the relatively simple behavior of increased student use of science materials and, apparently, there was no specific instruction in teacher use of "higher order questions," or encouragement of varied types of student statement or question. In the studies by Hunter and by Vickery the teachers may have modified their behavior exactly as they were trained; no more and no less. Similarly, in the other programs discussed above, the teachers were given training in specific instructional techniques. The teachers were free to vary their instruction, and they apparently did so.

One exception to these studies yielding no significant differences in teacher behavior, using different instructional materials, was obtained by Anderson, Walberg, and Welch (1969). Student ratings obtained on the Learning Environment Inventory indicated that the overall climate of classes using the Harvard Project Physics materials was different from that of the classes using other instructional materials. As the investigators predicted, students in the experimental classes rated their classes as significantly lower in Difficulty and higher on the Diversity scale. These two scales were specifically developed to evaluate the experimental program. All teachers using the experimental materials received special summer training.

In almost all of the studies discussed above there were wide variations in the classroom behaviors of teachers who were using the same instructional materials. Gallagher (1966, p. 33) concluded:

> The data would suggest that there really is no such thing as a BSCS curriculum presentation in the schools. . . . Each teacher filters the materials through his own perceptions and to say that a student has been through the BSCS curriculum probably does not give as much specific information as the curriculum innovators might have hoped.

Gallagher's conclusion might also be drawn from the other studies in this area. But if such an hypothesis is to be considered, then it is inconsistent to claim, as some have, that teachers are teaching the "new curriculum" in the same manner as they taught the "old." Perhaps the variation among teachers is so great that we cannot speak of an old or a new curriculum as a single instructional variable.

Although observational systems have been used to specify variability in behavior across classrooms, it is difficult to assess the importance of all these variations. Some of the behaviors may be important because their frequency or patterning may be related significantly to student outcome measures, and some of the behaviors may indicate classroom conditions within which other forces acted; but some of the behaviors may have no relevant educational meaning. At this time it is difficult to distinguish the relevant behaviors from the irrelevant ones.

Criterion-Referenced Instruction

A major use of an observational category system would be to determine whether the teachers are implementing an instructional package in an acceptable manner. The criteria for " acceptable" can come from the curriculum developers, the evaluators, or the teachers.

Those who developed a set of instructional materials seldom provided explicit guidelines on classroom behaviors pertinent to evaluating instruction. Gallagher (1968, p. 43) noted that:

> . . . those interested in curriculum development have not finished their job when they have packaged a cognitively valid and consistent set of materials. They must establish, in addition, how these materials are operationally introduced in the classroom environment. Otherwise, they will be left with certain unqualified assumptions as to how their package is unwrapped in the classroom.

In the above studies, three different category systems were used to observe instruction using the BSCS materials, but not one system was developed either for observing BSCS instruction or for assessing whether the teachers were performing in accordance with the BSCS design. If the developers of new instructional materials are accountable for the instructional results, perhaps they and the evaluation team should also determine whether the teachers are implementing the materials in an acceptable manner; perhaps they should also develop observational systems which can be used both in teacher training and in assessing whether the new curriculum is being given a fair trial.

Only one example was found of the use of "quality assurance" as part of curriculum implementation. This was the description of the Oral Language Program disseminated by the Southwestern Cooperative Educational Laboratory, Albuquerque, New Mexico (Olivero, undated). "Performance standards" were set for the teachers using the program. Teachers who were unwilling to accept the standards had the right to stop using the program;

they could also attend special in-service workshops, but "ultimately, if the teacher is unable or unwilling to perform, he or she will be asked to stop using the Oral Language Program" (Olivero, undated, p. 8).

Two experimental studies were found in which an observational system was used to determine fidelity to instructional specifications. In a study of two approaches to pre-school instruction, Katz (1969b) used the data obtained from her category system to determine that the three experimental teachers were not performing according to the predetermined criteria, and therefore she decided that the experiment was not a valid test of her hypothesis.

Worthen (1968a, 1968b) compared the effects of using a discovery and an expository approach to teach mathematical concepts. Model discovery and model expository teaching behavior on each of five characteristics was specified, and a paradigm of teaching techniques for each method was established. The eight participating fifth- and sixth-grade teachers received two to six hours' weekly training for thirteen weeks prior to and for seven weeks during the experiment. This training included use of two specific methods of instruction and familiarization with the mathematical concepts used in the instructional materials. Each teacher used an expository approach with one class and a discovery approach with another. An observer rating scale and a student questionnaire were used to assess the degree to which the teacher adhered to the prescribed teaching model. Mean scores on each instrument indicated that the teachers taught the two classes in distinctly different ways, and that the teachers varied their behaviors in a manner appropriate to each method.

The work by Worthen might serve as a model for research of this type because it included clear specification of behaviors, extensive training of teachers in the use of specific teaching behaviors, development of observational instruments specific to the instructional procedures, and use of these instruments by observers and by students. It is also the only study I found in which students were used as observers of teacher adherence to a specific instructional model.

Such an approach to performance standards might be

extended to the evaluation of other special curriculum projects. Classroom observational techniques can be used to determine whether the classroom instruction is continuing according to the plans of the curriculum developers. If it can be determined that some teachers are deviating from the intentions of the curriculum developers, the final report could have two sections, one for all the participating teachers and one for teachers whose behavior met specified criteria. The second section would represent the effects of the instructional materials under intended conditions; the first section would represent the effects under more general conditions. The number of teacher dropouts because of inability to meet performance specifications would be an additional measure of the amount of extra work necessary to implement the curriculum in accordance with the intentions of the designers.

Relating Observed Behaviors to Outcome Measures

Compared to the large number of descriptive studies, there have been relatively few studies of the relationship between measures obtained by the use of observational systems and measures of class achievement adjusted for initial aptitude or ability. Approximately forty studies were completed in this area. These studies are difficult to synthesize for at least three reasons: they varied widely in subject area, grade, and observational instruments; some studies used statistical procedures which were not appropriate; and in many studies the number of classrooms observed was less than twenty. Two attempts have been made to review some of the research relating classroom behavior to student achievement (Flanders, 1970; Rosenshine, 1969), but because of the above difficulties it is too early to identify relationships that can be stated with any confidence.

Most of these studies were investigations of teachers engaging in traditional instruction or using materials specially designed for use in the study. There were few studies relating teaching behaviors to student achievement within the context of special instructional packages such as the BSCS. An evaluator who has collected information on classroom behavior and student outcomes is in an excellent position to contribute to this research by attempting to relate the two.

Difficulties in Selecting and Using Observational Instruments

Selecting or Developing an Appropriate Observational System

In most instances, a teacher, administrator, or evaluator has little to guide him in selecting an observational instrument. Those who develop sets of instructional materials seldom provide guidelines specifying the classroom behaviors that are important in evaluating instruction. As discussed above, the category systems labeled as specific to a subject area include little to justify the label. Given these problems, evaluators frequently select a general category system which has been used in some other program in the hope that it will be useful for their specific purposes.

An alternative approach is first to identify the objectives of a program, then to study the instructional materials, and finally to identify a few behaviors or combinations of behaviors which seem most critical to the implementation of the materials and the achievement of the objectives. Once these performance criteria are identified, their frequency of occurrence could be assessed by using existing category systems or rating forms, by selecting relevant sections from existing instruments, or by modifying existing instruments to meet the specific purposes of the evaluation. Successive observations would then be made to determine how well these criteria are being met and to chart the results of a teacher's attempts to modify his behavior. Such procedures are detailed by Flanders (1970, Chapter 11).

Simple and Complex Observational Systems

Problems of cost may dictate that a relatively simple observational instrument be used. However, simple observational instuments may obscure important behaviors. For example, "student initiated talk" is easy to classify and record, but such talk may take place in a variety of contexts. Student initiated talk may be a contribution to a discussion, but it might also represent either persistent attempts to get the teacher to clarify what he said, or student outbursts in a disorganized classroom. If the category system is enlarged so each type of student initiated talk is considered separately, the system may become unmanageable. Enlarging the category system may be costly in training time and data processing, but such an enlargement may yield important data on variability among teachers, fidelity of instruction to an instructional model, and the relationship of teaching behaviors to student outcome measures.

One of the most difficult problems is choosing between a simple and a complex unit of measure (Biddle, 1967). In most category systems, frequency counts serve as the unit of measure, but some investigators have developed more complex units such as a topic (Gallagher, 1968), a venture (Smith *et al.*, 1964), or a teaching module (McNaughton *et al.*, 1967). These more complex units may be intrinsically more satisfying because they code patterns and sequences of classroom interaction; but typescripts are required to code these units and preparing typescripts and training observers is costly.

Description and Judgment

When an investigator presents observational data on instruction, the descriptive statements are frequently accompanied by judgments of the behaviors that a teacher "should" exhibit. Sometimes these judgments are softened by a statement such as "it would seem reasonable to expect that . . .," but the judgments remain and are frequently followed by prescriptions for teacher training.

For example, Hunter (1969, p. 42) noted that the teachers in her sample "do not give reasons for praising right answers or rejecting wrong ones." Morrissett, Stevens, and Woodley (1969, p. 269) reported a descriptive study in which "the tabulation showed an almost complete absence of teachers' accepting a student's feelings." Gallagher (1968, p. 44) stated that he "was disappointed at the relatively rare use, sometimes complete absence, of topics in the dimensions of Expansion and Evaluation." In all three studies the teachers were using instructional materials prepared by national curriculum groups.

It is difficult to justify the above use of implied "shoulds" on two counts. First, these evaluators were using general observational systems whose relevance to the instructional programs they were evaluating had not been established. Second, there were too few studies to date which attempted to establish the correlation between classroom behaviors and student criterion measures, and too little synthesis of this research; so the implied "shoulds" in the paragraph above do not rest on established empirical evidence. Even if consistent and significant linkages between classroom behavior and student outcome measures were established, one would need clear statements on the optimum frequencies for behaviors such as giving reasons for rejecting wrong answers, accepting students' feelings, or introducing Expansion or Evaluation topics.

Additional Sources for Observational Variables

Developers of observational systems appear to have made little use of the variables currently being investigated in laboratory research on instruction. Variables such as "organizers," relevant practice, promoting· learner interest, prompts and fading techniques, organization and sequence, and pacing have been studied using meaningful verbal materials, but in situations in which the instruction was mediated by written materials, films, and audio-tape recordings (see Anderson *et al.*, 1969; Popham, 1969; Tanck, 1969). The results of these studies do not appear in the observational instruments currently available, but there is nothing to prevent evaluators from including these variables in new observational systems.

One example of the inclusion of variables developed in laboratory studies in a classroom observational system is the study by Worthen (1968a, 1968b). In this study, a special rating system was used to determine whether the teachers were following the prescribed discovery and expository approaches. Rating systems appear quite appropriate for such initial ventures, and evaluators of programs which have a specific instructional focus might develop rating systems which include instructional variables developed in laboratory studies. Depending upon the purpose of the evaluation, the markings on the scale can require estimates of frequency as well as estimates of value.

Data Reduction and Consolidation

Because of the large number of variables in existing observational systems and the difficulty of comparing variables with similar sounding names in different observational systems, some reviewers suggested that the number be reduced and the variables compared by using data reduction techniques such as factor analysis or facet analysis (Biddle, 1967; Gage, 1969). Factor analytic techniques may be useful to the evaluator of a single program for which no replication is intended, but it would be hazardous to generalize from factor analytic results for three reasons: in most of these studies the number of classrooms is smaller than the number of variables; investigators using the same observational system, but in different locations, might not agree with others; and one does not know if the factor structure would be generalizable across different subject areas, different grades, or different curricula in the same subject area.

Several attempts have been made to reduce the data from two or more category systems using principal components factor analysis with varimax rotation (Soar, 1966; Wood *et al.*, 1969), but the results are not easy to compare, and in all three studies teachers were selected from a wide range of grade levels. The results are puzzling in the most comprehensive study (Wood *et al.*, 1969). For example, student statements coded as exhibiting application, analysis, synthesis, and evaluation all loaded on a factor devoid of any teacher behaviors; teacher behaviors such as amplification or extended amplification of student ideas loaded on a factor which did not contain teacher or student cognitive behaviors; and the factor labeled "teacher-student cognitive behavior" did not contain any student or teacher affective behaviors.

Solomon, Bezdek, and Rosenberg (1963) used factor analysis to consolidate information obtained from student ratings, observer ratings, and teacher questionnaires, with information obtained by coding each independent clause of classroom verbal behavior into a category system. Although the number of variables far exceeded the number of classrooms, such an approach might be useful for comparing observer and student perceptions and for discovering relationships between high-inference and low-inference variables.

Summary

Without adequate data on classroom transactions, it is difficult for an evaluator to make suggestions for the modification of an instructional program. Yet, researchers are only beginning to develop tools and concepts for the evaluation and study of instruction. Currently, three major needs are: greater specification of the teaching strategies to be used with instructional materials, improved observational instruments that attend to the context of the interactions and describe classroom interactions in more appropriate units than frequency counts, and more research into the relationship between classroom events and student outcome measures.

References

Amidon, E.J. and J.B. Hough (Eds.) *Interaction Analysis: Theory, Research and Application.* Reading, Massachusetts: Addison-Wesley, 1967.

Amidon, E.J. and A. Simon. "Teacher-Pupil Interaction," *Review of Educational Research*, 25, 1965, pp. 130-140.

Amidon, E.J., P. Amidon and B. Rosenshine. *Skill Development in Teaching Work Manual.* Minneapolis, Minnesota: Association for Productive Teaching, 1969.

Anderson, G.J. "Effects of Classroom Social Climate on Individual Learning." Doctor's thesis. Cambridge, Massachusetts: Harvard University, 1968. (ERIC: ED 015 153.)

Anderson, G.J. and H.J. Walberg. "Classroom Climate and Group Learning," *International Journal of Educational Sciences*, 2, 1968, pp. 175-180. (ERIC: ED 015 156.)

Anderson, G.J., H.J. Walberg, and W.W. Welch. "Curriculum Effects on the Social Climate of Learning: A New Representation of Discriminant Functions," *American Educational Research Journal*, 6, 1969, pp. 315-329.

Anderson, R.C. *et al.* (Eds.). *Current Research on Instruction.* Englewood Cliffs, New Jersey: Prentice-Hall, 1969.

Balzar, LeV. "Nonverbal and Verbal Behavior of Biology Teachers," *American Biology Teacher*, 31, 1969, pp. 226-230.

Belgard, M., B. Rosenshine, and N.L. Gage. "The Teacher's Effectiveness in Explaining: Evidence on Its Generality and Correlation With Pupils' Ratings and Attention Scores,"

Explorations of the Teacher's Effectiveness in Explaining. Technical Report No. 4. Stanford, California: Stanford Center for Research and Development in Teaching, Stanford University, 1968, Ch. 2, pp. 9-20. (ERIC: ED 028 147.)

Bellack, A.A. "Methods for Observing Classroom Behavior of Teachers and Students." Paper presented to the conference on "Methods of Determining Criteria for the Evaluation of Comprehensive Schools" sponsored by Padagogisches Zentrum, November, 1968. New York: Teachers College, Columbia University. (Mimeo.)

Biddle, B.J. "Methods and Concepts in Classroom Research," *Review of Educational Research*, 37, 1967, pp. 337-357.

Biddle, B.J. and R.S. Adams. "Teacher Behavior in the Classroom Context." In L. Siegel (Ed.) *Instruction: Some Contemporary Viewpoints*. San Francisco: Chandler, 1967.

Bloom, R. and H. Wilensky. "Four Observation Categories for Rating Teacher Behavior," *Journal of Educational Research*, 60, 1967, pp. 464-465.

Campbell, W.J. "Classroom Practices," *New Zealand Journal of Educational Studies*, 3, 1968, pp. 97-124.

Cicirelli, V. *The Impact of Head Start: An Evaluation of the Effects of Head Start on Children's Cognitive and Affective Development*. Washington, D.C.: Office of Research, Planning, and Program Evaluation, Office of Economic Opportunity, 1969.

Conners, C.K. and L. Eisenberg. *The Effect of Teacher Behavior on Verbal Intelligence in Operation Headstart Children*. Baltimore: Johns Hopkins University, School of Medicine, 1966. (ERIC: ED 010 782.)

Davis, O.L., Jr. and D.C. Tinsley. "Cognitive Objectives Revealed by Classroom Questions Asked by Social Studies Student Teachers and Their Pupils," *Peabody Journal of Education*, 45, July, 1967, pp. 21-26.

De Landsheere, G. *Comment les Maitres Enseignent: Analyse des Interactions Verbales en Classe*. Liege, Belgium: Ministere de L'education Nationale et de la Culture, 1969.

Educational Product Report. Evaluation Kit: Tools and Techniques. Educational Product Report, Information Supplement, February, 1969, No. 5. New York: Educational Products Information Exchange (EPIE) Institute, 1969.

Evans, T.P. "A Category System for Teacher Behaviors,"*American Biology Teacher*, 31, 1969, pp. 221-226.

Flanders, N.A. *Teacher Influence, Pupil Attitudes, and Achievement.* Cooperative Research Monograph No. 12, OE-25040. Washington, D.C.: U.S. Government Printing Office, 1965.

Flanders, N.A. *Analyzing Classroom Interactions.* Reading, Massachusetts: Addison-Wesley, 1970.

Fortune, J.C. *A Study of the Generality of Presenting Behaviors in Teaching Preschool Children.* Memphis, Tennessee: Memphis State University, 1967. (ERIC: ED 016 285.)

Fortune, J.C., N.L. Gage, and R.E. Shutes. "The Generality of the Ability of Explain." Paper presented to the American Educational Research Association, February, 1966. Amherst: University of Massachusetts, College of Education. (Mimeo.)

Furst, N. "Systematic Classroom Observation." In L. Deighten (Ed.) *The Encyclopedia of Education.* New York: Macmillan, 1971.

Furst, N. and F.K. Honigman. "A Study of Pupil-Teacher Interaction in Experimental Communications Courses Compared With Traditional Junior High School Classes." Paper presented to the American Educational Research Association, February, 1969. Philadelphia: Temple University, College of Education. (Mimeo.)

Gage, N.L. "Teaching Methods." In R.L. Ebel (Ed.) *Encyclopedia of Educational Research*, Fourth Ed. London: Macmillan, 1969, pp. 1446-1458.

Gage, N.L. *et al. Explorations of the Teacher's Effectiveness in Explaining.* Technical Report No. 4. Stanford, California: Stanford Center for Research and Development in Teaching, Stanford University, 1968.

Gallagher, J.J. *Teacher Variation in Concept Presentation in BSCS Curriculum Program.* Urbana: Institute for Research on Exceptional Children, University of Illinois, 1966. (ERIC: ED 023 206.)

Gallagher, J.J. *Analyses of Teacher Classroom Strategies Associated with Student Cognitive and Affective Performance.*

Cooperative Research Project No. 3325. Urbana: University of Illinois, 1968. (ERIC: ED 021 808.)

Gallagher, J.J. and M.J. Aschner. "A Preliminary Report on Analyses of Classroom Interaction," *Merrill-Palmer Quarterly of Behavior and Development*, 9, 1963, pp. 183-194.

Harris, A.J. and B. Serwer. *Comparison of Reading Approaches in First Grade Teaching with Disadvantaged Children (The CRAFT Project).* Cooperative Research Project No. 2677. New York: City University of New York, 1966. (ERIC: ED 010 037.)

Harris, A.J. *et al.* *A Continuation of the CRAFT Project: Comparing Reading Approaches with Disadvantaged Urban Negro Children in Primary Grades.* Cooperative Research Project No. 5-0570-2-12-1. New York: Division of Teacher Education of the City University of New York, 1968. (ERIC: ED 010 297.)

Hughes, M. *Development of the Means for the Assessment of the Quality of Teaching in Elementary Schools.* Salt Lake City: University of Utah Press, 1959.

Hunter, E. "Talking in First Grade Classrooms," *Urban Review*, 4, October, 1969, pp. 39-43.

Hyman, R.T. (Ed.). *Teaching: Vantage Points for Study.* Philadelphia: Lippincott, 1968.

Katz, L.G. "Children and Teachers in Two Types of Head Start Classes," *Young Children*, 24, 1969a, pp. 342-349.

Katz, L.G. *Teaching in Preschools: Roles and Goals.* Document No. 70706-E-AO-U-26. Urbana: National Laboratory on Early Childhood Education, University of Illinois, 1969b. (Mimeo.)

Lawrence, P.J. "The Anatomy of Teaching," *Australian Journal of Education*, 10, 1966, pp. 97-109.

Lockard, J.D. (Ed.). *Sixth Report of the International Clearinghouse on Science and Mathematics Curricular Developments.* College Park: University of Maryland, 1968. (ERIC: ED 020 143.)

McNaughton, A.H. *et al.* "The Use of Teaching Modules to Study High-Level Thinking in the Social Studies," *Journal of Teacher Education*, 18, 1967, pp. 495-502.

Medley, D.M. and L.H. Smith. "Instructions for Recording Behavior With OSCAR R," *A Continuation of the CRAFT Project: Comparing Reading Approaches With Disadvantaged Urban Negro Children in Primary Grades.* (Written by Albert J. Harris.) Cooperative Research Project No. 5-0570-2-12-1. New York: Division of Teacher Education of the City University of New York, 1968. Appendix, pp. 355-366. (ERIC: ED 010 297.)

Morrissett, I., W.W. Stevens, Jr., and C.P. Woodley. "A Model for Analyzing Curriculum Materials and Classroom Transactions." *Social Studies Curriculum Development: Prospects and Problems.* Thirty-ninth Yearbook. Washington D.C.: National Council for the Social Studies, 1969, Ch. 8, pp. 229-276.

Morsh, J.E. *Systematic Observation of Instructor Behavior.* Development Report No. AFPTRC-TN-56-52. San Antonio, Texas: Air Force Personnel and Training Research Center, Lackland Air Force Base, 1956.

Morsh, J.E., G.G. Burgess, and P.N. Smith. *Student Achievement as a Measure of Instructor Effectiveness.* Project No. 7950, Task No. 77243. San Antonio, Texas: Air Force Personnel and Training Research Center, Lackland Air Force Base, 1955.

Mouly, G.J. "Research Methods." In R.L. Ebel (Ed.) *Encyclopedia of Educational Research*, Fourth Ed. London: Macmillan, 1969, pp. 1144-1152.

Nelson, L.N. *The Nature of Teaching.* Waltham, Massachusetts: Blaisdell, 1969.

Nuthall, G.A. "An Experimental Comparison of Alternative Strategies for Teaching Concepts," *American Educational Research Journal*, 5, 1968, pp. 561-584.

Nuthall, G.A. "A Review of Some Selected Recent Studies of Classroom Interaction and Teaching Behavior. Classroom Observation." American Educational Research Monograph No. 6. Chicago: Rand McNally. Also in *New Zealand Journal of Educational Studies*, 3, 1968, pp. 125-147.

Olivero, J.L. *Developing the Oral Language Program.* Albuquerque, New Mexico: Southwestern Cooperative Educational Laboratory, undated.

Openshaw, M.K. and F.R. Cyphert. *The Development of a Taxonomy for the Classification of Teacher Classroom Behavior.* Columbus: Ohio State University Research Foundation, 1966.

Parakh, J.S. "A Study of Teacher-Pupil Interaction in High School Biology Classes: Part II. Description and Analysis," *Journal of Research in Science Teaching*, 5, 1967-1968, pp. 183-192.

Parakh, J.S. "A Study of Teacher-Pupil Interaction in BSCS Yellow Version Biology Classes," *American Biology Teacher*, 30, 1968, pp. 841-848.

Popham, W.J. "Curriculum Materials," *Review of Educational Research*, 39, 1969, pp. 283-375.

Raths, J., J.R. Pancella, and J.S. Van Ness. *Studying Teaching.* Englewood Cliffs, New Jersey: Prentice-Hall, 1967.

Rosenshine, B. "A Review of Process-Criteria Research." In I. Westbury and A.A. Bellack (Eds.) *Research into Classroom Processes.* New York: Teachers College Press, 1969a. A condensed version is available in *Classroom Interaction Newsletter*, 5, 1969, pp. 4-18. (Offset.)

Rosenshine, B. "The Effects of Enthusiastic and Animated Teacher Behavior Upon Student Achievement," *School Review*, 1969b.

Simon, A. and E.G. Boyer (Eds.). *Mirrors for Behavior: An Anthology of Classroom Observation Instruments*, Vols. 1-6. Philadelphia: Research for Better Schools, 1967a.

Simon, A. and E.G. Boyer (Eds.). *Mirrors for Behavior: An Anthology of Classroom Observation Instruments*, Vols. 7-15. Philadelphia: Research for Better Schools, 1967b.

Smith, B.O. *et al. A Tentative Report on Strategies of Teaching.* Urbana: Bureau of Educational Research, College of Education, University of Illinois, 1964. (ERIC: ED 029 165.)

Soar, R.S. *An Integrative Approach to Classroom Learning.* Public Health Service Grant No. 5-R11 MH 01096 and National Institute of Mental Health Grant No. 7-R11-MH 02045. Philadelphia: Temple University, 1966.

Solomon, D., W.E. Bezdek, and L. Rosenberg. *Teaching Styles and Learning.* Chicago: Center for the Study of Liberal Education for Adults, 1963.

Spaulding, R.L. *Achievement, Creativity, and Self-concept Correlates of Teacher-Pupil Transactions in Elementary Schools.* Cooperative Research Project No. 1352. Hempstead, New York: Hofstra University, 1965. (ERIC: ED 024 463.)

Tanck, M.L. "Teaching Concepts, Generalizations, and Constructs." *Social Studies Curriculum Development: Prospects and Problems.* Thirty-ninth Yearbook. Washington, D.C.: National Council for the Social Studies, 1969, Ch. 4, pp. 99-138.

Torrance, E.P. and E. Parent. *Characteristics of Mathematics Teachers that Affect Students' Learning.* Cooperative Research Project No. 1020. Minneapolis: School Mathematics and Science Center, Institute of Technology, University of Minnesota, 1966. (ERIC: ED 010 378.)

Travers, R.M.W. "Educational Psychology." In R.L. Ebel (Ed.) *Encyclopedia of Educational Research*, Fourth Ed. London: Macmillan, 1969, pp. 413-419.

Vickery, R.L. "An Examination of Possible Changes of Certain Aspects of Teacher Behavior Resulting from Adoption of Individualized Laboratory Centered Instructional Materials." Doctor's thesis, Tallahassee: Florida State University, 1968.

Walberg, H.J. "Teacher Personality and Classroom Climate," *Psychology in the Schools*, 5, 1968, pp. 163-169.

Walberg, H.J. "The Social Environment of Learning as a Mediator of Classroom Learning," *Journal of Education Psychology*, 60, 1969a, pp. 443-449.

Walberg, H.J. "Predicting Class Learning: A Multivariate Approach to the Class as a Social System," *American Educational Research Journal*, 4, 1969b, pp. 529-543.

Walberg, H.J. and G.J. Anderson. *Learning Environment Inventory.* Cambridge, Massachusetts: Harvard Project Physics, 1967.

Walberg, H.J. and G.J. Anderson. "Classroom Climate and Individual Learning," *Journal of Educational Psychology*, 59, 1968a, pp. 414-419.

Walberg, H.J. and G.J. Anderson. "The Achievement-Creativity Dimension and Classroom Climate," *Journal of Creative Behavior*, 2, 1968b, pp. 281-291.

Wallen, N.E. *Relationships Between Teacher Characteristics and Student Behavior: Part Three.* Cooperative Research Project No. SAE OE5-10-181. Salt Lake City: University of Utah, 1966. (ERIC: ED 010 390.)

Wallen N.E. and K.H. Wodtke. *Relationships Between Teacher Characteristics and Student Behavior: Part One.* Cooperative Research Project No. 1217. Salt Lake City: Dept. of Educational Psychology, University of Utah, 1963.

Welch, W.W. "Curriculum Evaluation," *Review of Educational Research*, 39, 1969, pp. 429-443.

Wood, S.E. *et al.* "A Factor Analysis of Three Sets of Simultaneously Collected Observational Data: Theory and Implications." Paper presented to the American Educational Research Association, February, 1969. Morgantown: University of West Virginia. (Mimeo.)

Worthen, B.R. "A Study of Discovery and Expository Presentation: Implications for Teaching," *Journal of Teacher Education*, 19, 1968a, pp. 223-242.

Worthen, B.R. *Discovery and Expository Task Presentation in Elementary Mathematics.* Journal of Educational Psychology Monograph Supplement, Vol. 59, No. 1, Part 2. Washington, D.C.: American Psychological Association, 1968b.

Wright, E.M.J. and V. Proctor. *Systematic Observation of Verbal Interaction as a Method of Comparing Mathematics Lessons.* Cooperative Research Project No. 816. St. Louis, Missouri: Washington University, 1961. (ERIC: ED 003 827.)

Zahorik, J.A. "Classroom Feedback Behavior of Teachers," *Journal of Educational Research*, 62, 1968, pp. 147-150.

Zahorik, J.A. "Teacher Verbal Feedback and Content Development." Paper presented to the American Educational Research Association, February, 1969. Milwaukee: University of Wisconsin. (Mimeo.)

15.

The Instructional Effectiveness Quotient

J.E. Bicknell

In any discussion of the measurement of instructional effectiveness the first question which should be settled is: What is the purpose of the assessment? There are many answers to this question; however, only one has validity: to provide information which can be used to improve the instructional programs which the school is providing for its pupils. Therefore, no assessment of the instructional effectiveness of teachers is justifiable unless the school carries it out in conjunction with an active program for instructional improvement.

This statement may be modified a bit, insofar as the recruitment and selection of new teaching staff is concerned. In this case it is incumbent on the candidate to convince the selection officials that he or she is an effective teacher, or has the potential of becoming one. Therefore, it is important for the individual teacher to have a current, documentary assessment of instructional effectiveness in his or her professional personnel file.

Before instructional effectiveness can be assessed, it must be operationally defined and criteria must be established. But, even before that, it will be necessary to make an important distinction. Until now, no mention has been made of "teaching effectiveness" as such. In this discussion it is assumed that "teaching effectiveness" is a generic term which includes a great many characteristics, skills, and attributes among which are those primarily

This article was written at the special request of the editors of this book. The author is Research Professor, State University College, Fredonia, New York.

involved in the performance of instructional acts. Therefore, "instructional effectiveness" is a more specific term which includes the subset of characteristics, skills, and attributes which are involved directly in the performance of instruction.

Now, to return to the problem of definition of "instructional effectiveness." If instruction can be defined as a series of inter-related, purposeful acts through which a teacher attempts to influence the attainment of a prespecified set of instructional objectives by one or more pupils, then "instructional effectiveness" can be *operationally defined* as the degree to which the prespecified instructional objectives are attained by the pupils instructed. For example, let it be assumed that a particular pupil has been assigned to a teacher for a specified period of time. Let us further assume that a criterion-referenced pre-test has identified the pupil's initial status (OI) on a hierarchy of instructional objectives (O); knowing the pupil's ability level and previous learning rate, it is possible to estimate a terminal status (OE) for the pupil on the hierarchy. Then, at the end of the specified time period, another criterion-referenced test is used to identify the pupil's attained status (OA) on the hierarchy. With respect to this particular pupil the teacher's instructional effectiveness (IE) could be expressed by the equation:

$$IE_p = \frac{(OA) - (OI)}{(OE) - (OI)} \tag{1}$$

and the teacher's average instructional effectiveness ($\overline{IE}$) for a class having a number of pupils (N) could be expressed as:

$$\overline{IE} = \frac{\Sigma(OA) - (OI)}{\Sigma(OE) - (OI)} \tag{2}$$

The foregoing formulas express the instructional effectiveness of a teacher in terms of the proportion of reasonably expected pupil gains which were actually achieved during a specified time. Each may be multiplied by 100 to express instructional effectiveness as the percent of reasonably expected pupil gains which were achieved. As such, it becomes an "instructional effectiveness quotient."

It should be noted that equation (1) expresses the effectiveness of a teacher with a particular pupil and a particular set of instructional objectives. It is reasonable to suppose that, with reference to these same instructional objectives, the teacher's instructional effectiveness will vary from pupil to pupil. On the other hand, with reference to a particular pupil, the teacher's instructional effectiveness could vary from one specific set of instructional objectives to another. It is from these sources of variability that the most useful information for an individualized in-service training program can be obtained. Of course, in the calculation of equation (2), this type of information is lost through averaging out the important variability. A further discussion of this will be presented later in connection with the use of instructional effectiveness assessment in an in-service training program.

Simple as equations (1) and (2) appear to be, it is not possible to apply them unless certain prior steps have been taken. A brief discussion of these prior steps will facilitate later discussions of the use of the formulas in an in-service training program and their use in a program of instructional research and development.

The first and most important step which a school system must take is to specify the objectives of instruction in behavioral terms and to order these in a hierarchical sequence. It is not necessary that this be done for the entire curriculum at one time. For example, a school may wish to revise its program in reading by beginning with the early primary program first, and extending the development in later years as children proceed through successively higher levels. Furthermore, a school need not start from scratch in defining the sequence of instructional objectives. It may begin by adopting or adapting an existing sequence. The Wisconsin Research and Development Center has developed a hierarchy of reading objectives. These are printed on cards for each pupil. When a pupil attains mastery of an instructional objective, his card is punched in the corresponding space. In this system, key-sorting techniques assist in keeping track of which pupils have attained which objectives. The New York State Education Department has been working for a number of years on a Comprehensive Achievement Monitoring System in which criterion-referenced test items are used as pre- and post-tests. Pupils are placed in the instructional hierarchy according to performance on the pre-test and their progress with respect to the instructional objectives is assessed by periodic post-tests. A large bank of objectives and their associated test items in several subject areas are available from the New York State Education Department (O'Rielly and Hambleton, 1971). Another source of instructional objectives and criterion-referenced test items is the Instructional Objectives Exchange (1972).

The second step to be taken follows from the first. Once the instructional objectives for a segment of the curriculum have been defined and sequenced, it follows that some means must be provided to determine pupil attainment of them. This is a criterion-referenced testing program in which each of the instructional objectives is specifically tested. These tests, used as pre-tests before instruction on a particular unit is to begin, will allow the pupils to be placed in the work of the unit at points which are appropriate to their skills. It will also define their initial status (OI). Further testing, which is devoted largely to the determination of when pupils attain the latter objectives, can be incorporated into the instructional sequence. Pupils then can move through the sequence at a pace which is appropriate for them. When a pupil attains the criterion level of performance for an objective, that objective is checked off for him. At the end of the specified time period the last completed objective defines the pupils' attained status (OA).

Before concluding the discussion of criterion-referenced testing, a brief comment should be made concerning criterion levels for each instructional objective. Bloom (1968) suggests that mastery should be attained and defined this as eighty to ninety percent correct responses to the items associated with an objective. Such a level of performance may be too costly of time and effort to be attained by most pupils. Some pupils may never be able to reach such a rigidly defined mastery level. Others may succumb to boredom before attaining that level even though, through persistence, they could reach it. It is suggested that criterion levels for each objective be established by a committee of teachers. These would depend upon the educational importance of the objective and on the instructional sequence. Objectives which are concerned with key skills or concepts should require higher criterion levels; the less important objectives should require lower criterion levels. Also, a single criterion level may not be appropriate for all pupils. Therefore, a criterion range should be specified. The upper limit of this range could well be the mastery level of eighty to ninety percent correct responses. The lower limit should be defined in terms of the minimum level of the skill or concept development which is necessary before the next step in the instructional objective sequence can be undertaken profitably.

The third prior step is the development of a procedure for estimating the terminal status of each pupil on the objective sequence at the end of a specified learning period (OE). For obvious reasons, these estimates should be made by someone other than the teacher who is responsible for the instruction, and should be as reliable as it is possible to make them. Initially, a committee of teachers, each of whom is familiar with a pupil's performance, can make an estimate based upon the consensus of their subjective judgments. Thereafter, records of the pupils' attainment of objectives can be used to establish an attainment rate for each pupil. These rates can be successively adjusted after each unit of instruction in a manner similar to the handicapping systems used in golf or bowling. At the beginning of an instructional period, the attainment rate for a pupil would be projected over the specified time period to obtain an estimate of his or her terminal status on the objective sequence. If a concise pupil record system has been developed, these estimates can be calculated routinely by clerical aides.

It was mentioned earlier that the assessment of instructional effectiveness should be carried on in conjunction with an active program for instructional improvement. Through such assessment, diagnostic information can be obtained which is essential to the success of an in-service teacher training program. The data from the assessment program may be analyzed in a variety of ways to obtain a great deal of information. For example, they can be analyzed to show which instructional objectives are most consistently achieved by the pupils of a school. Other analyses can reveal the strengths, or weaknesses, of individual teachers in terms of the sets of objectives which are most or least consistently attained by their pupils. These kinds of information will enable the planners to focus the in-service training program on problem areas and, if necessary, to individualize it for the teachers. Although the scope of this article does not permit an exhaustive presentation of all of the ways by which effectiveness data may be analyzed, a brief discussion of the major ones may point the way to further, innovative analyses.

To begin, let it be assumed that instruction is a complex function involving many skills and several strategies (ways in which skills are combined and sequenced to attain an objective). No single teacher possesses all of these skills or has facility with each strategy. Rather, each has a repertoire of skills and a limited number of alternative strategies which can be applied in particular instructional situations. Thus, if a teacher can be assigned to instruct only those groups of pupils for whom he or she has an appropriate instructional strategy, in units of instruction for which the teacher has many highly developed skills, he or she probably would be rated as a highly effective teacher. However, if it were necessary, as it usually is in most schools, to assign the teacher to units of instruction for which the teacher is less skilled, with a heterogeneous group of pupils for many of whom he or she has no viable instructional strategy, the effectiveness ratings would be considerably lower. Thus, for a particular teacher, a multivariate analysis of variance of effectiveness scores by units and pupils would reveal his or her strengths and weaknesses with both.

For example, it might be found that a teacher was effective with one group of pupils in certain units of instruction, and with a different group of pupils in other units. The teacher's repertoires of skills and strategies to deal with these units are too narrow for the groups of pupils with whom the teacher must deal. A careful study of the characteristics of the pupils and units of instruction concerned, most likely will reveal the particular skills and strategies which are lacking from the teacher's repertoire. An in-service program can then be prescribed.

In most graded elementary schools each of several teachers at a particular grade level teach all subjects to a group of children for an entire year. In such situations, variability among teachers could become another main effect in a multivariate analysis of variance design. The term for teacher by unit interaction, if significant, would provide a school with information which could be valuable in creating teaching teams.

In a school which wishes to increase the degree to which instruction is individualized, instructional effectiveness can be increased in proportion to its success in diagnosing the needs, abilities, and interests of its pupils. Instructional effectiveness data can be analyzed to yield valuable information for such diagnoses. The among-pupils main-effect term in the multivariate analysis of variance and the pupil by unit interaction term, if significant, will allow pupils to be classified according to the units for which their instruction was most and least effective. Pupil data, such as scores derived from interest inventories, biographical inventories, aptitude tests, anecdotal records, etc., can be used in a discriminant function to identify the characteristics which distinguish the various groups. This information can then be used to prescribe teaching techniques and strategies for pupils having these characteristics.

Although many potential benefits can be obtained through the use of an instructional assessment program, they cannot be fully obtained immediately. The usefulness of the measure proposed here is dependent upon two conditions which each user must create over a period of time. The first, and controlling one, is the establishment of an instructional research unit in which the many analyses can be carried out. The second is the reliability of the measure itself. The concluding portion of this article is devoted to a brief discussion of these conditions.

In the few examples which were presented of ways in which the measures of effectiveness can be analyzed, some techniques of multivariate analysis were mentioned. Such analyses require highly specialized training. Only the largest school systems can afford to hire people who have the required training and experience. It is not necessary, however, for a school to institute immediately a highly sophisticated research unit to obtain the initial benefits of the program. A great deal can be learned by sorting the effectiveness scores and averaging them in various ways. Thus, for a particular teacher, the effectiveness scores of pupils could be sorted according to the units of instruction. An average for each of the resulting groups would show in which units the teacher was the most and least effective. Such analyses as these are within the capability of most school systems. Through simplified initial analyses, the user of the system will develop more intricate questions—the answers to which require more sophisticated analyses. For example, one may become interested in interaction effects or the results of a controlled experiment in terms of the effectiveness scores of pupils, teachers, or both. Such studies can be carried out through a contractual arrangement with a consultant or with a faculty member at a nearby college. If a number of schools within an area are interested, they might hire jointly a full-time research director and provide him with clerical assistants on their own staffs. Intermediate districts such as the Boards of Cooperative Educational Services in New York State might provide research services for the schools in their areas.

One of the early functions of a research unit should be to maximize the reliability of the measure of instructional effectiveness. Its reliability is dependent upon (1) the reliability of the prediction system through which the expected objective status (OE) of a pupil is estimated and (2) the reliability of the measure of pupil attainment of each instructional objective. The latter of these two is of prime importance because it is involved in two terms of equations (1) and (2); the measurement of the pupils' initial status (OI) and the measurement of the pupils' terminal status (OA). It has been suggested earlier in this paper that the prediction of expected status for a pupil (OE) can be made in terms of a moving average of the number of objectives attained by a pupil per unit of time. The research unit should undertake the calculation of these rates for each pupil and to "update" them at the conclusion of each instructional unit. It is suggested that the rates be calculated over the five most recently taught units in each subject area, thus minimizing the effect of temporary fluctuations in a pupil's learning rate.

The establishment of the reliability with which pupil status on the objective hierarchy can be measured is a more complex matter, which is beyond the scope of this paper. This would involve the analyses of test and item reliabilities and studies of the reliability of criterion-referenced testing. Classical test theory, which forms the basis for the traditional, norm-referenced tests, has little to offer in designing a program for studying or developing the reliability or validity of criterion-referenced measures. Kriewall (1972) proposed a criterion-referenced test theory which might be of value in planning reliability and validity research programs. Other approaches to the problem are appearing in the growing literature on criterion-referenced measurement.

The system for assessing instructional effectiveness which is suggested here must be validated through use in each school where it is introduced. This may be a lengthy process. At first, the benefits of the system may be discouragingly small; if earnest and continued efforts are devoted to it, the benefits will increase rapidly.

References

Bloom, B.S. "Learning Mastery," *Evaluation Comment*, Vol. 1, No. 2, May, 1968.

Instructional Objectives Exchange. P.O. Box 24095, Los Angeles, California, 90024, 1972.

Kriewall, T.E. *Aspects and Applications of Criterion-Referenced Tests*. Institute for Educational Research, Downers Grove, Illinois, April, 1972.

O'Reilly, R.P. and R.K. Hambleton, *ACMI Model for an Individualized Learning Program in Ninth Grade Science*. ERIC Document TR-NO-14, 1971.

16.

Performance Tests of Teaching Proficiency: Rationale, Development, Validation

One of the most elusive targets in the history of educational research is a valid index of teacher effectiveness. Since the turn of the century, literally hundreds of investigations have probed the question of teacher competence assessment and most of them have produced little, if any, significant progress.

In the last few years, however, evolving conceptions of the nature of instruction seem to offer promise to teacher effectiveness researchers. In most of the early investigations in which measures of teacher competence were sought, there was an almost exclusive focus on the instructional means employed by teachers. Researcher after researcher attempted to identify "good teaching procedures" for, should such procedures be discovered, they would obviously have implications for teacher education as well as for the evaluation of teachers on the job. Only recently have many educators come to accept the proposition that there are diverse instructional means which can be used to bring about a single instructional end. Teacher effectiveness research based on this assumption will tend to focus on the results achieved by instructors, not merely the means they employ.

When Morsh and Wilder (1954) in their definitive review of teacher effectiveness research during the first fifty years of this

Reprinted from *American Educational Research Journal*, Vol. 8, No. 1, Copyright © January, 1971. Reprinted with permission of the author and the publisher. The author is Professor of Education, Graduate School of Education, University of California, Los Angeles.

century indicated that no single teaching act had been discovered which was invariably associated with learner achievement, teacher competence researchers should have been more attentive. We should have first focused our efforts on identifying teachers who could produce superior growth in learners, leaving aside for the moment the question of how such improvements were brought about. If one can identify satisfactory measures of pupil attainment, then the next step is to identify the complicated procedures by which such achievements are attained. It is important to emphasize the complexity of this task. The undoubted reason that reviewers such as Morsh and Wilder find few descriptions of "good teacher procedures" is that effective instruction represents a series of subtle interactions among a given teacher, his particular students, the instructional goals he is attempting to achieve, and the instructional environment.

Of course, there have been researchers who have employed the criterion of learner growth as an index of a teacher's proficiency. Such efforts would seem to represent proper attention to instructional ends rather than means. Most of these investigations relied upon the use of standardized achievement tests which, while comprehensive, rarely took into consideration the particular instructor's expectations regarding the outcomes to be measured. Further, the standardized measures employed were typically based on norm-referenced rather than criterion-referenced approaches to test construction (Glaser, 1963) and, as a consequence, were often inappropriate to measure group progress toward specified instructional goals.

Since the early 1960s we have witnessed a marked increase in research employing systematic classroom observation techniques. These efforts, perhaps best typified by the use of Flanders' Interaction Analysis procedures, have too frequently attended to classroom process variables without consideration of resulting modifications in learner behavior. Only recently (Campbell and Barnes, 1969) have a number of these investigations undertaken to report relationships between observation indices and learning outcome variables.

Because of the methodological difficulties encountered to date by teacher effectiveness researchers, a heretofore untried procedure for assessing teaching competence was conceived at the University of California, Los Angeles, during 1964, involving the use of performance tests of teaching proficiency. Support was secured from the U.S. Office of Education for a four-year investigation designed to develop and subsequently test the validity of performance tests in the fields of social science, electronics, and auto mechanics.

Rationale

In brief, the general approach used in the performance tests of teaching proficiency calls for the development of a set of explicitly stated instructional objectives to cover a specified instructional period, in this case approximately ten hours. Coupled with such objectives are examinations based exclusively on the objectives. In addition, a collection of possible instructional activities and references is provided in a form comparable to the resource units found in so many curriculum libraries. The procedure for using such performance tests requires that an instructor be given the objectives and resource materials well in advance of instruction. He is told to devise a sequence of instruction suitable for accomplishing the objectives and then allowed to teach to the objectives using whatever instructional procedures he wishes. In other words, only the ends are specified—the pedagogical means are left to the instructor. A teacher would be obliged, therefore, to accomplish the pre-specified objectives, but would have freedom to choose instructional procedures which, to him, seemed likely to achieve those goals.

It is difficult, of course, to validate the merits of such an approach to the assessment of teaching competence. One does not have readily available the already established criterion measures which can be used to calculate concurrent validity coefficients. A construct approach to validation, therefore, appeared to be more appropriate. It seemed, considering the nature of the performance tests, that these measures ought to be able *at least* to distinguish between credentialed, experienced teachers and those who were neither credentialed nor experienced. In other words, if one were to take a group of credentialed, experienced teachers and ask them to teach to the objectives, in contrast to asking a group of "people off the the street" to teach to the same objectives, the experienced teachers ought to out-perform their inexperienced counterparts. In order to test this validation hypothesis, it was proposed that performance tests be developed in the three fields previously mentioned and that the ability of the tests to discriminate between experienced teachers and non-teachers be determined. Results of developmental work and field tests will be described in the remainder of this paper. More detailed descriptions of the research are available elsewhere (Popham, 1967; 1968).

Development

The developmental phase of this project involved the selection of a topic, statement of objectives, assembly of resource materials, and construction of test items. Any topic chosen had to meet several requirements. First, it should take ten hours or less to teach, hopefully permitting us to secure cooperation from public school personnel who might be willing to devote two weeks of normal class time to our field trials but would be loath to give longer periods to the research. Second, to reduce the likelihood of previous student exposure to the material, the topic should not be currently taught in the schools. Third, the topic should require no specified set of student entry behaviors dependent upon previous instruction. Fourth, the topic should be able to be inserted logically at any point in the curriculum. A last requirement for the topic was that it be so acceptable to teachers that they would feel it important enough to employ.

Developmental work on the three performance tests, two in vocational education and one in the social sciences, occurred in the following pattern. First, topics meeting the above criteria which might be covered in two or three weeks were selected. These were then submitted to several subject-matter specialists who served as consultants during the project. From these tentative topics, three were selected and instructional objectives were prepared which were also screened by consultants. A preliminary set of these objectives was agreed on, and test items based directly on the objectives were developed. In addition, possible learning activities and reference materials were assembled. In some instances, these learning activities were designed to be particularly pertinent to the given objectives. In other cases, the activities were planned to be appealingly exotic but not germane to the objectives. It was thought that less experienced instructors might be attracted to the irrelevant activities, but that the sophisticated teacher would tend to use the pertinent activities. These materials were revised several times prior to initial trials. Of course, it was possible that a teacher might choose to develop his own instructional activities without any reliance on the materials provided in the resource unit.

The early forms of the post-tests were given to several teachers for administration to classes of beginning and advanced students currently taking related vocational or social studies courses. Resulting data underwent item analysis procedures which led to the revision of many test items. When ready for the first field trial, all three performance tests consisted solely of objectives which were measurable by paper-and-pencil tests.

After extensive field trials with preliminary versions of the materials, one of the two vocational education tests was completely abandoned and a new topic selected. The other two tests, though seriously revised, were retained. When finally ready for the validation phase of the research, the following three performance tests were available:

- *Social Science Research Methods.* This test, dealing with basic research techniques employed by social scientists, consisted of thirteen specific instructional objectives, a ninety-one-page resource unit, a thirty-three-item pre-test, and a sixty-eight-item post-test.
- *Basic Power Supplies.* This test in the field of electronics consisted of twenty-three specific instructional objectives, a thirty-page resource unit, a twenty-item pre-test, and a forty-six-item post-test.
- *Carburetion.* This test in the field of auto mechanics consisted of twenty-nine specific instruction objectives, a twenty-seven-page resource unit, a twenty-item pre-test, and a ninety-nine-item post-test.

Validation

As indicated previously, we wished to test the hypothesis

that the performance tests *at least* ought to be able to discriminate between experienced teachers and non-teachers with respect to their ability to accomplish prespecified instructional objectives. Thus, after developing the performance test materials, the next task was to locate a suitable number of teachers and non-teachers.

Subjects

The recruitment of subjects proved to be the most time-consuming operation of the entire research project. We solicited the cooperation of major metropolitan districts in which there would be a large number of teachers in the desired fields as well as numerous non-teachers who would have sufficient subject-matter backgrounds to teach the units, but no prior teaching experience. In the case of the performance test for auto mechanics, we anticipated using garage mechanics from service stations, auto agency service departments, etc. For the electronics performance test, we hoped to recruit individuals such as television repairmen and workers in the electronics industries. The non-teachers for the social science performance test might be drawn from housewives or college students with a social science background. Of all the large districts contacted throughout the state, only the San Diego City Schools agreed to participate in the project.

Beyond the location of school officials who would participate, there was also the problem of locating teacher volunteers as well as non-teachers who would agree to teach in the schools. Because of their extra effort involved in this project, an honorarium (for social science: $25; for electronics and auto mechanics: $50) was given to each participating teacher. A similar honorarium was given to each non-teacher participant.

Locating a sufficient number of non-teachers for the two vocational performance tests presented a considerable challenge. Personal contact with local industries failed to yield enough non-teachers who were both willing to participate in the project and could arrange their schedules in order to teach in the schools. We finally relied on saturation newspaper advertising in order to attract the attention of the non-teachers. After several months of proselytizing, a sufficient number of teachers and non-teachers were located so that we had twenty-eight pairs (teacher and non-teacher) for the auto mechanics field test and sixteen pairs for the electronics field test.

There was far less difficulty encountered in locating non-teachers for the social science performance test field trials. The performance of thirteen experienced teachers was contrasted with thirteen San Diego State College students who had completed at least two years of college with a major or minor in social science.

All of the thirteen social science teachers possessed a California teaching credential and a minimum of four years' teaching experience, several of them having taught for more than ten years. All of the twenty-eight auto mechanics teachers and the sixteen electronics teachers possessed a California teaching credential and had taught for at least two years, with a mean of five years of teaching experience for both types of vocational education teachers. None of the non-teachers in any of the three comparison groups possessed formal teaching experience or had completed previous teacher education coursework.

Procedure

All three performance tests were subjected to validation contrasts in on-going school situations involving 2,326 public school students. There were slight differences between the procedures employed for the two vocational education tests and the social science test. Because of the necessity of controlling the potential influence of school effects in the data analysis, we located a non-teacher "match" for every teacher who agreed to participate in the project. For the two vocational education tests, teachers were selected who had at least two sections of a class in which the unit could be taught for approximately nine hours. For electronics, the following kinds of classes were usually involved: first and second year electronics and introductory electricity. For auto mechanics the following kinds of classes were generally involved: first and second year auto mechanics and power mechanics.

For the vocational education tests one of the classes was randomly designated as that which would be taught by the teacher. We were anxious to avoid the possibility that a teacher would select one of his best classes and, consciously or unconsciously, give a less able group to the non-teacher. In some instances, of course, the availability of a particular non-teacher dictated the selection of a certain class hour for him. In this instance, if more than one class remained which could be assigned to the regular teacher for the purposes of this project, the selection was made at random.

In general, the procedure for the electronics and auto mechanics tests involved giving the teacher and non-teacher sets of the instructional materials, that is, objectives and resource unit, approximately two weeks prior to the time when instruction was to commence. The non-teacher generally arrived at the school for the first time on the day instruction was to commence. He was introduced to the regular teacher by a member of the project research staff who then administered the pre-test to all students at the beginning of ten hours reserved for the project. The pre-test took approximately fifteen to twenty minutes to complete. The regular teacher and non-teacher then, in their separate classes, taught for approximately nine hours. They attempted to achieve the objectives specified in the unit but, as indicated before, were free to use any instructional methods they wished. For legal purposes, while the non-teacher instructed, the regular teacher remained at the rear of the classroom but was directed not to interfere with the non-teacher's efforts or to collaborate in any way with the non-teacher in planning his instruction. At the conclusion of the nine hours of instruction, a member of the project staff administered the post-test to all students. A brief student questionnaire and instructor questionnaire were also filled out at the conclusion of the unit. In completing their questionnaires, the experienced teachers reported that they had refrained from involvement in the instructional activities of the non-teachers.

The tryout of the social science test, while essentially the same as for the two vocational education tests, was carried out somewhat differently. First, the instructional time allowed was only four hours. Second, the experienced teacher's regular class was randomly divided into two groups, one of which was taught in a separate room by the non-teacher. Again, for legal purposes, a credentialed substitute unobtrusively remained at the rear of the non-teacher's classroom as he instructed the group. At the close of the four-hour instructional period the post-test and questionnaire were administered to all students. Because of the random assignment to the two groups no pre-test was used.

Analysis

Because of the interaction among pupils in given classes, it was considered appropriate to treat the data in terms of classroom units rather than individual pupils. Accordingly, the first step in the analysis called for the calculation of classroom means for each of the variables involved in the investigation. These means constituted the data for subsequent analyses. The principal analysis concerned the prediction that teachers would significantly out-perform non-teachers. The first analysis conducted to test this hypothesis was a correlated t test using the gross post-test score as the criterion. The correlated t model was employed because of the probable relationship associated with a teacher and non-teacher pairs being drawn from the same school. The correlation coefficients were .76, .60, and .23 for electronics, auto mechanics, and social science, respectively. For the auto mechanics and electronics data, an analysis of covariance was computed in which pre-test scores and students' expressed interest in the topic (on a five-point scale as reported in the questionnaire administered at the close of instruction) served as covariates. Due to the absence of pre-test data, no analysis of covariance was computed for the social science data. Results of pupil affective data on the post-instruction questionnaires were compared by analysis of variance. These analyses also involved classroom means rather than data for individual pupils.

Results

Results of the three contrasts involving t test comparisons of gross post-test scores are presented in Table 1, where it can be seen that differences of only a small magnitude existed between the teacher and non-teacher groups. Only in the case of the electronics data was the difference significant ($p < .05$, one tailed) on the basis of a correlated t test. A subsequent analysis of covariance in which post-test means were adjusted for initial pre-test differences (favoring the teacher group) failed to confirm this significant difference. The adjusted electronics means were almost identical, i.e., teachers: 23.9; non-teachers: 23.1. Analysis of covariance results for the auto mechanics and electronics contrasts are present in Tables 2 and 3, respectively. Thus, in all three instances, there were no significant differences between the ability of teachers and non-teachers to promote learner attainment of prespecified instructional objectives.

Table 1

Means, Standard Deviations, and Correlated t Test Results for Teacher and Non-teacher Classes

Test	Subjects	n	x^*	s	t
Social Science	Experienced Teachers	13	33.4	2.2	.6
	College Students	13	32.3	3.0	
Auto Mechanics	Experienced Teachers	28	48.2	6.5	1.4
	Tradesmen	28	46.5	6.8	
Electronics	Experienced Teachers	16	24.3	4.5	2.0
	Tradesmen	16	22.7	3.8	

*Points possible: Social Science, 50; Auto Mechanics, 99; Electronics, 46.

Table 2

Analysis of Covariance of Auto Mechanics Classes (Teachers Versus Non-teachers) Post-test Performance, Using Pre-test Scores and Pupils' Expressed Interest in Auto Mechanics as Covariates

Source	df	SS	MS	F
Between	1	22.7	22.7	.84
Within	52	1405.6	27.0	
Total	53	1428.3		

	Control Variables		Criterion Variables	
Group	Pre-test X	Interest X	Unadjusted Post-test X	Adjusted Post-test X
Teachers	9.8	3.6	48.2	48.0
Non-teachers	9.7	3.6	46.5	46.7

Table 3

Analysis of Covariance of Electronics Classes (Teachers Versus Non-teachers) Post-test Performance, Using Pre-test Scores and Pupils' Expressed Interest in Electronics as Covariates

Source	df	SS	MS	F
Between	1	5.3	5.3	.72
Within	28	205.9	7.3	
Total	29	211.2		

	Control Variables		Criterion Variables	
Group	Pre-test X	Interest X	Unadjusted Post-test X	Adjusted Post-test X
Teacher	6.9	3.6	24.3	23.9
Non-teachers	6.8	3.5	22.7	23.1

Analysis of variance tests of the difference between affective reactions of pupils, as reflected by responses to the student questionnaire, failed to reveal any significant differences between teacher classes and non-teacher classes. Measures involved in these analyses included responses to such questions as: "After this unit how would you rate your interest in the specific topic of carburetion?"

Discussion

Results of all three validation replications failed to confirm the prediction that experienced teachers would promote significantly better achievements of given instructional objectives than would non-teachers. In dealing with such results, one must consider the possibility of measurement or methodological deficiencies in order to explain away the unsupported hypothesis. The measuring instruments, however, appeared to be quite satisfactory. They satisfied criterion-referenced validity standards, that is, the test items were judged by a number of experts to be congruent with the stated objectives. There was certainly sufficient test ceiling in all three instances, with post-test performance never reaching seventy percent correct.

Methodologically, because of the desire to conduct the investigation in on-going school situations, the teachers had several clear advantages over their non-teacher counterparts. The teachers were familiar with the school setting, e.g., classroom facilities, resource materials, etc. They knew their students, having worked with them for a number of weeks prior to the time the field tests were conducted. Couple these rather specific advantages with those which are typically attributed to teaching experience (such as skill in attaining classroom discipline, ease of speaking before students, sensitivity to the learning capabilities of particular age groups, etc.) and one might expect the teachers to perform much better on this type of task. The question is "Why not?"

Although there are competing explanations, such as insufficient teaching time, the explanation that seems inescapably probable is the following: *Experienced teachers are not particularly skilled at bringing about prespecified behavior changes in learners.* When it comes to a task such as that presented by the performance test in which they must promote learner attainment of specific instructional objectives, perhaps most experienced teachers are no better qualified than a person who has never taught. To realize why this might be so, one needs only to speculate on the typical intentions of most public school teachers. They wish to cover the content of the course, to maintain classroom order, to expose the student to knowledge, and so on. Rarely does one find a teacher who, prior to teaching, establishes clearly stated instructional objectives in terms of learner behavior and then sets out to achieve those objectives. Only recently, in fact, do we find many teachers who are even familiar with the manner in which instructional objectives are stated in measurable form.

Lest this sound like an unchecked assault on the teaching profession, it should be pointed out that there is little reason to expect that teachers should be skilled goal achievers. Certainly they have not been trained to be; teacher education institutions rarely foster this sort of competence. Nor is there any premium placed on such instructional skill after the teacher concludes pre-service training. The general public, most school systems, and professional teachers' groups rarely attach special importance to the teacher's attainment of clearly stated instructional objectives.

To the extent that the foregoing analysis is accurate, the attempt to validate the performance test of teaching proficiency by contrasting the accomplishments of teachers and non-teachers was probably ill conceived. It may have been wishful thinking to believe that experienced teachers would perform better. But the fact that this validation scheme was injudiciously selected does not mean that the performance test approach is unworkable, nor that such tests cannot be validated.

This validation effort was an attempt to supply construct validity evidence. Another more reasonable construct validation approach could be based on a contrast between (a) instructors who had manifested measurable skill in promoting learner attainment of prespecified objectives and (b) instructors who had not manifested such skill. The initial group of instructors could be trained on comparable teaching tasks until they could show that when presented with instructional objectives specified in terms of learner behavior, they could accomplish such objectives. Then both the skilled and unskilled group could be given other performance tests such as those described in this report. The prediction would be, of course, that the skilled instructors display their generalized teaching proficiency by out-performing the unskilled instructors. In a similar vein, two investigators (Connor, 1969; Justiz, 1969) recently reported high positive correlations between teachers' achievements on two different short-term performance tests comparable to those described here. Such results are, of course, encouraging.

An additional caveat should also be mentioned. At the earliest conception regarding the use of these performance tests as measures of teaching competence, it was assumed that we could develop a sufficiently sensitive index of a particular teacher's ability to accomplish instructional objectives so that this measure might be used in evaluating individual instructors. The idea, for example, of using results of one or more performance tests in teacher merit-rating schemes appeared possible. Granted that problems of variability among different teachers' classes existed, it was thought that this might be adequately compensated for through sensitive weighting procedures or other forms of statistical adjustment. It now appears, in light of the grossness of the measurement devices likely to be available in the near future, that we shall be pleased even if the performance tests are suitable for use only with groups. In other words, it will be a sufficient advance to develop a reliable group criterion measure which could be used in myriad educational situations such as to assess the efficiency of teacher education programs.

The principal conclusion of this project was that in three separate instances teachers were not able to perform better than non-teachers in their ability to promote learner attainment of prespecified instructional objectives. Obviously, generalizations beyond the types of teachers and non-teachers involved in the investigation, as well as the teaching task and pupils, should be undertaken cautiously. The explanation offered for these results was based on the teachers' lack of skill in achieving present behavioral changes in learners.

References

Campbell, J.R. and C.W. Barnes. "Interaction Analysis—A Breakthrough?" *Phi Delta Kappan*, 50, 1969, pp. 587-590.

Connor, A. "Final Report: Cross-validating Two Performance Tests of Instructional Proficiency." Office of Education Project No. 8-1-174, Grant No. OEG 9-9140174-0011 (057), University of California, Los Angeles, December, 1969.

Glaser, R. "Instructional Technology and the Measurement of Learning Outcomes: Some Questions," *American Psychologist*, 18, 1963, pp. 519-521.

Justiz, T.B. "A Method for Identifying the Effective Teacher." Doctoral dissertation, University of California, Los Angeles. Ann Arbor, Michigan: University Microfilms, No. 29-3022-A, 1969.

Morsh, J. and E. Wilder. *Identifying the Effective Instructor: A Review of the Quantitative Studies, 1900-1952.* Research bulletin AFPTRC-T-54-55. Texas: Lackland Air Force Base, 1954.

Popham, W.J. "Final Report: Development of a Performance Test of Teaching Proficiency." Office of Education Project No. 5-056602-12-1, Contract No. OE-6-10-254, University of California, Los Angeles, August, 1967. (ERIC No. ED 013242.)

Popham, W.J. "Final Report: Performance Tests of Instructor Competence for Trade and Technical Education." Office of Education Project No. 5-004, Contract No. OE-5-85-051, University of California, Los Angeles, June, 1968. (ERIC No. ED 027418.)